Wiltshire Record Society

(formerly the Records Branch of the Wiltshire
Archaeological and Natural History Society)

VOLUME XXXI
FOR THE YEAR 1975

Impression of 450 copies

POVERTY IN
EARLY-STUART SALISBURY

EDITED BY
PAUL SLACK

DEVIZES
1975

THIS VOLUME IS PUBLISHED WITH THE HELP OF A
GRANT FROM THE BRITISH ACADEMY

Set in Times New Roman 10/11pt.

PRINTED IN GREAT BRITAIN BY
WARWICK PRINTING COMPANY LTD.
WARWICK

CONTENTS

CONTENTS

PREFACE

This volume contains editions of seven complete documents, extracts, complete in themselves, from a further four documents, and a reprinted 17th-century pamphlet. It is unusual for the Society to publish extracts of documents and to reprint. It feels justified in doing so now, however, because the documents and complementary extracts, enlivened by the contemporary commentary of an extremely rare pamphlet, combine so well to establish the theme of the book.

The Society is indebted to the former Town Clerk of Salisbury for granting Dr. Slack access to the documents and to the Chief Administration Officer of the Salisbury District Council for permission to publish them. It warmly records its thanks to the Research Fund Committee of the British Academy for a contribution to the cost of publishing them. Dr. Slack wishes to thank the Librarian of the Wiltshire Archaeological and Natural History Society (Mr. R. E. Sandell) for his kindness in making available the library's copy, the only one known, of the pamphlet. He also wishes to thank Miss Pamela Stewart of the Wiltshire Record Office, Mr. R. W. Chell of the Hampshire Record Office, Miss Elizabeth Rainey, and Dr. Claire Cross for their help and advice.

DOUGLAS CROWLEY
July 1975

ABBREVIATIONS

Asz. 24	Public Record Office: Assizes, Miscellaneous Books
C 93	Public Record Office: Proceedings of Commissioners for Charitable Uses, Inquisitions and Decrees
C.P. 40	Public Record Office: De Banco Rolls
Hants R.O.	Hampshire Record Office
Hist. MSS. Com.	Historical Manuscripts Commission
S.C.A.	Salisbury Corporation Archives
Sar. Dioc. R.O.	Salisbury Diocesan Record Office
V.C.H.	*Victoria County History*
W.A.M.	*Wiltshire Archaeological and Natural History Magazine*
W.R.O.	Wiltshire Record Office

INTRODUCTION

The documents and extracts from documents printed below have been chosen from the Salisbury Corporation archives to illustrate the nature and problem of poverty and the efforts to deal with it in early-17th-century Salisbury. Partly because the corporation then initiated an ambitious experiment to relieve the poor, which, in its idealism and scope, was matched in few other towns, the documents concerned with poverty in Salisbury exist in a quantity and are of a quality rarely found elsewhere. Those printed are the register of passports for vagrants 1598–1669 (I: S.C.A., vol. Z 225 [ff. 12–45]) and surveys of the poor 1625 (II: S.C.A., vol. S 162, ff. 25–[108v.]) and c. 1635 (III: S.C.A., misc. papers, box 6; IV: ibid. box 6, M 36); a project for the relief of the poor c. 1613 (V: S.C.A., misc. papers, box 6, O 7) and orders for the poor 1623 (VI: S.C.A., Ledger C, f. 291) and 1626 (VII: S.C.A., misc. papers, box 6); and extracts from the monthly overseers' accounts for July–December 1635 (VIII: S.C.A., S 162 [ff. 224v.–227v.]), a file of overseers' papers for 1635–6 (IX: S.C.A., misc. papers, box 2, O 2), and extracts from the workhouse accounts for 1627–30 (X: S.C.A., Y 211 [ff. 156v.–159v.]). A contemporary pamphlet describing the Salisbury experiments, John Ivie's *Declaration* of 1661, has been printed as an appendix.

THE PROBLEM OF THE POOR

Most social commentators, legislators, and magistrates of 16th- and early-17th-century England viewed poverty as a two-sided problem. Destitute but able-bodied vagabonds moving to towns in search of employment or charity were condemned and punished, but paupers resident in a town or parish, most of them in some sense impotent, were generally acknowledged to have legitimate claims to public relief. [1]

Vagrants
According to the vagrancy statute of 1598 [2] rogues, vagabonds, and sturdy beggars over the age of 7, found 'begging, vagrant, wandering, or misordering themselves', were to be whipped by the order of any justice of the peace or constable and immediately sent back to their parish of birth, or, if that could not be discovered, to the place where they last lived for a year or more. They were in theory to be handed over from constable to constable along the road, and they had to carry with them a testimonial,

---

1 Poverty in Salisbury is discussed in greater detail in P. Slack, 'Poverty and Politics in Salisbury 1597–1666', *Crisis and Order in English Towns 1500–1700*, ed. P. Clark and P. Slack, 164–203; and vagrancy in 'Vagrants and Vagrancy in England 1598–1664', *Econ. Hist. Rev.* 2nd ser. xxviii. 260–79.
2 39 Eliz. I, c. 4, *Statutes of the Realm*, iv. 899–902.

signed by the justice or constable and the minister of the parish where
they were found, recording the date and place of their punishment, their
destination, and the number of days allowed to them for their journey. Their
passports were to be registered by the minister in a book provided for that
purpose.

The register of passports issued in Salisbury between 1598 and 1669
(document I) is one of the very few such records surviving for the early
17th century and it appears to be unique in its coverage of a whole town for so
long a period. Although there were three parishes in Salisbury the administration of poor relief in them was centralized under the supervision of the town's
justices from 1598 and the enforcement of the vagrancy statute was similarly
controlled by municipal and not by parish officers. That the register of
passports was kept with the poor relief records of the corporation is suggested
by the fact that it was compiled in a volume which also contains the names of
those who annually benefited from the clothing charity administered by the
city council. Since very few of the Salisbury quarter sessions records survive
for the early 17th century, however, the exact method of dealing with vagrants
is unclear. It is probable that they were normally apprehended by the constables
(no. 506) and their punishment and passport ordered by two justices (no. 88),
or occasionally by only one (nos. 507-8). There are cases early in the register
where the whole quarter sessions approved the punishment (nos. 26-9, 34),
but that seems to have been the usual procedure only when the vagrant was
presented on suspicion of theft or some other criminal offence, in which case
a record of the examination sometimes survives in the fragmentary quarter
sessions records (e.g. nos. 185-6, 307). The vagrants in those cases, like a
few other offenders (e.g. no. 518), were kept in custody between apprehension
and punishment, but the normal practice was for the two to follow closely on
one another (e.g. no. 527). In one or two instances the Salisbury justices went
beyond the letter of the law. They assumed in the case of Aplyn Pryor (no. 20),
for example, that three years' residence was needed to establish settlement, as
under the 1572 statute,[1] whereas the Act of 1598 shortened the required
period to a year. In general, however, they adhered closely to the provisions
of the statute and like other local authorities relied on the judges on assize
to determine cases of disputed settlement (e.g. no. 9).

The form of the entries in the register is not entirely uniform. The passport
itself is mentioned in the early entries but sometimes omitted after 1602.
Sometimes the vagrants are expressly described as being whipped, at other
times as being simply punished or spared punishment when pregnant or infirm.
Most of the entries nevertheless contain the basic information required by the
statute, including the number of days assigned for the vagrant's journey[2] and
the date when the passport was issued. It is probable, however, that the
entries were not made at the time of punishment, but entered at a later date
from slips of paper, some of which remain between the folios of the register
(nos. 223, 368, 385). As a result there are sometimes long intervals between

---

[1] 14 Eliz. I, c. 5, *Statutes of the Realm*, iv. 594.
[2] The authorities usually seem to have allowed a day for every 10–12 miles.

entries when passports were presumably not registered (e.g. nos. 404–5, 442–3). There is also a general decline in the annual number of passports from the beginning of the register until 1638, after which only a few cases from the 1660s were summarily entered. It seems evident from the continuing concern of the corporation with the problem of immigrant strangers that vagrants were punished after 1638, but if any continuous record was kept of them it has perished along with nearly all the town's quarter sessions records of that period.

Although it is a unique record, therefore, the Salisbury register is by no means a perfect one. It does not record the total number of vagrants in the town or show precisely how the number fluctuated. The constables probably apprehended only a small proportion of those wandering in, and the decline in the numbers punished after the initial activity inspired by the 1598 statute may indicate that the proportion gradually diminished. The large numbers of vagrants punished in 1598 and 1630 suggest increasing immigration into the town after periods of bad harvest, and the high numbers regularly taken in March and April confirm the view of contemporaries that vagrants began to move in the spring, but the precise number of vagrants entering Salisbury and their full impact on the life of the town cannot be measured from the register.

The register does, however, illustrate the nature of early-17th-century vagrancy. The most striking feature is the great distances which many of the 666 recorded vagrants had travelled before arriving in Salisbury. While a large proportion were returned to near-by Wiltshire parishes, many were sent to villages in the New Forest and to parishes dependent on the rural woollen industry of the Wiltshire–Somerset border. Several had wandered even further, arriving in Salisbury from Ireland, the West Country, or the North. Some 20 per cent of those sent away had travelled more than 100 miles to Salisbury as the crow flies, but the real distance was probably much greater since vagrants often followed well established itineraries and some of them had been wandering months or even years (nos. 139, 230, 319, 385). The high number of vagrants punished more than once shows how constables could little control that sort of mobility and even the Salisbury justices were reluctant to brand, rather than only to whip, such incorrigible offenders as a statute of 1604[1] prescribed (nos. 238, 268, 270).

In their habitual and extensive mobility the Salisbury vagrants fit the stereotypes made familiar by the rogue literature of the period,[2] but they conform less closely to contemporary models in other respects. They usually seem to have wandered singly or in pairs, not in large vagrant bands. They included men who practised the picturesque trades of fortune-telling or morris-dancing and others who learned the arts of forging passports or counterfeiting illness (e.g. nos. 142, 164, 262, 288, 295, 516), but they were a small minority. Most were probably victims of underemployment or over-population in the countryside, moving to towns in search of casual work and

---

[1] 1 Jas. I, c. 7, iii, *Statutes of the Realm*, iv. 1025.
[2] Some of the literature is printed in *The Elizabethan Underworld*, ed. A. V. Judges.

only later learning new ways of making a living. The respectable origins and the personal tragedies which possibly preceded their vagrancy are, however, rarely recorded (nos. 130, 289, 422). There is similarly little information about vagrants' ages, but it is striking that more than half those punished were unmarried men and another quarter were single women. They were perhaps young adults who, in the prevailing conditions of industrial depression, were competing for employment with natives of the town and who were likely to burden the parishes with poor children. It is not surprising therefore that, while ever ready to pass vagrants back to their parishes of origin, the justices found excuses not to accept those returned to Salisbury from elsewhere (nos. 71, 160, 188, 308, 462, 552).

The whipping and expulsion of vagabonds was not the only way in which the Salisbury authorities could prevent the problem of poverty being exacerbated by immigration. Some immigrants had to be accepted, as in all towns with high mortality rates, but sureties were often demanded from the friends or landlords of strangers to guard against their becoming a charge on the parish. Other newcomers, often tradesmen with wives and children, were simply ordered to leave the town. [1] The men and women named in the register were probably only those thought to deserve severe punishment because their behaviour, age, or status seemed a threat to social stability and public order. The runaway apprentice, the 'lewd' couple claiming to be married, and those 'not able to give an account of their lives' were the wanderers who attracted attention. For the Salisbury justices vagrancy was essentially a police matter.

'Native' Poor

Having thus tried to dispose of the immigrant poor, the Salisbury authorities could turn to what they saw as the essence of the problem of poverty, the relief of the native poor of the town. The poor relief statute of 1598 empowered the churchwardens and overseers of each parish to raise a poor-rate to provide funds for three carefully defined purposes: for paying masters who would take poor children as apprentices, for a dole to be paid weekly to the old, blind, or otherwise impotent, and for materials on which the unemployed could be set to work, usually in practice in a workhouse. [2] Under the supervision of the justices at monthly meetings the overseers of the three Salisbury parishes undertook all three tasks. In the early 17th century, however, as it became increasingly difficult to find masters to take on poor apprentices, as the number of the unemployed outgrew the facilities of the small workhouse, and as many in employment also came to require public alms to support their families, the burden on the poor-rate became unmanageable. [3] Outdoor household relief was gradually extended beyond the impotent, for whom it was originally intended, to the unemployed and underemployed.

The increasing cost led to the taking of surveys of the poor in 1625 and 1635 (documents II–IV) which showed clearly how poverty affected the

[1] e.g. see pp. 94, 98; S.C.A., S 162, ff. 1, 2; P/125, ff. 68v., 75.
[2] 39 Eliz. I, c. 3, *Statutes of the Realm*, iv. 896.
[3] See pp. 8–9.

able-bodied as well as the impotent inhabitants of the town. The first listing (document II), entered at the beginning of a volume of overseers' accounts for the period 1629–94, was ordered by the council on 18 March 1625 and completed by 4 April. [1] It was part of a new scheme to arrange employment in the town for those poor who could not be absorbed by the workhouse or by the ordinary mechanism of pauper apprenticeship. The survey was made possible by the subdivision of the town and parishes into 'chequers', the topographical divisions based on the regular street plan of Salisbury which were used for various administrative purposes from the early 17th century. [2] The poor were listed in three categories under the names of the chequers and of the aldermen and their assistants who were responsible for surveying them. Each section concluded with the names of the impotent poor requiring relief, half of whom were aged 70 or over, and of the poor apprentices, half of them under the age of 15; but the principal object in compiling the survey was to record those poor who could not be bound out as apprentices but who might be employed and trained for shorter periods by masters in the town. In their case the entries were tabulated in columns giving in turn the master's name, his occupation, the names of the poor employed by him, their ages, their work, the wages they earned, the amount of money allowed to them or their master out of the workhouse funds for their expenses, and in some cases the amount of work to be completed in a week. Two-thirds of those employed in this way were under 15 years old, like many of the poor apprentices, but some of them were adults who could not be classed as impotent. The census also listed married women who had to have employment arranged by the corporation and complete families requiring materials or masters to provide them with work. [3]

The surveys of 1635 recorded the names of the poor receiving relief in the town ten years later. The census of the poor in St. Edmund's and St. Thomas's parishes (document III) is contained in a small stitched file of ten paper membranes. [4] It has no heading and is not dated, but comparison with a list of householders receiving poor relief in April 1635 [5] shows that it is of similar date and that it lists all those then receiving the dole in the two parishes. The aim of the survey was clearly to gather information about the families and incomes of those householders. Although recording only those receiving relief, it may be a product of the injunction given to the aldermen and their assistants on 9 December 1635 to 'examine every house in their division, what persons are there, how many children, of what ages, and how

1 S.C.A., Ledger C, ff. 315v., 317v.
2 *Churchwarden's Accounts of S. Edmund and S. Thomas Sarum*, ed. H. J. F. Swayne, 194; S.C.A., S 162, f. 189v.; Ledger C, ff. 233v.–234v. Most of the chequers may be identified from the map in *Historic Towns*, ed. Mary D. Lobel, i, Salisbury. At least two of the chequers in St. Edmund's parish, possibly the later 'Three Cups' and 'Vanners', are not mentioned in this survey, but the coverage of the other two parishes appears complete.
3 See pp. 68, 70.
4 The MS. resembles an earlier census of the poor taken in Ipswich in 1597: *Poor Relief in Elizabethan Ipswich*, ed. J. Webb (Suff. Rec. Soc. ix), 121–40.
5 S.C.A., misc. papers, box 6, O 3.

they are employed to get their livings'. [1] The St. Edmund's parish listing, though not that of St. Thomas's, surveys the poor by chequer, ending with the names of the old men and women in the alms-houses in Bedwin Row. The survey of the poor in St. Martin's parish (document IV) is in a small paper book headed 'St. Martin's relief book' in a later hand. It appears to be of the same date since those named in it as receiving alms were also listed in the relief book of April 1635. The alms-people were described in less detail than in the survey of the other two parishes: wives, for example, seem to have been noted only when there were no children. The survey includes, however, the names of many not on relief. That they were also poor is suggested by the naming of many of them in a list of those receiving a charitable dole in the parish in the same year. [2] Since there are too few names in the manuscript to suggest that a complete census of the parish was attempted, it seems that only those considered poor were listed and that the sums given weekly to those of them on relief were later added to the finished document.

The three listings of 1635, which between them cover the whole town apart from the cathedral Close, show that the attempt to provide employment for the able-bodied poor in 1625 had failed to solve the problem and that many of them were by 1635 receiving household relief. A quarter of the alms-people recorded in St. Edmund's and St. Thomas's parishes were between the ages of 15 and 60, men and women who might have been expected to support themselves. Some were sick, crippled, or blind but others were simply 'miserable poor' or 'wanted work'. More significantly, the survey shows that poor relief was being used to supplement wages. In aggregate the poor in the two parishes were earning 75s. each week and receiving 71s. from the dole. Half the families on relief had earned income of some kind. As in Norwich in 1570 and Ipswich in 1597 the poor-rate was being used to support many more than the disabled, orphan children, and the unemployed. [3]

The three 1635 surveys make it possible to estimate the numbers of poor on relief in the town and their relationship to the total population. [4] A total of 315 people received parish relief in 1635, perhaps nearly five per cent of the population. That may have been a tolerable figure, but it was subject to fluctuations and there was no obvious dividing line between those on relief and other persons who might be considered poor. The unrelieved poor as well as the alms-people seem to have been listed for St. Martin's, the two groups together amounting to perhaps as much as a third of the parish population. The ways in which such additional numbers could become a burden on the poor-rate were described in trenchant if exaggerated terms in John Ivie's pamphlet and in the notes among the overseers' papers

[1] See p. 99.

[2] S.C.A., misc. papers, box 6, M 39.

[3] *Norwich Census of the Poor 1570*, ed. J. F. Pound (Norf. Rec. Soc. xl); *Poor Relief in Ipswich*, ed. Webb (Suff. Rec. Soc.), 121–40.

[4] Slack, 'Poverty and Politics', 173–7. In these calculations presumed wives have been added to the St. Martin's figures where the listing apparently omits them.

for 1635–6. [1] The Salisbury authorities were constantly subjected to appeals both from within the town and from outside for relief for special cases. They had to pay extraordinary sums to those who fell ill, as in Greencroft Street in 1635, and they were presented with new claims for support in the notes of overseers from particular chequers. Once the payment of relief was extended beyond the impotent there seemed no limit to the demand.

The numbers of poor were particularly likely to increase at times of crisis. Bad harvests in the middle 1590s, early 1620s, and later 1640s all raised the price of grain and therefore both the number needing help and the cost of their relief. [2] The most serious crises were caused by outbreaks of plague. An epidemic in 1604 removed perhaps a sixth of the total population of the town and left others impoverished. A further visitation in 1627 caused fewer deaths, perhaps some eight per cent of the population dying in the year, [3] but the strains it imposed on the administrative machinery of the town were as marked. A series of regulations had to be issued for the quarantining of houses, the burial of the dead, and the support of the sick and their families. [4] The social crisis caused by the plague was described by Ivie in his pamphlet. [5] In letters written to the recorder during the epidemic Ivie presented a more immediate picture of the situation, describing not only the disorder which followed the flight of the richer citizens but also the threat of starvation because of the disruption of local trade. He wrote, 'I do think upon my conscience here are in the city at the least two thousand sick of the famine and many of them begin to look as green and pale as death'. [6]

The 1627 epidemic was the climax to a decade of industrial depression in the town. The Cockayne project, European currency manipulations, the disruption of overseas markets caused by the Thirty Years War, and bad harvests at home successively hit the West Country cloth industry and by 1623 had brought unemployment to most centres of the old draperies. [7] By 1626, on the eve of the plague, accounts of the state of Salisbury could put the number of citizens requiring relief at no less than 2,700, probably more than a third of the population. [8] The slump in the textile industry explains why so much attention was paid to poor relief in the 1620s, not only in Salisbury, but also in many other clothing towns.

---

1 See pp. 100–4, 113–14.
2 Consequences of high food prices are referred to in S.C.A., Add. 40, doc. 8, 9; N 100, letter, 31 Dec. 1625; Ledger D, f. 39.
3 Slack, 'Poverty and Politics', 169–71.
4 S.C.A., N 101, plague orders, 1625–7.
5 See pp. 117–28.
6 Hants R.O., J. L. Jervoise, Herriard Coll. 44M69/S6/XXXVII. 29.
7 G. D. Ramsay, *Wilts. Woollen Industry in the Sixteenth and Seventeenth Centuries*, 71–81; B. E. Supple, *Commercial Crisis and Change in England 1600–42*, 53–8.
8 Hants R.O., J. L. Jervoise, Herriard Coll. 44M69/S6/XXXVIII. 61; S.C.A., N 100, letter, 31 Dec. 1625; N 101, letter, 16 Jan. 1626. The 1635 census of the poor in St. Martin's parish suggests that the estimates may not have been grossly exaggerated.

POOR RELIEF

In the first decade of the 17th century the mayor and council of Salisbury had at their disposal the instruments for poor relief sanctioned by Elizabethan legislation, a weekly poor-rate, a workhouse, and a system of poor apprenticeship. The administration of poor relief in the three parishes of the town was centralized after the statute of 1598. The overseers of the poor and churchwardens of each parish appeared before the justices of the peace at monthly meetings, where their accounts were examined and where funds from the richest parish, St. Thomas's, were transferred to the two poorer parishes. [1] The Close, however, remained a separate jurisdiction and the question of its contribution to municipal poor relief a source of dispute and confusion. By 1600 the poor-rate in the town brought in £187 a year, [2] which was redistributed in weekly payments to those poor who were accepted as meriting relief every Easter. In 1564 the council already planned to establish a house of correction in Winchester Street for the employment of the 'able poor' and in 1602 a workhouse with beds for a dozen inmates was set up in St. Thomas's churchyard, financed by rents from the London property given to the town by Joan Popley in 1571. [3] In the early years of the 17th century the parish overseers were in addition spending small sums binding out poor children as apprentices and the corporation could also draw on charitable bequests providing loans for poor tradesmen. [4] It was quickly apparent, however, that these facilities were inadequate. In the epidemic of 1604 the cost of poor relief was three times the income from the poor-rate, and even in normal years the number of able-bodied beggars in the town excited comment and was a bone of contention in the disputes between the bishop and the town which preceded and followed incorporation in 1612. [5]

From 1597, therefore, there was a series of municipal projects and committees for relieving and employing the poor which, although they achieved little in practice, revealed the scale of the problem. [6] One set of suggestions (document V) is entered in a small paper book, headed in a later hand 'Orders about Vagrants' but undated and unsigned. In this project the definition of the poor was extended beyond the conventionally impotent and the unemployed to include those engaged in occupations like spinning who did not earn enough to support their families. The author noted that the charitable loan funds which were intended, and might have been expected, to

---

1 S.C.A., S 161 records the earliest of these meetings.
2 Calculated from the accounts ibid.
3 R. Benson and H. Hatcher, *Old and New Sarum or Salisbury* (Hoare, *Modern Wilts.* iv), 283, 285; S.C.A., Ledger C, ff. 155v., 157v., 169v.; S 163 (reversed), accounts of the house of correction, 1602–12.
4 S.C.A., S 161, overseers' accounts; Slack, 'Poverty and Politics', 178–9.
5 Slack, op. cit. 169–70; S.C.A., N 101, letters on disputes with the bishop; misc. papers, papers about contributions by the lay inhabitants of the Close; Sar. Dean and Chapter Rec., press IV, letters on various subjects, 29 Dec. 1609.
6 e.g. S.C.A., Ledger C, ff. 155v., 157v., 169v., 274v., 275v.

help such poor tradesmen were being used for other purposes.[1] On 10 September 1613 the town council published a list of 'projects for the relief of the poor and avoiding of idleness' which in some respects followed the recommendations of the document.[2] The new regulations included the appointment of two beadles in every chequer to apprehend beggars and to set the poor to work, an order that those receiving any of the charitable loan stocks should employ the poor, and the nomination of Richard Sponder, one of the junior councillors, as 'surveyor for good government' to supervise the enforcement of the orders. Sponder may therefore have been the author of the undated project, which probably formed part of discussions on regulating the poor after the incorporation of the town and the reorganization of craft companies in 1612.[3] The discussions had little practical effect, however, and the problem worsened after 1613. Expenditure on the poor from the poor-rate, which had declined immediately following the years of high prices in the 1590s, had risen again to £170 by 1620.

The New Scheme

In the 1620s the problem of poverty was attacked in an original way by a determined group of Puritan councillors led by John Ivie and Matthew Bee and by Henry Sherfield, the recorder elected in 1623. They were inspired by a wish to discipline the poor and to eradicate the sin of idleness in order to achieve 'a true and real reformation of the city',[4] and the religious aspirations of the group are revealed in some of the orders for the poor as well as in the language of Ivie's pamphlet.[5] Not all their ambitions were put into effect. Ivie, for example, had plans to make the Avon navigable to Salisbury and hoped to obtain parliamentary support for a tax on all smokers of tobacco to pay for this and similar schemes.[6] The three innovations which were achieved, however, radically reshaped poor relief in Salisbury for twenty years. They required the co-operation or overriding of important private interests in the town and caused deep political divisions in the governing class.[7]

New machinery for poor relief was developed between 1623 and 1628 based on three institutions, a remodelled workhouse, a municipally owned brewhouse, and a storehouse. The orders for the poor of 1623 (document VI), taken from the council minutes of 6 June, reformed and enlarged the workhouse in St. Thomas's churchyard as a place where the poor could be taught a trade. Bee was appointed one of the governors and Ivie master of the works. The municipal brewery was set up in Milford Street.[8] Its profits, managed

---

1 See pp. 85, 132; cf. C 93/1/15.

2 S.C.A., Ledger C, ff. 233v.–234v.

3 In Mar. 1613 the justices were instructed by the council to consider new methods for relieving the poor: ibid. f. 231.

4 Hants R.O., J. L. Jervoise, Herriard Coll. 44M69/S6/XXXVIII. 54.

5 See pp. 88, 109, 123.

6 Hants R.O., J. L. Jervoise, Herriard Coll. 44M69/S6/XXXVII. 23.

7 Slack, 'Poverty and Politics', 183–9.

8 Tenements were leased from the dean and chapter and from Lawrence Horne, a councillor: S.C.A., S 179, ff. 5, 7.

initially by the workhouse authorities, were intended to set the poor to work wherever possible, not in the workhouse itself, but under masters in the town. In March 1625 clothiers, spinners, and knitters were asked to say how many poor children they were willing to employ, 6*d.* a week was to be paid by the town for their upkeep, and funds were made available to buy tools for them. [1] The 1625 listing of the poor shows that 100 children were provided with masters in that way.

By 1626 arrangements for the employment of poor children had thus been added to those for the workhouse and brewhouse and the details of the scheme were presented in a small paper book endorsed 'Orders touchinge the Poore' (document VII). The orders are the clearest surviving record of the idealism and administrative thoroughness which marked the new experiments, but their precise origin is obscure. There is no evidence that they were drawn up by the town council. They were more likely drafted by a smaller group, perhaps by the city's bench of justices, although no records of the quarter sessions survive to verify that. They were approved in their final form, however, at one of the monthly meetings of the justices, churchwardens, and overseers and signed by most of the aldermen and assistant councillors in order of seniority and by the churchwardens and overseers of the three parishes. On 5 October 1626 the council ordered their publication in the parish churches. [2]

In founding a brewery to pay for the employment of the poor the Salisbury corporation copied the action of the rulers of Dorchester in 1622. [3] Its initial cost was £1,500, a third of which was raised from gifts from councillors, companies, and other benefactors; the rest was borrowed at interest and an additional poor-rate levied towards its repayment. [4] Alehouse-keepers and innkeepers were urged to patronize it and, in order to protect it against the opposition of private brewers, attempts were made to have the establishment confirmed by Act of Parliament. Although a bill to encourage the erection of common brewhouses, to be called 'houses of the poor', failed to pass the House of Commons in 1626, the Salisbury brewhouse remained. [5]

The third institution, the storehouse, was Ivie's personal contribution. It was first set up as a means of provisioning the poor when normal trading was disrupted during the 1627 epidemic, but was continued afterwards. The initial costs were met by £100 collected throughout Wiltshire in 1627 towards the relief of the infected poor in Salisbury. [6] It was intended to provide victuals for the poor at cost price and also, since in future parish relief was to be given in the form of special tokens rather than in cash, to prevent them spending their dole entirely on drink. The dual motivation of so many

---

[1] S.C.A., Ledger C, ff. 312v., 313v., 315.

[2] Ibid. f. 330v.

[3] *Municipal Records of the Borough of Dorchester*, ed. C. H. Mayo, 525–9.

[4] S.C.A., tin box 4, file 'Various 1600–30', doc. 65A; tin box 4, doc. 40; S 179, ff. 30, 47, 58; tin box 9, doc. 1.

[5] Ibid. Ledger C, f. 314v., 323v.; Hants R.O., J. L. Jervoise, Herriard Coll. 44M69/S6/ XXI. 4.

[6] See p. 118; S.C.A., Y 216, storehouse accounts, 1628–9.

features of poor relief in Salisbury, the moral discipline of the poor and their effective relief, is as evident in this institution as in the earlier orders of 1626. Ivie described his ambitions in a letter to Sherfield in July 1628:

'There should be provided a storehouse. . . stored with wholesome provision for the poor as this year they have had it, which is, as I will prove, £100 saved in £300. And we would make certain tokens with the city arms in them. The tokens should be from a farthing to sixpence, and this money should be current nowhere but at the storehouse where they should have such diet as is fit for them, both for victual of bread, butter, cheese, fish, candles, faggots, and coals, and some butchers appointed to take their money for flesh if need be. And the old course of collecting the monies should stand as before only they [the collectors] should bring it to the mayor and take so much in [tokens] to pay the poor . . . So if they will needs be drunk they should either work for the money or steal it. In my opinion if this way take effect we shall avoid drunkenness and beggary.'

Like the rest of the poor relief scheme, this was intended to bring 'glory to God and profit to the city'. [1]

The way in which the new institutions worked is illustrated by the extracts from the records of the overseers and of the workhouse (documents VIII–X). The overseers' accounts of July–December 1635 (document VIII) are extracted from a large paper volume containing a record of business conducted at the monthly meetings of overseers and churchwardens before the justices between 1629 and 1694. The money collected from the poor-rate was paid directly to the storehouse and so not entered in the overseers' accounts presented at those meetings; but money for extraordinary needs, in cases of sudden sickness for example, was still given by the overseers to the poor themselves. That was taken from extraordinary revenues, from the collection boxes at the city's inns and churches, provided for in the orders of 1626, or from fines for tippling and swearing. The accounts show that the extraordinary expenditure grew to exceed income, a development which in the end vitiated the hope that the storehouse would lead to a reduction in the amounts spent on the poor. The extraordinary needs of the poor which made such cash payments essential are revealed in the overseers' papers for the same period (document IX). They are gathered together in the only surviving file recording extraordinary disbursements and other information presented to the mayor and justices at the monthly meetings, as provided for in the orders of 1626. Some of the documents add information about sums of money and individuals referred to in the overseers' accounts or in the surveys of the poor. Parts of the file were too badly damaged to be printed, but the remainder illustrate the day-to-day supervision on which the administration of poor relief depended.

The workhouse accounts for 1627–30 (document X) are taken from an unfoliated volume covering the period 1612–40. They record the continuing employment of the poor in the workhouse itself and also that of poor children in the town at a weekly cost of 6d. each. The expenses of the work-house continued to be met from the rents of Popley's tenements in London [2]

---

1 Hants R.O., J. L. Jervoise, Herriard Coll. 44M69/S6/XXXVIII. 20.

2 See p. 8.

and the cost of employing the children was partly met from the same source. It should also have been financed by a weekly payment of £1 from the brewhouse,[1] but exactly how those contributions were spent is not clear from the accounts. It is clear, however, that the organization of employment in the town by the workhouse authorities and the token system managed by the storehouse were the twin pillars of the new scheme of poor relief in Salisbury.

Failure of the Scheme

In spite of the enormous investment in the new institutions, however, profits did not materialize. The brewhouse, intended to fund much of the scheme, never succeeded in freeing itself from debts contracted when it was set up, which still amounted to almost £1,000 in 1627. Private brewers organized such a successful boycott of their municipal competitor that Henry Russell, a brewer from Andover, had to be brought in to run the new brewhouse and only half the innkeepers and alehouse-keepers of the town are recorded among its customers.[2] Even so, a considerable amount of beer was brewed there. On average it consumed 900 quarters of malt a year and produced more than 200 barrels of beer a week in the mid 1630s. It had over 800 customers, the most regular of them including Bee, Ivie, and Sherfield, but because the accounts, though voluminous, were never drawn up in a final form it is difficult to be precise about its financial affairs. The accounts suggest that in 1635, for example, there ought to have been a gross profit of £500, but the giving of extended credit to customers, perhaps the only means of attracting them away from private brewers, meant that such profits were rarely realized. The brewhouse succeeded in paying £1 a week to the workhouse or to the parishes for the employment of poor children and 12s. a week to the alms-houses at Winchester Gate, but no more.[3] By 1642 the debts were so great that brewing had stopped, and the brewery was wound up in 1646 when £450 was still owed to creditors.[4]

The machinery for the employment and training of children was similarly bedevilled by lack of co-operation from private interests. Except for the years when Ivie was mayor,[5] there is little evidence after the initial arrangements of 1625 that employers could be found who were willing to set poor children to work. The trend was rather back towards using the workhouse as a self-contained centre of employment. By December 1625 the corporation had already made an agreement with Philip Veryn, one of the masters named in the 1625 survey, for the instruction of children in dressing and spinning hemp inside the workhouse. The eight poor children and two adults he had agreed

[1] S.C.A., Ledger C, f. 312.
[2] Hants R.O., J. L. Jervoise, Herriard Coll. 44M69/S6/XXXVIII. 5; S.C.A., S 179, f. 61; N 101, list of innkeepers; S 181/1.
[3] This account of the brewhouse is based on its surviving stock books, debtors books, brewing and tunning accounts, and minutes in S.C.A., vols. S 180/1-3, 181/1-2, 182, 165, 179.
[4] Ibid. Ledger C, f. 413v.; D, ff. 10v., 17, 19-23.
[5] See pp. 107-8.

to employ earlier in the year may have moved in with him. [1] By November 1632 only five people were supported in the workhouse and only two masters outside it were being paid for employing children. [2] By then the workhouse had clearly reverted to its pre-1623 condition, and the ambitious attempt to provide large-scale employment had failed and was not revived. When the workhouse was again remodelled in 1638 room was provided in the new house in Crane Street for 30 poor children to be permanently housed there until they could be bound out as apprentices. The councillors contributed £110 of their own money towards the initial costs of the new house and charitable endowments, like the rents from Popley's lands, were drawn on for running expenses. In 1642 there were 20 children in the workhouse, and although the building itself had apparently fallen into decay by the end of the decade, it was restored and the 1638 orders were confirmed in 1657 [3] This, however, was a conventional workhouse like those in other towns and like that proposed by conservative interests in the 1620s as an alternative to the plans of Ivie and his colleagues. [4]

The most original part of the new experiment, the storehouse and token system, had also collapsed by 1640. The storehouse regularly provided enough bread and beer to support sixty or seventy people, [5] but the system was too inflexible. As Ivie stresses, its finances depended on restricting relief to those accepted at Easter each year. Even without the favouritism or corruption of the overseers, however, there were bound to be frequent new claims for alms which pushed up their extraordinary expenditure beyond the level of their income from the collection boxes at inns and churches. [6] There were also rapid fluctuations in the number of those supported by the token system which it could not easily cope with. In 1628, the first full year of the storehouse, the cost of the relief it provided amounted to £308, largely because of the destitution left by the 1627 epidemic. By 1630 it had been reduced to £187, only slightly higher than expenditure on outdoor relief in the years before 1627, but at the same time extraordinary payments increased. After 1632 normal expenditure rose again to reach £295 in 1636 and in the same year extraordinary disbursements reached a peak of £68, but the weekly poor-rate raised an annual income of at most £220. [7] To make up deficits of this kind unpopular additional rates had to be levied, or the assessment of the rate itself revised, as it was in 1631 and on two occasions in 1636. [8] Since the storehouse failed to reduce the cost of poor relief and made administration

---

[1] S.C.A., N 100, agreement, 11 Dec. 1625; and see below, pp. 65–7, 69, 72, 74.
[2] S.C.A., S 178/1, 26 Nov. 1632.
[3] Ibid. S 154, workhouse ordinances, 1639; S 157, New Workhouse Bk., 1638–77, ff. 3–24 and *passim*; Ledger C, ff. 400, 401v., 402v.; Ledger D, ff. 43v., 67v., 108.
[4] Hants R.O., J. L. Jervoise, Herriard Coll. 44M69/S6/XXXVII. 9; Slack, 'Poverty and Politics', 188.
[5] Slack, op.cit. 189.
[6] See pp. 6–7.
[7] These figures have been calculated from the storehouse accounts in S.C.A., Y 216 and N 98, and the overseers' accounts in S 162. They differ slightly from Ivie's: see below, pp. 128–9.
[8] S.C.A., S 162, Aug. 1631; Feb., Oct. 1636.

more complicated it was abolished in July 1640 and the cash in hand given to the new workhouse. [1]

After 1640, therefore, outdoor and household relief was administered as it had been before 1627, with expenditure hovering around £200 a year. When the figure rose slightly in 1648 and again to £295 in 1658 Ivie was recalled to revive the storehouse in attempts to reduce costs, [2]   but neither revival lasted long or succeeded. The token system again proved too rigid to be adaptable to short-term fluctuations in poverty in the town, and Ivie himself could balance the books in 1659 only by reducing allowances to the poor at the end of the financial year. [3]

As in the 1620s lack of co-operation from the overseers and political opposition from within the council were also important obstacles, although the exact course of the disputes which divided the governing class of Salisbury in 1659–61 is unclear. The controversy came to a head in the city sessions of 1659 when the overseers, led by John Harrison and supported by some of the councillors, were imprisoned for refusing to work the storehouse and token system. They then brought a suit against the mayor and justices alleging assault and false imprisonment, first in the bishop's court for civil pleas and later in the Court of Common Pleas, the latter case being heard at the Salisbury assizes in July 1661 under a writ of *nisi prius*. Although no record of the final judgment has been discovered, it seems clear that the jury found for the overseers. [4]

The controversy of 1659–61 inspired the pamphlet by John Ivie, *A Declaration*, published in London in 1661, which is reprinted below as an Appendix. [5] Ivie, mayor of Salisbury in 1627 and 1648, was the leading proponent of new schemes for poor relief from his election as chamberlain in 1620 until his death in 1666. His pamphlet, written in old age [6] when he saw his hopes for reform largely destroyed, provides a vivid commentary on the methods of poor relief recorded in the other documents. It describes the way in which the storehouse and the token system functioned and the ambitions behind them, neither of which is clear from the confused storehouse accounts which survive; [7] but its character as a political tract is more significant. Written by the most committed supporter of poor-law reform, it records the political obstacles to innovations, the idealism which nevertheless made them possible, and some of the reasons for their failure. With its breathless style and its unqualified moral judgements, it adds depth to the drier official records and provides a unique insight into urban government in the 17th century.

---

[1] S.C.A., Ledger C, f. 419.
[2] Ibid. Ledger D, ff. 42v., 107v., 108.
[3] Ibid. S 162, account, 1659–60.
[4] See below, pp. 110, 115–16, 133. There are references to the case in Asz. 24/35, 29 July 1661; C.P. 40/2741 rot. 1306d.; S.C.A., N 98, 9 Nov. 1659.
[5] The only copy known to survive is in the library of the Wiltshire Archaeological and Natural History Society, Devizes. It was reprinted by the Salisbury Field Club in 1900.
[6] Ivie was married in 1612: Sar. Dioc. R.O., St. Edmund's par. reg. 23 Feb. 1612.
[7] S.C.A., Y 216, storehouse accounts, 1628–39.

The rigidity of urban administration and the irreconcilable conflict between municipal, parochial, and private business interests in Salisbury seriously impeded the new institutions. Even their initial contribution to the relief of the poor in the 1620s and 1630s was limited. The occupations in which children were trained under the new employment arrangements, such as spinning and bonelace-making, were those most vulnerable to economic depression and therefore unlikely to rescue them from poverty. The immediate effects of the experiments on the living standards of the poor are less easy to determine. The total amount spent on the poor in the 1630s was double what it had been in the first decade of the century, although prices had risen by perhaps no more than 25 per cent. [1] On the other hand, although it is not clear how many were being supported by the town before 1635, it is probable that the numbers of the poor had increased since 1610 and that the rising expenditure on poor relief did no more and possibly less than keep pace. The average weekly income per head, including earnings, of those receiving relief in St. Edmund's and St. Thomas's parishes in 1635 was only 7½d., barely enough for subsistence at a time when the wages of labourers and apprentices in the town were set at 10d. a day. [2] The experiments of the 1620s arose less from increased generosity on the part of the Salisbury authorities than from the unprecedented size of the problem.

There can be no doubt, however, about the effort with which the Salisbury councillors met the challenge after 1620 and before 1640. It is the aspiration rather than the final achievement which commands respect. Charitable benefactions, the pockets of councillors, and local industries were all exploited, if only temporarily, in an attempt to reduce the number of native poor and thus to reform society in the town. But the achievement was inevitably limited by the two overriding aims of the magistrates, to discipline the poor and to reduce the cost of their relief. Both implied a return to old methods when expensive experiments failed; and neither was practicable, granted the extent and complexity of the problem of poverty in the town.

EDITORIAL METHOD

The aim in editing the various documents has been to produce modernized and readily intelligible transcripts. Spelling, punctuation, capitalization, and figures have therefore been modernized and abbreviations extended. Surnames have been left in the original form but forenames have been modernized where possible. The original spelling of place-names has been retained except that the Latin forms for Winchester, Exeter, Shaftesbury, Oxford, and Salisbury have been translated. Where possible the places have been identified in the index. Dates have been altered to accord with the modern

---

[1] E. H. Phelps Brown and S. V. Hopkins, 'Seven Centuries of the Prices of Consumables compared with Builders' Wage-Rates', *Essays in Economic History*, ed. Eleanora M. Carus-Wilson, ii. 195.

[2] Slack, 'Poverty and Politics', 175.

reckoning of the beginning of the year. Marginations have been printed in italic. Editorial interpolations are enclosed in square brackets, description and comment being additionally in italic. Folio numbers are enclosed in rounded brackets where present in the original, in square brackets where the original is unfoliated.

The documents have been transcribed in full, with one major and some minor exceptions. The heading to the register of vagrants' passports and the first entry have been given in full, but the remaining entries have been summarized since they follow a regular pattern. Individual details, such as the description of the vagrant, have, of course, always been noted. The dates which form the subheadings are those when the passports which follow them were issued. The name of the county has been added, in square brackets where necessary, except for places in Wiltshire, some large towns, and places near London. The passports have been numbered.

The arrangement of the surveys of the poor and overseers' and workhouse accounts has been slightly altered to save space. The parts of the 1625 survey given in tabular form in the original have been rearranged into paragraphs under the heading '*Masters and workfolk*'. Each begins with the name of the master followed by the names of the workers, their ages, enclosed in round brackets, and the details of their work. In the 1635 survey of St. Edmund's and St. Thomas's parishes the tabular form of the original has been retained except that the 'employment' and 'ability' columns have been combined. The lists of names in the 1635 survey of St. Martin's and the entries in the overseers' and workhouse accounts have been arranged in paragraphs. The orders for the poor of 1623 and 1626 and the overseers' accounts, overseers' papers, and workhouse accounts have all been slightly abbreviated by the omission of such recurrent words as 'item' and 'paid' where they are super-fluous. Documents on the file of overseers' papers which were illegible or badly torn have been omitted, and the remainder numbered consecutively. The punctuation of Ivie's *Declaration* has required extensive revision. The use of italics for added emphasis, sometimes in complete paragraphs, has not been reproduced. The punctuation in passages of direct speech, inconsist-ently punctuated in the original, has been revised. Apart from punctuation and spelling, however, the text is as printed in 1661 and additions necessary to make grammatical sense or elucidate the text are enclosed in square brackets.

THE POOR

I REGISTER OF PASSPORTS FOR VAGRANTS 1598–1669

[f. 12] 20 April 1598
Directions taken and put in execution on the day and year above written as touching certain articles made in the last parliament concerning vagrant and wandering idle persons and their punishment and passport to the places where they were born, according to the statute made in the last parliament A.D. 1597–8, [1] *tempore* Ephraim Uvedall, *maior civitatis Nove Sarum.*

20 April 1598
1. A passport is made unto Margery Lane, the daughter of William Lane of Humington in the county of Wilts., who was taken within this city as a vagrant person and hath had and received punishment of whipping according to the statute made in the last parliament in that behalf, by which passport she is appointed to go and travel to Homington aforesaid where she was born, there to be employed in work or otherwise as in the same statute is provided, and two days is assigned for her passage &c.
2. Elizabeth Synderburye, daughter of Richard Synderburye, late of Strowdewater, Glos., taken as a vagrant and idle person and a rogue, was punished. Passport to Strowdewater where she was born; 6 days assigned.
3. [f. 12v.] John Hall, a vagrant and idle person, a rogue and sturdy beggar, was punished. Passport to Corcke in Ireland where he was born; 20 days assigned.
4. Walter Woodall, a vagrant and idle person, a rogue and sturdy beggar, was punished. Passport to Warwicke where he last dwelt for one whole year; 20 days assigned.

21 April 1598
5. James Stoakes, a vagrant and idle person and a beggar, was punished. Passport to Brokenhurste, Hants, where he was born; 3 days assigned.
6. John Langton and Elizabeth Langton, vagrant and idle persons and beggars. Passport to Byrtford where they were born; 1 day assigned.
7. Sarah Poore, a child of 3 years of age not having remained in this city for one year. Passport to Deverell Longbridge where she was born; 3 days assigned.
8. John Wilkins, an idle and vagrant person and sturdy beggar, was punished. Passport to Lye in Westburye parish, where he was born; 3 days assigned.
9. [f. 13] Joan Bull, widow, an idle person, wandering as a rogue and sturdy beggar with Katherine her child, was punished. Passport to Mylford where Joan last dwelt and where Katherine was born; 1 day assigned. *The said Joan Bull has a passport to go to Brixton Deverell where she was born and*

---

[1] 39 Eliz. I, c. 4, *Statutes of the Realm,* iv. 899–902.

her child under 7 years is sent with her, by the Lord Chief Justice's order; 4 days for her passage. [1]

22 April 1598

10. John Knighte and Welthye his wife, idle wandering and vagrant persons, not resident in this city for one year, were punished. Passport to Wilton where they were born and lived for more than three years past; 2 days assigned.

11. Hugh Pritchett and Morgan Ryce, idle wandering vagrant persons and rogues, were punished. Passport to Whitchurche, Herefs., where they last dwelt; 12 days assigned.

12. John Hill, an idle wandering vagrant person and a rogue, was punished. Passport to Elme, Som., where he was born; 6 days assigned.

24 February [*recte* April] 1598

13. Joan Carde, daughter of Thomas Carde, deceased, an idle wandering vagrant person and a rogue, was punished. Passport to Mownckton Deverell where she was born; 3 days allowed. [Cf. no. 221]

[f. 13v.] 25 April 1598

14. Nicholas Hyllis, an idle wandering vagrant person and a sturdy beggar, was punished. Passport to Steple Langford where he was born; 2 days assigned.

15. Edward Goodricke, an idle wandering vagrant person and a sturdy beggar, was punished. Passport to Malmesburye where he was born; 5 days assigned.

16. Elizabeth Goodricke, an idle wandering person and a sturdy beggar, was punished. Passport to Houms Padymore, Yorks., where she was born; 40 days assigned.

26 April 1598

17. Edmund Vye, an idle wandering person and a rogue, was punished. Passport to Colyton, Devon, where he was born; 10 days assigned.

18. John Tyncker, an idle wandering vagrant person and a rogue, was punished. Passport to Sutton where he was born; 4 days assigned.

[f. 14] 27 April 1598

19. Thomas Lugge, son of George Lugge, an idle wandering person, was punished. Anne Lugge, his mother, is appointed by passport to carry and guide him to Argesson, Berks., where he was born; 6 days assigned.

20. Aplyn Pryor has not been resident in this city for the last 3 years but has lived in West Wellowe for 7 years. Passport to West Wellowe; 2 days assigned.

21. Dorothy Batter and Agnes Batter, vagrant wandering idle persons and rogues, were punished. Passport to Sutton Manfeilde where they were born; 2 days assigned.

---

[1] Cases like this in which the settlement of a vagrant was disputed or unclear were sometimes referred to judges on assize: cf. *Som. Assize Orders 1629–40*, ed. T. G. Barnes (Som. Rec. Soc. lxv), 7, 42, 43.

22. Margaret Juges, a vagrant wandering idle person and a rogue and sturdy beggar, was punished. Passport to Wylton where she was born; 1 day assigned.

[f. 14v.] 1 May 1598
23. Mary Hooper, an idle vagrant person and a rogue, was punished. Passport to Babcarye, Som., where she was born; 4 days assigned.
24. Sarah Bayley, an idle vagrant person and a rogue, was punished. Passport to Wynforde, Som., where she was born; 8 days assigned.

28 April 1598
25. Margaret Edwardes, an idle person, was punished. Since it appears that she was not born within this city and she confesses that she was resident in Bath for 3 years past, she has a passport to Bath [Som.]; 6 days assigned. [Cf nos. 63, 92]

29 April 1598
26. John Willyams, an idle vagrant wandering person and rogue, was punished. Passport to Downton where he was born; 1 day allowed. *By order of the sessions in Salisbury, 28 Apr. 1598.*
27. Ralph Jervis, *alias* Jackson, an idle wandering vagrant person and rogue, was punished. Passport to Fordingebridge, Hants, where he was born; 2 days assigned. *By order of the sessions as above.*
28. [f. 15] Joan Jervis, an idle wandering rogue, was punished. Passport to Fordinbridge, Hants, where she was born; 2 days assigned. *By order of the sessions as before.*
29. William Coxe, an idle wandering rogue and sturdy beggar, was punished. Passport to Godishill in Fordingbridge, Hants, where he was born; 2 days assigned. *By order of the sessions as before.* [Cf. no. 32]
30. Magdalen Lewes with her child, *Purnell*, aged 4 years, helping Margaret Evans, a sick woman, from King's Somborne, Hants, to this city. Passport to Romesey, Hants, where she was born; 2 days assigned.
31. Elizabeth Forde, an idle wandering person, a rogue and sturdy beggar, was punished. Passport to Kcynton, Devon, where she was born; 12 days assigned.

2 May 1598
32. William Coxe, a rogue and idle person, was punished. Passport to Godshill in Fordingbridge, Hants, where he was born; 2 days assigned. [Cf. no. 29]
33. John Pytman, an idle vagrant rogue, was punished. Passport to Rushon, Dors., where he was born; 3 days assigned.
34. Charles Reynolds, a rogue, was punished. Passport to Devizes where he was born; 3 days assigned. *By order of the sessions.* [Cf. no. 170]
35. [f. 15v.] Christopher Forde, a wandering child, is given a passport to Grymsted where he was born as we are informed by his mother; 1 day for his passage.

3 May 1598

36. John Browne, an idle person, a vagrant and rogue, was punished. Passport to Barcklye Horne, Glos.; 8 days appointed.

37. John Pepper, an idle person and a rogue, was punished. Passport to Chesselborne, Dors.; 4 days assigned.

38. Piers Phillippes, an idle person and a rogue or vagrant, was punished. Passport to Sutton Mannfeilde where he was born; 2 days appointed.

39. Margery Aysheton, an idle person and a rogue or vagrant, was punished. Passport to Devizes Green where she was born; 3 days appointed.

40. Joan Skynner, an idle vagrant and wandering person, was punished. Passport to East Grymsteed where she was born; 2 days assigned.

6 May 1598

41. Alice Erney *alias* Erlie, an idle person and a vagrant, was punished. Passport to Pytton where she was born; 1 day assigned.

[f. 16] 3 May 1598

42. John Holman, a vagrant and idle person, was punished. Passport to Alford near Castell Carye, Som.; 3 days appointed.

43. Margaret Brooke, an idle person, was punished. Passport to Armitage, Dors.; 4 days assigned.

44. Joan Collyns, a vagrant and idle person begging, was punished. Passport to Wynecaunton, Dors. [*recte* Som.], where she was born; 3 days assigned.

45. Edith Lansdall (*Lansdon*), a vagrant idle begging person, was punished. Passport to Nether Woodford where she was born; 1 day assigned.

46. Ellen Jefferye, a vagrant idle begging person, was punished. Passport to Ebbesborne where she was born; 2 days assigned.

47. James Lewes, a vagrant begging idle person, was punished. Passport to Over Stowye, Som., where he was born; 5 days assigned. *Mr. Thomas Eyer has undertaken that he shall not charge this city.*

48. Joan Primerose, a vagrant begging idle person, was punished. Passport to Wargrove, Berks., where she was born; 15 days assigned.

49. [f. 16v.] Joan Hewlett, a vagrant begging idle person, was punished. Passport to Wolver, Som., where she was born; 5 days assigned.

50. Thomas Preston, a begging vagrant, was punished. Passport to Wanborowe where he was born; 4 days assigned.

51. Katherine Beassante, wandering and begging, was punished. Passport to Mylford where she was born; 2 days assigned.

52. Joan Bakehowse, wandering and begging, was punished. Passport to Bulford where she was born; 2 days assigned.

53. Anne Whyte, wandering and begging, was punished. Passport to Sopley, Hants, where she was born.

54. Katherine Smythe *alias* Hodges, wandering and begging, was punished. Passport to Hanginge Langford where she was born; 3 days assigned.

4 May 1598

55. Alice Sylvester, wandering and begging, was punished. Passport to Readinge, Berks., where she was born; 15 days assigned.

56. Richard Purdewe, wandering and begging, was punished. Passport to Houghton, Hants, where he was born; 4 days assigned.

57. [f. 17] Philip Mamfeilde, wandering and begging, was punished. Passport to Gussage All Saints, Dors., where he was born.

58. Thomas Lyner, wandering and begging, was punished. Passport to Queene Hyve, Midx., where he was born; 6 days for his passage.

59. Phyllis Cooke, wandering and begging, was spared punishment because of impotence. Passport to Fovante; 3 days assigned.

60. William Harford, wandering and begging, was spared punishment because of his sickness. Passport to Bishopston; 2 days assigned. By order of the Lord Chief Justice he has taken with him his wife and one child under the age of 7 years.

5 May 1598
61. William Adlington, an idle wandering person and a rogue, was punished. Passport to Longe Southwark in St. Mary Overies parish, Surr.; 5 days assigned.

6 May 1598
62. Elizabeth Browne, an idle wandering person and a rogue, was punished. Passport to Harlington, Beds., where she was born; 20 days assigned.

63. Margaret Edwardes, an idle wandering person and vagrant, cannot declare where she was born but says that she dwelt at Havant, Hants, for two years with William Edwardes her uncle. Passport to Havant; 4 days assigned. [Cf. nos. 25, 92]

64. [f. 17v.] Morgan Jeanes, a vagrant wandering person and a rogue, was punished. Passport to Durryson, Dors., where he was born; 2 days assigned.

65. Juliana Purchis, wandering and vagrant, was punished. Passport to Burchalke where she was born; 2 days assigned.

66. Sibyl Newman, wandering and begging, was punished. Passport to Brodechalke where she was born; 2 days assigned.

67. Joan Shereman, wandering and begging, was punished. Passport to Fornissfell, Lancs., where she was born; 50 days assigned.

11 May 1598
68. Joan Ellyott, wandering and begging, was punished. Passport to Allhallows parish, Oxford, where she was born; 10 days assigned.

16 May 1598
69. Anne Hollowaye, begging, was punished. Passport to Fisherton Anger where she was born; this present day assigned for her passage.

26 May 1598
70. Nicholas Smythe, an idle person wandering and begging, was punished. Passport to Durington where he was born; 3 days assigned. By order of the Lord Chief Justice he has taken with him his wife and one child under the age of 7 years.

[f. 18] 26 July 1598
71. Robert Nelson was sent to this city from Hackney parish, Midx., with a passport made by the curate and constable there alleging that he was born

in this city, but no mention is made in it that he was a rogue, vagrant, or begging or that he was punished according to the statute. Therefore Mr. Mayor and Mr. Bower, by a passport under their hands and seals, sent him back to Hackney again, since he dwelt there for 8 years past; 10 days assigned.

21 August 1598
72. George Davis, an idle vagrant person, was punished. Passport to Wyne Cawnton, Som., where he was born; 3 days assigned.

4 October 1598
73. William Noble, an idle vagrant person and a minstrel, was punished. Passport to St. Sidwell's without Eastgate in the suburbs of Exeter, Devon, where he was born; 4 days for his passage.
74. Mary Ramson, an idle vagrant person, was punished. Passport to Corselye where she was born; 2 days assigned. [Cf. no. 90]
75. Grace Cutberd and Joan Bassett, idle and vagrant persons, were punished. Passport to Winchester, Hants, where she [sic] was born; 2 days for their passage. [Cf. no. 91]

 October 1598
76. Margaret Vaughan, wife of Griffin Vaughan of Bristol, was found idle and vagrant and punished. Passport to St. James's parish, Bristol, where she says her husband lives; 4 days appointed.

[f. 18v.] 24 November 1598
77. Grace Martyn, wandering and begging, was punished. Passport to Lawnsowe, Cornw., where she says she was born; 1 month allowed. By order of the Lord Chief Justice she has taken her 3 children, William, Agnes, and Jane Martyn, being under the age of 7 years, with her. [Cf. no. 78]
78. John Martyn, *son of Grace aforesaid and of the age of 14 years*, was taken begging and punished. Passport to Meare, Som., where he says he was born; 10 days allowed. [Cf. no. 77]

25 November 1598
79. Elizabeth Eagebrowe, wandering and begging, was punished. Passport to Bewdlye, Worcs., where she says she was born; 10 days allowed.

29 November 1598
80. Joan Pytford, wandering and vagrant, was punished. Passport to Kinsburye, Som., where she was born.
81.   Agnes Shaller, wife of John Shaller, was found as a vagrant person and punished.   Passport to Hartelerewe, Hants, where she feels sure she will be received and entertained by her friends and kinsmen dwelling there.

4 December 1598
82. William Jone (*Jones*), who termed himself a petty chapman, and Anne his alleged wife, were found as wandering idle persons and punished. Passport to Southewerke, Surr., where they say their dwelling is; 6 days allowed.

[f. 19] 11 December 1598
83. George Kytchen and Timothy Kytchen his son, wandering idle and

vagrant persons, were punished. Passport to Christechurche, [Hants], where they say their dwelling is; 3 days allowed.

10 January 1599
84. John Chrowche and Elizabeth his wife, idle wandering persons, were punished. Passport to Fordington, Dors., where their dwelling is; 3 days allowed. [Cf. no. 87]
85. John Williams and Mary his wife, idle wandering persons, were punished. Passport to Marston, Som., where John says he was born and lives; 4 days allowed.

11 January 1599
86. Thomas Coward, an idle vagrant person, was punished. Passport to Mylton, Hants, where he says he was born and lives; 4 days allowed.

26 January 1599
87. John Heyward *alias* Chrowche *alias* Hancock, an idle vagrant person [and Elizabeth his wife *deleted*] was punished. Passport to Fordington, Dors., where his dwelling is. [Cf. no. 84]

1 February 1599, before Zachary Lyninge, mayor, and Giles Hutchins, gent., justices.
88. Joan Grobbyn is to be whipped openly since she was lately delivered in St. Edmund's parish Salisbury of a third bastard child, begotten upon her as she affirms and confesses by one Thomas Wyatt, late servant to John Vaucher of Salisbury. She says that one Battyn, a joiner, deceased, is father of the first child, a son yet living, and that she does not remember the father of the second child, a daughter, because he was a stranger to her. Also she says that she had no punishment for the same.

[f. 19v.] 10 February 1599
89. Morgan Percyvall, an idle person, and one Rebecca, to whom he says he was married in St. Peter's in the Baylie, Oxford, were punished. Passport to Oxford where they say their dwelling is; 4 days assigned. They have taken their daughter Alice with them.

21 March 1599
90. Mary Ramson, an idle person and a rogue, was punished. Passport to Corsley where she says she was born; 2 days assigned. *She was whipped before in October.* [Cf. no. 74]
91. Joan Bassett, an idle person and a rogue, was punished. Passport to Mylton, Hants, where she says she was born; 3 days appointed. *She was whipped in October last.* [Cf. no. 75]
92. Margaret Edwardes, an idle person and a rogue, was punished. Passport to Mylton, Hants, where she says she was born; 3 days appointed. *She was whipped in May last.* [Cf. nos. 25, 63]

19 April 1599
93. Michael Servington, an idle person and a rogue, was punished. Passport to Birtford where he says he was born; 2 days appointed. *By order of the sessions.*

94. Agnes Hooper, an idle person and a rogue, was punished. Passport to Warmester where she says she was born; 2 days allowed. *By order of the sessions.* [Cf. no. 98]

24 April 1599
95. Jenkyn Jones, an idle person, was punished. Passport to Cardiffe, Glam., where he says he was born; 10 days allowed. *By order of the sessions.*

[f. 20] 28 April 1599
96. Robert Langham, late of Uxbridge, Midx., tinker, was found an idle person and a rogue and was punished. Passport to Branckcton, Hunts., where he says he was born; 8 days assigned.

30 April 1599
97. Bridget Parson (*Parsons*), an idle person and a vagrant, was punished. Passport to Beryton, Hants, where she says she was born; 4 days assigned.

2 May 1599
98. Agnes Hooper, a rogue, wandering as an idle person, was punished. Passport to Warmester where she says she was born; 4 days appointed. [Cf. no. 94]

11 May 1599
99. Edmund Breade *alias* Sampson, a vagrant, was punished. Passport to Malmesburye, where he says he was born; 3 days assigned.

12 May 1599
100. Richard Manninge, a vagrant, was punished. Passport to Grigory Stoake, Som., where he says he was born; 3 days assigned.
101. John Bassett and Agnes his wife, vagrants, were punished. Passport to Pensaunce, Cornw., where he says he was born; 30 days assigned.
102. Thomas Saunders and Jane his wife, vagrants. Thomas was punished but Jane was spared because she is distracted. Passport to Hunnington, Devon, where he says he was born; 6 days assigned.
103. William Kinge, a vagrant, was punished. Passport to Corffe Castle in the Isle of Purbecke, Dors., where he says he was born; 3 days assigned.

[f. 20v.] 14 May 1599
104. Thomas Acrofte, an idle person and a vagrant, was punished. Passport to Okington, Devon, where he says his dwelling is; 6 days appointed.

11 June 1599
105. Thomas Arnoll, an idle vagrant, was punished. Passport to Teverton, Devon, where he says he was born; 8 days appointed. [Cf. nos. 107, 126, 185]

20 June 1599
106. Thomas Wheler, a wandering vagrant, was punished. He terms himself a glass-bearer, not having any licence for his travel, and is accompanied by Elizabeth Carpenter, a lewd woman, whom he alleges to be his wife, which appears on examination to be altogether untrue. Passport to Rumsey, Hants, where he says he was born; 2 days appointed.

13 July 1599

107. Edith Arnoll, a vagrant and wandering person, was punished. Passport to Teverton, Devon, where she says her husband Thomas dwells; 10 days assigned. [Cf. nos. 105, 126, 185]

108. John Gate, an idle person, was punished. Passport to Coventrye, [Warws.], where he says he was born; 8 days assigned.

11 August 1599

109. John Winge, an idle person, was punished. Passport to Shrewton where he says he was born; 2 days assigned.

13 August 1599

110. Peter Jackeson, an idle person, was punished. Passport to Fulham, Midx., where he says he was born; 3 days assigned.

111. [f. 21] Peter Constantyn, an idle person and a vagrant, was punished. Passport to Moresteed, Hants, where he says he was born; 2 days appointed.

14 August 1599

112. Humphrey Pearce and Margaret Hooper, living lewdly together and not married, as they confessed, were punished. Passport to Southampton where they say their dwelling is; 2 days appointed.

16 August 1599

113. Mary Payne, an idle person and a vagrant, was punished. Passport to Warmester where she was born; 3 days appointed.

114. Thomas Rose, an idle person and a vagrant, was punished. Passport to Carlile, Cumb., where he was born; 15 days assigned.

18 August 1599

115. Edith Wylles, an idle person wandering and vagrant, was punished. Passport to Abbott Searne, Dors., where she says she was born; 3 days assigned.

23 August 1599

116. Richard Markham, an idle wandering person, is given a passport to Oxford where he has friends by whom he hopes to be relieved; 4 days assigned. *He exercises a kind of music on bells in churches.*

24 August 1599

117. Anne Moyle, an idle wandering person, was punished. Passport to Altam, Kent, where she says she was born; 10 days assigned.

27 August 1599

118. George Massey, a gent., as he says, who was lately employed in service in the Isle of Wight under the conduct of Henry Dabridgecourte, esq., is given a certificate to Westchester, [Ches.], where he says he was born; 12 days assigned. *He says he was allied to Mr. Ed. P.* [1]

[f. 21v.] 4 October 1599

119. Robert Lowe, an idle person and a vagrant, was punished. Passport to

---

[1] Possibly Edward Penruddocke of Compton Chamberlayne, a justice, deputy lieutenant, and sheriff 1599.

Burporte where he says he was born; 4 days assigned.

5 October 1599

120. John Vacher, an idle person and a vagrant, was punished. Passport to Hunington, Devon, where he says he dwells; 7 days assigned. *By order of the sessions.*

6 October 1599

121. Richard Irishe, an idle person and a vagrant, was punished. Passport to Downeton where he was born; 2 days assigned. *By order of the sessions.*

122. Bartholomew Birche, wandering and using the art of a minstrel, was punished. Passport to Sherborne, Dors., where he dwells; 6 days assigned. *By order of the sessions.*

26 October 1599

123. Eleanor Dawton, an idle person who came since Whitsuntide from Bassington, Cumb. [*recte* Northumb.], where she says she was born, was punished. Passport to Bassington; 40 days assigned.

Tempore David Eaton, mayor.

8 December 1599

124. Anne Mathewe, wife of John Mathewe of Sherborne, Hants, was found as an idle wandering person and a vagrant and punished. Passport to Sherborne; 5 days assigned.

14 December 1599

125. Edith White and Thomas White her son, idle persons, were punished. Passport to Bristoll, where their dwelling is; 4 days assigned.

15 January 1600

126. Edith Arnoll, wife of Thomas Arnoll, butcher, of Tyverton, Devon, was found as an idle person and punished. Passport to Tyverton where her dwelling is; 12 days assigned. *By order of the sessions.* [Cf. nos. 105, 107, 185]

127. Henry Neale, an idle person, was punished. Passport to Wotton Bassett where his dwelling is; 4 days assigned.

[f. 22] *Tempore* William Holmes, mayor.

9 February 1600

128. George Williams and John Pearce, idle persons who say they came from Ireland and landed at Dover, were punished. Passport for one to go to Chynlye, the other to Barstable, Devon, where they were born; 10 days assigned.

16 February 1600

129. John Heyward, an idle person wandering and begging, was punished. Passport to Brecknocke where he says he was born; 20 days assigned.

28 March 1600

130. Richard Walker, who says he lost his leg in Plymouth, had a passport from the mayor there to be conveyed to where he was born and lost his passport by the way. Passport to go to Dover, [Kent], with Margery Walker as his guide; 30 days assigned.

9 May 1600
131. Thomas Gardner, an idle person and a vagrant, was punished. Passport to Glastonburye, Som., where he says his dwelling and his wife and children are; 3 days assigned.

10 May 1600
132. John Smyth, a wandering vagrant, was punished. Passport to Wolverhampton, Staffs., where he says his dwelling is; 8 days assigned.
133. Robert Johnson, a vagrant, was punished. Passport to London where he says his dwelling is; 5 days assigned.

31 May 1600
134. Katherine Jones and William her son, vagrant wandering persons, were punished. Passport to St. Giles's parish, London, where they were born; 20 days assigned.

5 June 1600
135. Edward Clarke, a vagrant and wandering person, was punished. Passport to Brickesworth, Northants., where he was born; 10 days assigned.

23 August 1600
136. Simon Reeves, junior, a vagrant and wandering person, was punished. Passport to Ringwood, Hants, where he was born; 2 days assigned.

[f. 22v.] 6 September 1600
137. John Bassett, an idle person and a vagrant, was punished. Passport to Penreese, Glam., where he says he was born; 8 days assigned.

7 October 1600
138. John Smythe, a vagrant person, was punished. Passport to St. Peter's in the Isle of Tenett, Kent, where he says he was born.

24 October 1600
139. Anne Standley was taken as a vagrant and she confesses she has been a wanderer for the last year, has been punished three times before, and had passports accordingly. She says she has a husband who dwelt last in Sherborne, Dors., where she was born. Passport to Sherborne; 3 days assigned.

Tempore Matthew Bee, mayor.
19 November 1600
140. John Fowler, a vagrant disturbing the queen's people in this city, was punished. Passport to Sandwiche, Kent, where he says he was born and where he was impressed for her Majesty's service in the Low Countries; 12 days assigned.

22 November 1600
141. Joan Jones, a vagrant, was punished. Passport to St. Giles's near London where she says she was born; 7 days assigned.

6 December 1600
142. Richard Wood, a vagrant, was punished. Passport to West Cooker, Som., where he says he was born. He had a counterfeit passport. [The counterfeit

passport, or a copy of it, is loosely held between the folios of the register. It reads: 'To ballis Constables hedborowgs & all other her Ma[jes]tes ofycers what soeuer to whome yt shall app[er]teyne for asmouch as the barer heare of Richard Wood ys lycenced to departe from his Father [to] serue eles wher acordyng to the statute, he wase borne in Westcoker and hath dwylled ther all the dayes of his lyfe & hathe ben Juste & trew in all his delinges. Ther fore to wyll & Requer you and euery of you to home yt shall app[er]tayne quyetle to p[er]myt sofer & let pase the sayd Rychard Wood demeaninge hemsselfe well & onestly, geuen at Westcoker, xiiij of october, in wytnes hereof I Walter Apsey, constable, hathe put my h[a]nd & sealle, the day & yere aboue wryten. [Signed] Phellip Edmondes, curet there.']

[f. 23] 11 December 1600

143. Thomas Powell and Anne his wife, idle and vagrant persons, having a passport which was contrary to the statute for wanderers, were punished. Passport to Malpasse, Ches., where they say their dwelling is; 20 days assigned.

14 December 1600

144. Robert Hodges, Elizabeth his wife, and William their son, idle vagrant persons using the trade of petty chapmen, were punished. Passport to Glassenbery, Som., where they say their dwelling is; 4 days assigned.

145. Anthony Hooper, pretending to be a glassman but having no licence to that effect according to the statute, [1] was punished. Passport to Newbery, Berks., where he and one Tesser, to whom he is apprentice, live; 2 days assigned.

19 December 1600

146. Richard Gyles, a vagrant, was punished. Passport to Hartlerewe, Hants, where his last dwelling was; 2 days assigned.

14 December 1600

147. Elizabeth Parker, wife of John Parker, was taken as a vagrant and punished. Passport to Christchurche, Hants, where she says her husband dwells.

148. Joan Jeames, wife of Robert Jeames, was taken as an idle person and vagrant and punished. Assigned [blank] days to go to Christchurche, [Hants], where she says her husband lives.

17 December 1600

149. Mary Edwardes, an idle person and a vagrant accompanied by Richard Grene, was punished. Passport to Arneton, Berks., where she was born and whence she was allured by Grene; 4 days assigned. [Cf. no. 151]

[f. 23v.] 22 December 1600

150. Leonard Watson, an idle and vagrant person, was punished. Passport to London where he says he has a brother living; 5 days assigned.

1 39 Eliz. I, c. 4, xv, *Statutes of the Realm*, iv. 902.

20 December 1600

151. Richard Grene, an idle person and a vagrant, terming himself a minstrel, accompanied by Mary Edwardes and having a false passport, was punished. Passport to Steventon, Berks., where he says his dwelling is; 3 days assigned. [Cf. no. 149]

21 February 1601

152. Thomas Griffyn, terming himself a petty chapman, found wandering, was punished. Passport to Blacke Fryers in London where he says Thomas Griste his master lives and where his dwelling is; 4 days assigned.

153. Thomasin Ridgeway, an idle person and a vagrant accompanied by Robert Jones, was punished. Passport to Thorneford, Dors., where she was born; 3 days assigned. Jones alleged that Thomasin was his wife but on examination she confesses that they were never married and that they have been together for half a year. [Cf. no. 155]

154. Stephen Wood, a rogue, had a passport in January last. He named himself Thomas Wellard and said he was robbed of divers goods and apparel at the park corner; on examination this was found to be false and he was punished. Assigned 6 days to go to Gothurste, Kent, where he last dwelt.

28 February 1601

155. Robert Jones, a vagrant accompanied by Thomasin Ridgeway, confesses on examination that she is not his wife. He was punished. Passport to Caunterburye, [Kent], where his dwelling is. [Cf. no. 153]

3 March 1601

156. John Butcher, a vagrant terming himself a petty chapman, was punished. Passport to Exeter, [Devon], where his dwelling is; 8 days assigned.

[f. 24] 7 March 1601

157. Agnes Gerrett, an idle person, pregnant, says she dwelt last Michaelmas with Mr. Richard Pottycarye where she stayed one quarter and since has wandered from place to place, and that she came from Brodechalke to this city. Passport to Brodechalke where she says she was born; 2 days assigned.

21 March 1601

158. Joan Maddocke, an idle person accompanied by Ralph Johnson to whom she affirmed that she was married, which she confessed on examination to be untrue, was punished. Passport to St. Albons, Herts., where she says her dwelling is; 10 days assigned. [Cf. no. 159]

24 March 1601

159. Ralph Johnson, a vagrant, was found with Joan Maddocke in a kind of lewd life, alleging her to be his wife, which on examination appears untrue. They lived in this kind of lewd life about one month and met together in Hertfordshire. Passport for him to Bristol and from there to the sea coast and so to return to Ireland to serve again under Sir Francis Shane, one of her Majesty's captains there;[1] 4 days assigned to Bristol. [Cf. no. 158]

---

[1] For Shane's activities in Ireland see *Cal. State Papers Ireland*, 1600, pp. 83–5 and *passim*.

28 March 1601

160. Richard Guye, widow, was sent here from Lee where she was taken as a vagrant and punished. Passport to South Cheryten, Devon, where she says she was born; 12 days assigned.

6 April 1601

161. Cecily Musprett, daughter of Thomas Musprett of Laverstocke, an idle person having no abiding place, is spared her punishment because of her sickness. Passport to Laverstocke where she says she was born; 1 day assigned.

18 April 1601

162. Isaac Neale, an idle person, confesses that he ran away from George Waters of Gosporte, Hants, a cooper with whom he is bound apprentice. He is to go back; 2 days assigned.

163. [f. 24v.] John Wescott, an idle person and a wanderer, was punished. Passport to Nuyington, Surr., where he says he lives; 7 days assigned.

17 July 1601

164. Thomas Williams, a vagrant, was punished. Passport to Landalo Garsanno, Mon., where his dwelling is; 8 days assigned. *He offered brass rings coloured with quicksilver.*

20 July 1601

165. William Greene was punished on his conviction at the quarter sessions on 17 July. Passport to Horningsham where he says he was born; 2 days assigned.

12 September 1601

166. Rebecca Wilkes *alias* Seymor *alias* Anne Wilkes, a vagrant accompanied by four other idle persons, who confesses that she travels from fair to fair, was punished. Passport to Twyfford, Hants, where she says she was born; 2 days assigned. *Margaret Goslyn was one of the four.* [Cf. no. 167]

167. Mary Bowden, wife of Thomas Bowden, a vagrant accompanied by the said Rebecca and others, was punished. Passport to St. Ives, Cornw., where her dwelling is; 12 days assigned. [Cf. no. 166]

Tempore Henry Byle, mayor.

19 November 1601

168. Richard Ogborne, a vagrant person, was punished. Passport to Fisherton where he says he was born; 1 day allowed.

1 December 1601

169. Humphrey Saunders *alias* Alexander Humfrey, an idle person vagrant and begging, was punished. Passport to Sandwiche, Kent, where he was born; 30 days allowed.

[f. 25] 12 February 1602

170. John Reynoldes, son of Joan Reynoldes, a vagrant about the age of ten years, wandering with Simon Tucke and his wife and Olive Hallame, was punished. Passport to St. Mary's parish, Devizes, where he says he was born and where his mother lives; 3 days assigned. [Cf. nos. 34, 171–2]

171. Simon Tucke and Anne his wife, idle wandering persons yielding no good account of their life, were punished. Passport to Kingeton, Dors., where they say their dwelling is; 4 days assigned. [Cf. nos. 170, 172]

172. Olive Hallame, a wandering person using the trade of a petty chapman, selling small wares contrary to the statute, was punished. Passport to St. James's parish, Bristoll, where she says her dwelling is; 5 days assigned. [Cf. nos. 170–1]

17 February 1602
173. Elizabeth Clarke, wandering, was punished. Passport to Wymborne, [Dors.], where her last dwelling was; 2 days appointed.

12 March 1602
174. William Wilcockes and Jane his alleged wife, idle vagrant persons, having a counterfeit passport under the seal of Richard Williams, mayor of Harwiche, Essex, were punished. Assigned 4 days to go to Goddishill in the Isle of Wight where he was born.
175. Thomas Morris and Lucy his alleged wife, vagrant and wandering persons, were punished. Assigned 4 days to go to Newe Towne in the Isle of Wight where Morris was born.

16 March 1602
176. Matthew Mackeris, a vagrant person travelling with a counterfeit passport under the hand of Sir John Byron,[1] was punished. Passport to Popplewicke, Notts.; 10 days allowed.

6 April 1602
177. Margaret Paige, vagrant, daughter of Thomas Paige, was punished. Passport to St. Mary Borne, Hants.
178. Gregory Jarvis, vagrant, was punished. Passport to Hynton in Christ-churche parish, [Hants].

[f. 25v.] 3 April 1602
179. Richard Thomson of the parish of Byglesworthe, Beds., a vagrant chapman with a counterfeit passport, was punished. Assigned [blank] days to go to Byglesworthe. [Cf. nos. 182–4]

9 April 1602
180. Thomas Cooper, vagrant, was punished. Passport to Atherston, Warws., where his dwelling is; 9 days assigned.
181. Joan William, wandering, was punished. Passport to Cardiffe, [Glam.], where she says her dwelling is; 10 days assigned.

13 April 1602
182. Richard Thomson, vagrant, was punished and is to go to Biglesworth, Beds., by order of the sessions; 16 days assigned. [Cf. nos. 179, 183–4]
183. William Hopkins, a rogue, was punished. Passport to Potton, Beds.; 14 days assigned. By order of the sessions. [Cf. nos. 179, 182, 184]

---

[1] A Notts. J.P.

184. Christopher Halfehead, a rogue, was punished. Passport to Hoggington, Cambs.; 15 days assigned. By order of the sessions. [1] [Cf. nos. 179, 182–3]

185. Edith Arnoll, a vagrant, wife of Thomas Arnoll, was punished. Passport to Bristol, where her husband dwells; 8 days assigned. She has a young child. [2] [Cf. nos. 105, 107, 126]

186. Thomas Dearinge, a vagrant, was punished. Passport to Tingemouth, Devon, where he was born; 8 days assigned. *Indicted for felony at the sessions, 13 Apr. 1602.* [3]

27 April 1602

187. Francis Crome, son of John Crome, an idle person and a vagrant, was punished. Passport to Brenspiddle, Dors., where he says he was born; 3 days assigned. *He deceived Mr. Wallis with a false message and so by that means got from him 18d.*

3 May 1602

188. John Hill, who came to this city supposing that he was born here, which cannot be confirmed, confesses that he dwelt 15 years or thereabouts at Burnewood, Essex, where he has an aunt named Joan Hill. He is spared punishment in regard of his weakness. Passport to Burnewood; 40 days assigned. *Katherine Hill and he came from Barstall.*

[f. 26] 28 June 1602

189. Humphrey Sadler, an idle vagrant person, was punished. Passport to Gravesend, Kent, where he was born; 20 days assigned.

190. Valentine Johnson, vagrant, was punished. Passport to Rockeborne, Hants, where he last dwelt; 2 days assigned.

26 July 1602

191. Christopher Harris, a vagrant rogue and begging wanderer, was punished. Passport to Thorpe, Devon, where he was born and last dwelt; 18 days assigned.

9 November 1602

192. Roger Jones and Eleanor his wife, wandering vagrant persons and chapmen, having certain rings of copper slightly gilded, were punished. Passport to Winckley, Devon, where their last dwelling was; 16 days assigned. *One Russell [John Payne, deleted], a glover dwelling in Wimborne Minster, made a counterfeit passport for the persons abovenamed and had 2s. from them for it.*

---

[1] On the examinations of Thomson (nos. 179, 182), Hopkins (no. 183), and Halfehead before quarter sessions (S.C.A., Q 136b) Hopkins and Halfehead alleged that they were impressed to serve in Ostend, where Halfehead was wounded. On their return they obtained payments from various county treasurers for maimed soldiers and met each other at Basingstoke (Hants). On re-examination, however, they confessed that their soldier's passports were forged by a man in Shoreditch (Mdx.). They met Matthew Mackeris (no. 176) in Andover (Hants).

[2] On examination by the justices on suspicion of stealing cloth (S.C.A., Q 136b) Edith said she had not seen her husband for 3 weeks. Her child was kept in Salisbury by Elizabeth Brodripp while Edith lodged at John Love's house in Tanner St.

[3] Dearinge, said to have served in Ireland under Sir George Carew, was indicted for theft: S.C.A., Q 136b.

Tempore James Haviland, mayor, 1602.

193. Alice Vyney, servant to Thomas Atwaters of Flameston in Bishopston parish, lately travelling through this city, was there casually delivered of a bastard child. The justices were given to understand that she dwelt last at Flameston for about 6 years. Passport to Flameston.

15 January 1603

194. Henry Fairlye, a tinker and vagrant, was punished. Assigned 8 days to go to Dunstable, Beds., where he says his dwelling is.

4 March 1603

195. Elizabeth Welles, vagrant, was punished. Assigned 3 days to go to Newton where she says she was born.

16 March 1603

196. Ambrose Brookebancke and Edith his wife, late of Upper Teffante in Dynton parish, brought with them to this city 3 children born in Teffante as they affirm, and have been here harboured for a season without the knowledge of the mayor and justices. Having no house or certain abode here they desire to go to the place where they lately dwelt. Passport to Teffante.

197. Henry Powell, wandering and idle, is found on examination to be the lawful apprentice of John and Agnes Light of Whiteparish by indenture for divers years yet to come, and to be in no way lawfully discharged. Passport to go back to his master.

[f. 26v.] 30 June 1603

198. Amy Moore, an idle person and vagrant, was punished. Passport to Wareham, Dors., where she was born; 2 days assigned. [Cf. nos. 226, 268, 270]

10 July 1603

199. Margaret Vynsent, a vagrant, wife of John Vynsent, was punished. Passport to Dorchester, [Dors. *or* Oxon.], where she says her husband lives; 5 days assigned.

Tempore William Eton, mayor.

13 December 1603

200. Patience Fortescue *alias* Foscue, a vagrant, was punished. Passport to Stoke, Devon, where she was born; 13 days assigned.

11 December 1603

201. George White, a vagrant, was punished and is to go to Perrye, Som., where he was born; 4 days allowed. *He was indicted for felony at the quarter sessions in October 1603 for [stealing] oxen.*

20 January 1604

202. Francis Symes and Richard Symes, vagrant persons, were punished. Assigned 1 day to go to Pytton, where they say they were born.

21 March 1604

203. Robert Rode, an idle person and vagrant, who has been loitering about this town three days, was punished. Assigned 6 days to go to Plymoth, [Devon], where he says his dwelling is.

3 May 1604

204. Richard Parker, begging and vagrant, was punished. Assigned 6 days to go to Little Hempson near Totnes, Devon, where he says his dwelling was.
205. William Blakemore, begging and wandering, was punished. Assigned 4 days to go to Cowstone near Exeter, Devon, where he says his last dwelling was.

Tempore Robert Banes, mayor.

4 February 1605

206. Anthony Kerlye, begging and wandering, was punished. Passport to Shaftesbury, [Dors.], where he was born, as he says, in St. James's Street; 3 days assigned.

[f. 27] 5 March 1605

207. William Davis, an idle wandering person and a vagrant from place to place, was punished. Passport to Malmesburye where he says he was born; 3 days assigned.

19 March 1605

208. Richard Goffeydge, vagrant, was punished. Passport to Marston in Potterne parish where he says he was born; 2 days assigned.

8 April 1605

209. Dorothy Grene *alias* Percye, a wanderer, was punished. Passport to Manson, Dors., where she says she was born; 3 days assigned. *First she was found lying at the Lamb and so sent away without punishment and shortly after she came again and was taken and so had her passport. She is not able to give account of her life.*

10 April 1605

210. Anne Hamersley, wandering and a vagrant, confesses that she was in Fisherton gaol and was discharged out of the prison at the last assizes at Marleboroughe, and so came wandering to this city. She was punished. Assigned 8 days to go to St. John's Street, London, where she says she last dwelt.
211. Agnes Jones *alias* Symes, with her two children Bennett *Jones* and James *Symes*, was taken vagrant and wandering. She has been in Fisherton gaol for two years as a condemned person and was freed at the Marleboroughe assizes and came back to this city. She was punished. Passport to Frome Sellwood, Som., where she was born and last dwelt; 3 days assigned.

16 April 1605

212. William Maior, wandering and a vagrant, having two counterfeit passports, was punished. Assigned 12 days to go to Ashe near Sandwiche, Kent, where his last dwelling was.

18 April 1605

213. Agnes Ellyott *alias* Davys was taken in this city on suspicion of felony and at the sessions on 12 Apr. was ordered to have a passport to Easton Graye where she says she last dwelt; 4 days assigned.

3 May 1605

214. Chester *alias* Christopher Harris, wandering and begging, was punished. Passport to Moreton, Devon, where he says he was born.

[f. 27v.] 28 May 1605

215. Simon Tooke, a vagrant, was punished. Passport to Calne where his last dwelling is; 2 days assigned.

216. John Mundye, vagrant, was punished. Assigned 2 days to go to Wymborne, Dors., where he last dwelt.

11 June 1605

217. Thomas Pistoe and Joan his wife were taken idle, wandering, and using the trade of a tinker. He was punished and she was spared because she was great with child. Assigned 6 days to go to Wynscombe, Glos. [*recte* Som.], where their dwelling is.

218. John Hodson, a vagrant and tinker, was punished. Assigned 4 days to go to the backsides in Southwarke near London where he dwells.

17 June 1605

219. Dorothy Lyminge, an idle wanderer and vagrant, wife of John Lyminge, was punished. Assigned 3 days to go to Marleboroughe where she dwells and she is to carry with her a child which she says she left at Fisherton Anger.

20 June 1605

220. John Sellavand, born an Irishman as he says, was found wandering and begging disorderly, and associated with lewd company, viz. the hangman or topman. He was formerly taken in Readinge where he had a passport to be conveyed to Bristoll without any time limit for his travel. Notwithstanding he wandered out of his way. He was punished. Passport to Bristoll and from there to Ireland; 20 days assigned.

221. Joan Carde, a vagrant and wanderer, daughter of Thomas Carde of Mounton Deverell, was punished. Assigned 5 days to be conveyed to Mounton Deverell where she says her parents dwell. [Cf. no. 13]

24 July 1605

222. Richard Barrett, an idle wandering person, alleged that he travelled from place to place to seek his wife who left him. Here he persuaded one Feltam's daughter that he would marry her but on examination it appeared that he had a wife living. Assigned 8 days to go to Mytche Markelle, Herefs., where he says he last dwelt. [Cf. no. 397]

5 July 1605

223. Philip Trume, a vagrant with a counterfeit passport, alleged that he came lately from the sea and that he was a soldier. He was punished and assigned 24 days to go to Mylford Haven, Pembs., where he says he was born. [A loose MS. note of this and the following passport remains in the register.]

224. Samuel Clarke, a vagrant, was punished. Assigned 4 days to go to Islyngton near London. [Cf. no. 223]

[f. 28] 19 August 1605

225. John Jefferye, an idle person and a wanderer from place to place who

was drunk at the time of his apprehension, was punished. Passport to Malmesburye where he last dwelt; 3 days limited.

24 August 1605

226. Amy Moore, wandering, was spared her punishment because she is with child and near her time of delivery. She confesses that William Hardinge, son of Eleanor Hardinge, widow, of Mountague, Som., is the father of her child. Assigned 3 days to go to Chesselbury, Som., where she says she was born and lives. [Cf. nos. 198, 268, 270]

31 August 1605

227. John Grymes, together with Frances his alleged wife, brought to this city William Grymes his brother, a cripple. They have wandered together from Belford, Northumb., where they say their habitation was, and they had no passport. John and his wife were punished. Assigned 2 months to go to Belford.

9 November 1605

228. Barnaby Bennett, a vagrant accompanied by one naming himself William Saunders, having a counterfeit passport confessed by them to be made by Thomas Paule, dwelling in the soke near Winchester, was punished. Assigned 2 days to go to Tisburye where he was born. [Cf. no. 229]

229. One naming himself William Saunders, wandering with a counterfeit passport, was punished. Assigned 6 days to go to Bradlinche *alias* Bradlich, Devon, where his last dwelling is. [Cf. no. 228]

Tempore Thomas Hancocke, mayor.

2 December 1605

230. Blanche Fowler, late wife of John Fowler, was found wandering with other wanderers and confessed that she had been in the counties of Oxford and Dorset and was previously sent by passport from Wareham, Dors., to St. Sidwell's, Exeter. She was punished. Assigned 8 days to go to St. Sidwell's.

3 December 1605

231. Owen Dallabye was found as a wanderer with Susan Crebron *alias* Jenkyn, and they lay together or were found abed together. He was punished. Assigned 2 days to go to Steple Asheton where he says his dwelling is. [Cf. no. 232]

23 December 1605

232. Susan Crebron *alias* Jenkyn, wandering with Owen Dallabye, was punished. Assigned 8 days to go to St. Sidwell's, Exeter. [Cf. no. 231]

[f. 28v.] 12 December 1605

233. George Norkett, who was freed from Fisherton gaol last Monday, came wandering into this city and uttered lewd and false speeches. He was punished. Assigned 3 days to go to Pelsford, Som., where he was born. *He uttered words against Thomas Gorges and Richard Grobham, knights.* [1]

---

[1] Local J.P.s. A man imprisoned by Grobham petitioned for relief in 1603: Hist. MSS Com. 55, *Var. Coll.* i, p. 76.

3 January 1606

234. One naming herself Elizabeth Sherwood, wife of George Sherwood of St. Philip's parish, Bristoll, was found wandering and because she is with child her punishment was spared. Assigned 5 days to go to Bristoll. *She stole venison from Mr. Sidenham's house.*

7 January 1606

235. One naming himself Leonard Dyton, a vagrant and wanderer, was spared punishment because of his impotence. Assigned 5 days to go to Brode Hynton where his last dwelling was.

14 January 1606

236. John Younge, an idle person and vagrant, was whipped by order of the sessions. Assigned 12 days to go to [*blank*] where he was born.

17 January 1606

237. Bridget Wylmotton, vagrant, says that she came lately from Pitton where she dwelt about half a year and where she was begotten with child by Peter Frye. She confesses that she dwelt last at Horsington, Som., where she lived 16 years. Assigned 6 days to go to Horsington. [Cf. no. 238]

22 February 1606

238. The said Bridget, because of negligence of officers under the former passport, was not sent to Horsington but suffered to return to Mylford near this city where she has hidden and kept herself in secret manner until last night when she was apprehended. She has another passport under the hand of Mr. Mayor, Sir Edward Penruddock, Edward Estcourt, esq., and Mr. Thomas Eyer, to be sent to Horsington; 6 days assigned. [Cf. no. 237]

7 April 1606

239. One naming himself Thomas Carter, an idle person and a vagrant not able to yield any account of his idle course of life, was punished. Assigned 10 days to go to Caster, Lincs., where he says he was born. *Taken drunk in Griffin Jones's house.*

17 May 1606

240. One naming himself William Coxe, tinker, wandering and misdemeaning himself, was punished. Assigned 3 days to go to Sherborne, Dors., where he was born.

11 June 1606

241. Peter Gill, idle and begging, was punished. Assigned 13 days to go to Tharverton, Devon, where he says he was born.

[f. 29] 20 September 1606

242. George Michell, an idle person wandering and using a kind of play upon bones and bells and other idle course of life, was punished. Assigned 30 days to go to Edenboroughe, Scotland, where he says he was born.

243. James Lyllington, vagrant, was punished. Assigned 2 days to go to Blandford, [Dors.], where he was born.

Tempore Roger Gauntlett, mayor, 1606.

28 November 1606

244. Thomas Anthonye, a vagrant going about with a kind of stuff called black lead, was punished. Assigned 6 days to go to Highgate, Midx.

12 December 1606

245. Andrew Mould, vagrant, was punished. Assigned 14 days to go to Wilkinson near Exeter, Devon, where he says he was born.

14 January 1607

246. Ralph Bowden, wandering, was punished. Assigned 10 days to go to St. Nicholas, Kent, where he was born. *He had a counterfeit passport.*

28 January 1607

247. Robert Lowell, wandering, was punished. Assigned 2 days to go to Mayden Bradlye where he says he was born. [Cf. nos. 275, 278]

248. Margaret Farr, daughter of Thomas Farr, deceased, of Horton, Dors., whose last dwelling was with Jane Norris, widow, at Whit Waltham, Hants [*recte* Berks.], where she was begotten with child by Wilding Norris, son of Jane, and who was delivered of the child at Wotton Bassett about three weeks ago, came to this city last Saturday to Elizabeth Wheler, a poor woman, her mother-in-law, and brought with her the bastard child named Jeremy. Margaret affirmed that Wilding Norris is her husband. Because she was not dwelling here and her mother is unable to relieve her, she has a passport to Waltham to her pretended husband.

31 January 1607

249. Hugh Plattyn, idle and vagrant and misdemeaning himself, was punished. Assigned 3 days to go to Evill, Som., where he says he last dwelt for 26 years.

250. Kiffin Taylor, idle and vagrant, was punished. Assigned 7 days to go to St. Marye Overyes near London.

[f. 29v.] 7 February 1607

251. Joseph Griffyn, idle and wandering, was punished. Assigned 2 days to go to Christchurche, Hants, where he says he was born and dwelt.

252. Robert Pitcher, wandering, was punished. He is to go to Brode Searne, Dors., where he says he last dwelt.

20 February 1607

253. Francis Cope was found wandering, begging, and vagrant, having two passports, one of them written in Somerset by a person unknown to him. He confesses that he has been wandering about this city and Fisherton for three days and that he brought here rapiers and a dagger and sells them for profit. Assigned 20 days to go to Carleton, Yorks., where he says he was born.

3 March 1607

254. William Jefferye *alias Virye*, wandering and vagrant, and Mary Scott *alias* Washbeard were apprehended by the constable, Charles Jacob, in a house privately together very suspiciously. He is assigned 1 day to go to Rumbridge in Wayehill parish, [Hants], where he says he last dwelt. [Cf. no. 255]

4 March 1607
255. Mary Scott *alias* Washbeard, vagrant, is assigned 1 day to go to Appleshowe, Hants, where she last dwelt. [Cf. no. 254]

26 March 1607
256. John Swyfte, vagrant, is assigned 2 days to go to Motcombe, Dors., where he says he was born and last dwelt. *He was delivered out of prison at the last assizes before Sir Walter Long, Baron.*

10 April 1607
257. William Kerrye, idle and wandering as a vagrant, servant to John Beckington, siever, of Eastdeane, Wilts. [*recte* Hants], was punished. Assigned 2 days to go to Eastdeane to his master.

20 April 1607
258. John Squier, begging, wandering, and vagrant, was punished. Assigned 12 days to go to Pemsey, Suss., where he says he was born.

9 June 1607
259. Alice Evans, begging and misbehaving herself, was punished. Assigned 13 days to go to Lanporte, Som., where she was born. *Misbehaved and abused Mr. Hancock* [1] *and she was taken vagrant in Alton.*

30 June 1607
260. Agnes Beale, vagrant, was punished. Assigned 5 days to go to Youron, Dors., where she was born.

[f. 30] 10 July 1607
261. Gabriel Jones, wandering as a rogue, was punished. Assigned 20 days to go to Swynishe, Glam., where he says he was born.

11 July 1607
262. John Myllett, wandering as a vagrant, having bells for his legs and using a kind of dancing, was punished. Assigned 2 days to go to Warmester where he says he was born.

20 July 1607
263. Maurice Harris, wandering and begging, was punished. Assigned 6 days to go to Crokanpill, Som., where he says he was born.

29 July 1607
264. Thomas Bennett, using a fantastical play with his mouth and hand, wandering with an idle woman, was punished. Assigned 10 days to go to Chidley, Devon, where he says he was born.

26 August 1607
265. Bridget Parsons, wandering as a vagrant with a bastard child, was punished. Assigned 2 days to go to Winchester where she says she dwelt for the last 7 years.
266. Joan Welshe *alias* Potter, wandering, was spared punishment because she is with child and near her time of delivery. Assigned 12 days to go to Bridgewater, Som., where she says she was born.

[1] Thomas Hancock, mayor of Salisbury 1605.

27 August 1670

267. Katherine Burges, wandering, was punished. Assigned 10 days to go to Dartmouth, Devon, where she says she was born.

268. John Hancocke was taken wandering with a lewd woman named Amy Moore, alleging her to be his wife and that he was married to her at Dorchester, [Dors.], by one Mr. Harvye. On examination he confessed that he was not married and that she had been taken as a vagrant in this city in 1604 and 1605. He was punished. Assigned 6 days to go to Bramsgrove, Worcs., where he says he was born. [Cf. nos. 198, 226, 270]

269. Eleanor Vaughan, a cook, wife of Roger Vaughan, wandering with a lewd person, was punished. Assigned 10 days to go to Ludlowe, Salop., where she says her dwelling is.

31 August 1607

270. Amy Moore, wandering with John Hancocke, was punished. Assigned 3 days to go to Dorchester, [Dors.], where she says her dwelling is. [Cf. nos. 198, 226, 268]

[f. 30v.] 10 October 1607

271. Richard Pearce, who is in years and likely to be chargeable to the place where he shall be settled, had a passport from the churchwardens and overseers of Nonney parish, Som., to get work.[1] Since it appears by that passport that he was formerly settled for eight years in Nonney, he is sent back there.

Tempore Richard Payne, mayor, 1607.

17 November 1607

272. Edward Weekes, vagrant, was punished. Assigned 8 days to go to Ferris, Suss., where he says he was born.

273. Elizabeth Wells, wandering, was punished. Assigned 4 days to go to Cicester, Glos., where she was born.

22 December 1607

274. John Thurdon, wandering as a vagrant, was punished. Assigned 8 days to go to Exeter where he was born.

23 December 1607

275. Robert Lovell, idle, wandering as a vagrant, was punished. Assigned 3 days to go to Mayden Bradley where he was born. [Cf. nos. 247, 278]

24 December 1607

276. Samuel Vynson, wandering as a vagrant using divers false sleights and shifts, was punished. Assigned 2 days to go to Mudford, Som., where he says he was born.

30 January 1608

277. Richard Bradwell, vagrant, son of John Bradwell, clerk, was spared punishment because of sickness and infirmity. Assigned 4 days to go to Wodborowe where he says he was born.

---

[1] The Statute of Artificers, 1563, required anyone leaving his parish in search of work to carry a certificate: 5 Eliz. I, c. 4, *Statutes of the Realm*, iv. 416; P. Styles, 'Evolution of the Law of Settlement', *Birm. Univ. Hist. Jnl.* ix. 49.

3 February 1608

278. Robert Lovell, wandering, was punished. Assigned 3 days to go to Mayden Bradleye where he says he was born. He was taken before in December. [Cf. nos. 247, 275]

4 February 1608

279. Robert Baskume, wandering in the company of Hugh Sharpe, was punished. Assigned 3 days to go to Bell Chavell, Dors., where he was born.

12 February 1608

280. William Ogborne, wandering and found in Benedict Swayne's backside, was punished. Assigned 2 days to go to Brigmelston where he was born.

[f. 31] 22 February 1608

281. William Davis and Jane his wife, wandering as vagrant persons, were punished. Assigned 40 days to go to Withington, Salop., where they say their dwelling was.

3 March 1608

282. Thomas Nott, wandering as a vagrant accompanied by two women, was punished. Assigned 14 days to go to Witheridge, Devon, where he says he was born.

283. John Pyke, a wandering vagrant, was punished. He is to go to Highe Littleton, Som., where he says he was born; 12 days assigned because his wife is great with child.

284. Thomas Pepper, wandering and travelling with small wares as a chapman, was punished. He is to go to Much Holland, Essex, where he was born and dwelt; 28 days allowed in respect of his lameness.

18 April 1608

285. Simon Thresher was found wandering.

286. John Thomas *alias* Hardinge, idle and wandering as a vagrant very suspiciously, was taken at Dixon's house. He frequented this city three times this month, staying two or three days at a time, and resorted to Henry Grafton's. At one time he brought a young woman and caused her to sell her apparel in this city and he cannot say what is become of her. He was punished. Assigned 3 days to go to Draton, Suss., where he says he was born.

13 June 1608

287. Edith Smythe, widow, was found wandering as a vagrant with Robert Williamson and Bridget his alleged wife, who have been at Exeter and further westward. She was punished. Assigned 4 days to go to St. Nicholas's parish, Cheapside, London, where she last dwelt. [Cf. no. 288]

14 June 1608

288. Robert Williamson was found wandering as a vagrant with Edith Smythe and Bridget his alleged wife. He says he is an embroiderer by trade and now sells small wares and that Bridget tells fortunes. He was punished and Bridget was spared on account of her pregnancy. He is assigned 6 days to go to Pickle Heringe, Southwark, London, where he says his dwelling is. [Cf. no. 287]

2 July 1608

289. Joan Hickes, sometime servant of John Cuckney of this city, butcher, was found wandering after her departure from her master and punished, though in some sort spared because she was with child and supposed to be begotten with child whilst she was dwelling with John Cuckney. Assigned 1 day to go to South Newton where she was born.

3 August 1608

290. Alice Ingram, wife of John Ingram of Lymington, Hants, was found wandering and affirming herself to have the plague, and she runs into divers houses to the great terror of many people. She was punished. Assigned 3 days to go to Lymington to her husband. [Cf. no. 387]

11 August 1608

291. John Peters, wandering, was punished. Assigned 5 days to go to Chichester, Suss., where he was born.

[f. 31v.] 3 September 1608

292. Andrew Lock, servant and apprentice of Peter Bawden *alias* Bowden of Barstable, Devon, weaver, unlawfully ran away from his master and was found wandering and begging in this city. He was punished. Assigned 16 days to go to his master.

Tempore Edward Rodes, mayor, 1608–9.

31 December 1608

293. John Monginge, vagrant and wandering, affirming himself to be a chapman and a traveller, was punished. Assigned 2 days to go to Wymborne Mynster, Dors., where he says he was born.

20 January 1609

294. Alice Smythe, wandering with others, was presented as a rogue to the sessions on 16 Jan. 1609, and there ordered to be whipped and sent to her birthplace. She was punished. Passport to North Bradleye where she says she was born; 3 days assigned.

16 January 1609

295. Humphrey Reade and Anne his wife, wandering, were presented at the same sessions as rogues and had a counterfeit passport, as he confesses, which was made by a stranger under a hedge. There was found about him a seal of his own carving and divers purses. They were ordered to be whipped and sent to their birthplace. It appears by their examinations at the sessions that they have wandered many years and have no place of habitation. [Cf. no. 319]

15 July 1609

296. Sarah Evans, daughter of William Evans, wandering as a vagrant, was punished. Assigned 3 days to go to Mudford, Dors. [*recte* Som.], where she says she was born.

15 August 1609

297. Francis Burroughes, wandering as a vagrant, was punished. Assigned 10 days to go to Plymouth, Devon, where he says he was born. He can give no reason for his wandering but follows the court.

298. *John Johnson was found wandering. Assigned 12 days to go to* [blank], *Hunts.*

25 August 1609
299. Ralph Greivell, wandering as a vagrant, was punished. Assigned 2 days to go to Trowbridge where he says he has a mother dwelling. [Cf. no. 300]
300. Mary Baylye, wandering as a vagrant with other idle and wandering persons, was punished. Assigned 4 days to go to Caresbrooke in the Isle of Wighte where she says she lives. She had a girl which she said was her child and was accompanied by Christopher Nevell, who confessed that he had made a false passport for Ralph Greivell. [Cf. no. 299]
301. [f. 32] Eleanor Stourton, wandering, was punished. Assigned 3 days to go to Tynhed in Edington parish where she was born.
302. Elizabeth Pawlyn, wandering, was punished. Assigned 4 days to go to Preston, Som., where she was born.

12 October 1609
303. George Medley, wandering, was punished. Assigned 15 days to go to Elford, Worcs. [*recte* Staffs.], where he was born.

14 October 1609
304. John Sympson, wandering as a vagrant showing no cause of his wandering, was punished. Assigned 14 days to go to Lanham, Suff., where he was born.

Tempore Richard Gauntlett, mayor, 1609–10.
5 January 1610
305. Stephen Bytton *alias* Bickey, wandering, was punished. Assigned 10 days to go to Plymouth, [Devon], where he was born.

11 January 1610
306. Richard Rabbettes *alias* Roberts, wandering and begging, was punished. Assigned 6 days to go to Arsson, Glos., where he was born.
307. Margaret Legge *alias* Jackson *alias* Smyth was found wandering as a vagrant, not giving any reason or account of her wandering, and was accompanied by William Legg, affirming him to be her husband, but they differ on their place of marriage and dwelling. She is spared punishment because she is pregnant, as the justices are informed. Assigned 10 days to go to the Mynoryes near Tower Hill, [London], where she says her habitation is.[1] [Cf. no. 315]

18 January 1610
308. Thomasin Barrett was sent here from Wells by a passport dated 12 Jan. under the hands of Hugh Walter and William Atwell, constables there, suggesting that she was born in this city. It appears on examination of

[1] On examination before the justices in Jan. 1610 (S.C.A., Q 136b) William alleged that he was a freeman of the London Cordwainers Company and that his wife was widow of a London barber surgeon. He said they were married in St. Bride's by Mr. Holland, the minister there, and that he brought tobacco to sell in Salisbury. When examined about a stolen cloak Margaret said they were married at Kingston on Thames and that she was a chapwoman, but had been so beaten by her husband that she was unable to practise her trade.

Elizabeth Feltham, wife of Peter Feltham, and of Dixon's wife, with whom Thomasin's sister is living, that Thomasin was born in the Lion near the New Inn in Sherborne, Dors. Passport to Wells; 6 days assigned.

25 January 1610
309. Henry Waker *alias* Walker, wandering, was punished. Passport to convey him to his master, Robert Suckett, gent., of Stuckton near Fordingbridge, [Hants], where he says his dwelling is; 1 day assigned.

6 February 1610
310. Francis Browne, wandering, was punished. Assigned 12 days to go to Aepson, Suss. [*recte* Surr.].

[f. 32v.] 22 February 1610
311. Mary Crosse *alias* Wells, wandering as a vagrant, was spared her punishment because she is great with child and near her time. Assigned 6 days to go to Charleton, Som., where she says she was born and dwelt. [1]

9 March 1610
312. Henry Coles, wandering and begging, has a passport to Gosporte in Alwardstock parish, Hants; 10 days assigned in respect of his age.
313. Grace Carter, wandering, was punished. Assigned 30 days to go to Dartmouth, Devon, in respect of her lameness.

22 March 1610
314. Nicholas Reade, begging and wandering, was punished. Assigned 20 days in respect of his lameness to go to Plymouth, Devon, where he says he was born.

2 April 1610
315. Margaret Legg *alias* Jackson *alias* Smythe, wandering, was formerly sent by passport on 16 Jan. and was again punished. Assigned 6 days to go to the Mynoryes near Tower Hill, London, where she says she last dwelt. [Cf. no. 307]

3 April 1610
316. Lucy Bluntt, wife of John Bluntt, wandering, is spared her punishment because she is pregnant. Assigned 2 days to go to Winterborne Stooke where she says her husband lives.

Tempore Thomas Eyer, mayor, 1610.
11 April 1610
317. David Arnold was found wandering as a vagrant with Anne Fowell. They have lain together and confess that they are not married. He was punished. Assigned 10 days to go to Penbreek, Carms., where he says he was born. [Cf. no. 318]
318. Anne Fowell, wandering, was punished. Assigned 4 days to go to St. Augustyne's near or in the city of Bristoll. [Cf. no. 317]

---

[1]Mary Wells *alias* Cross *alias* Andrews *alias* Farewell was punished as a vagrant a Hindon: W.R.O., Q. Sess. R., Hil. 1610, Kalendar.

3 May 1610
319. Humphrey Reade and Anne his wife were found wandering as vagrants not having any certain place of dwelling and having wandered many years. They were taken as rogues on 16 Jan. 1609. They have been punished and are assigned 5 days to go to Old Wyndsor, Berks., where he says he was born. [Cf. no. 295]

[f. 33] 16 June 1610
320. Ralph Tendringe, wandering as a vagrant, using fantastical means and practices with rings of copper or brass and other things to deceive his Majesty's subjects, was punished. Assigned 10 days to go to Borom, Essex, where he says he was born.

7 July 1610
321. John Earle was found wandering and begging, pretending to have suffered shipwreck at sea which on examination appears to be untrue. He was punished. Assigned 5 days to go to St. Katherine's by Tower Hill, London, where he says he was born.

Tempore Bartholomew Tookye, mayor, 1611.

17 November 1610
322. Margaret Arnold was found wandering and begging having no apparel about her, alleging that she was robbed of it, which on examination appears to be false. She was punished. Assigned 3 days to go to Bramshawe, Hants, where she says she was born.

15 May 1611
323. John Utislans, clerk, who had formerly been in the county gaol and had a passport from the county justices, says he lost it, and afterwards was taken idle and drunk in the city. He was committed to prison and punished. Assigned 10 days to go to [Sout]hampton to the Dutch church there where he hopes to have some relief, and from there to travel to London where he says he has friends.

16 May 1611
324. John Nypperell, terming himself a metal-man and a bellows-coverer, was found wandering with a lewd woman named Edith Barnard. They met at East Meane, Hants, a week after Christmas, and he travelled with a counterfeit passport. He was punished. Passport to Ichenwell in Kingesclere parish, Hants, where he says he was born; 2 days assigned. [Cf. no. 325]

18 May 1611
325. Edith Barnard, wandering with John Nypperell, was punished. Assigned 2 days to go to Subberton, Hants, where she says she last dwelt and where her mother is. They affirmed that they were married at Winchester by Mr. Bawes, minister in the soke, and afterwards they confessed the contrary and their lewd living and wandering. [Cf. no. 324]

18 July 1611
326. John Martyn and Elizabeth his wife, wandering as vagrants, were punished. Assigned 2 days to go to Hampreston, Dors., where they last dwelt. [Cf. no. 371]

[f. 33v.] 2 August 1611

327. Matthew Bendle, wandering as a vagrant, was punished. Assigned 4 days to go to Asheweeke near Wells, Som., where he says he was born.

6 August 1611

328. Robert Ellis, apprentice to Edward Jones, dwelling in Barnaby Street, Southwark, confesses that he ran away from his master and was taken wandering in this city. He was punished. Assigned 3 days to go to his master.

29 October 1611

329. Thomas Lawe, terming himself a petty chapman, was found wandering with a woman naming herself Eleanor. On examination they differ in their affirmation of their marriage. They were punished and are assigned 6 days to go to Seale, Surr., where his dwelling is.

Tempore Thomas Raye, mayor, 1611.

12 December 1611

330. Richard Coller *alias* Cooke, wandering and begging with a counterfeit passport, was punished. Assigned 2 days to go to Orchard, Dors., where he was born and where his father lives.

15 January 1612

331. Jane Gilbert, wife of Thomas Gilbert, was indicted for petty larceny at the sessions on 13 Jan. for selling a gown of Elizabeth Brockwaye's. Passport to Quene Camell, Som., where she says she last dwelt; 6 days assigned because of her weakness.

24 January 1612

332. Sibyl Kingman, wandering and vagrant, was punished. Passport to Lake in Willeford parish where she says she was born; 2 days assigned.

333. William Hixon, wandering as a vagrant, was punished. Assigned 1 day to go to Downton where he says he was born.

[f. 34] 25 February 1612

334. Robert Hotchins, wandering as a vagrant, was punished. Passport to Tilberye, [Essex], where he says he was born; 8 days assigned.

10 March 1612

335. Christopher Wyllen, wandering as a vagrant, was punished. Passport to St. Peter's [*recte* St. Petrock's] parish, Exeter, where he says he was born; 6 days assigned.

336. Robert Fludd, wandering, was punished. Passport to Hanyehanger, Ang., where he says he was born; 12 days assigned.

18 March 1612

337. Richard Tippes, a minstrel, and Margaret his wife, wandering, were punished. Passport to Bristoll where they say their dwelling is; 6 days assigned.

25 May 1612

338. William Robertes, wandering, confesses that he ran away from his master John Ovell, saddler, of Wymborne Mynster, Dors., to whom he was

bound apprentice, and that he was born at South Lytchett, Dors. He was punished; 3 days appointed to go to Wymborne.

27 May 1612
339. Hugh Halles, son of Bartholomew Halles, wandering, was punished. Assigned 4 days to go to Fyvefield, Som.

6 June 1612
340. Thomas Wynestopp, son of John Wynestopp of Southampton, wandering and begging, was punished. Assigned 2 days to go to Southampton

11 June 1612
341. Jane Childe, supposed wife of Thomas Childe, wandering, was punished. Assigned 12 days to go to Atherley, Devon.

31 July 1612
342. Thomas Thursbye, wandering as a vagrant having no testimonial nor showing any cause of his wandering, was punished. Assigned 3 days to go to Chichester, Suss., where he was born.

28 August 1612
343. John Parker, wandering as a vagrant, was punished. Assigned 20 days to go to Warton, Lancs., where he says he was born.

[f. 34v.] 8 September 1612
344. Bernard Barrye, terming himself a petty chapman, wandering as a vagrant, was punished. Assigned 10 days to go to Bratton, Devon, where he says his dwelling is. He says he has a wife and child wandering about Dorchester, [Dors. or Oxon.]. [Cf. no. 345]
345. John Graunt, wandering as a vagrant with the said Bernard Barrye, misdemeaned himself in this city towards the constable and officers and secretly took away a leg of mutton. He was punished. Assigned 1 day to go to Houghton, Hants, where he says his dwelling is. [Cf. no. 344]

21 September 1612
346. Agnes Symons, wandering as a vagrant, was punished. Assigned 3 days to go to Wareham [Dors.] where she says she was born.

24 September 1612
347. Honour Humber, wandering as a vagrant, was punished. Assigned 7 days to go to Tyverton, Devon, where she says she lives.

30 September 1612
348. Humphrey Bate, found wandering as a vagrant and taking fruit from a garden or orchard, was punished. Assigned 3 days to go to Hackfeild, Hants, where he says he was born and lives.

Tempore Lawrence Horne, mayor.
29 December 1612
349. Alice Barley, widow, wandering, was spared her punishment because of her weakness and feebleness. Assigned 3 days to go to Upper Walloppe, Hants, where she says she was born.

25 January 1613

350. Anthony Basse, wandering, was punished. Assigned 20 days to go to St. Thomas's parish, Exeter, where he was born. He is very weak and sick.

9 March 1613

351. Henry Jones and Joan Thomas, widow, found wandering as vagrants and drunk, were punished. Assigned 4 days to go to Bristoll where they say they live. [Cf. no. 403]

[f. 35] 29 April 1613

352. Robert Hulett, found wandering and behaving himself lewdly with Magdalen Masters, was punished. Assigned 1 day to go to Dorneford where he says he was born. *They abused themselves in the fields on Thursday last and at Seywell's.*

25 June 1613

353. Joan Powell, wandering, was punished. Assigned 10 days to go to Wellington, Herefs., where she says she was born.

12 July 1613

354. Margery Clyfford, a wanderer and vagrant, was punished. Assigned 2 days to go to North Tydworth where she says she last lived.

4 September 1613

355. Amy Smythe, wandering as a vagrant, was punished. Assigned 8 days to go to St. Giles's parish near Holborne, London, where she says she last lived.

Tempore Mr. Alexander Alford, [mayor].

13 January 1614

356. Philip Williams, indicted and convicted of petty larceny at the sessions, was ordered to be whipped and sent to Killingworth, Warws. He was punished and is to go there.

3 May 1614

357. Jane Norris, daughter of John Norris and Grace his wife. Passport to Martyn where she says she was born; 2 days assigned.

30 May 1614

358. John Burnett, wandering and vagrant. Passport to Hixon, Cornw., where he says he was born.

359. William Walden, wandering, is assigned 3 days to go to Winchester, where he says he was born.

14 June 1614

360. John Crosse, wandering. Passport to Woodbery, Devon, where he says he last lived; 10 days assigned.

18 June 1614

361. John Dybbe, wandering, was punished. Assigned 2 days to go to Fordingbridge, Hants, where he last lived.

[f. 35v.] 23 July 1614

362. William Smythe, wandering, was punished. Assigned 30 days to go to Newcastle, Yorks. [*recte* Northumb. *or* Staffs.].

363. William Courtney, wandering, is assigned 8 days to go to Exeter.

Tempore Henry Pearson, mayor, 1615.

8 June 1615

364. Mary Saunders, widow, wandering as a vagrant, was punished. Assigned 2 days to go to Devizes where she says she last lived.

Tempore Henry Dove, mayor, 1615.

15 December 1615

365. Edward Browne, wandering and begging, was punished. Assigned 1 day to go to Wilton where he was born.

19 December 1615

366. John Rundle, a petty chapman, wandering idly with Dorothy Orpyn, was punished. Assigned 2 days to go to Shaftesbury, Dors., where he lives. [Cf. no. 367]

367. Dorothy Orpyn, wandering with John Rundle, was punished. Assigned 1 day to go to Amesburye where she lives. [Cf. no. 366]

9 April 1616

368. Henry Whyte, indicted for felony at the sessions, was ordered to be burnt in the hand and given a passport to Kylve, Som., where he was born; 5 days assigned. [A loose MS. note of this passport remains in the register.]

10 April 1616

369. Anne Benberye, spinster, wandering as a vagrant, was punished. Assigned 6 days to go to Wymborne Mynster, Dors., where she says she lived for 15 years.

[f. 36] 3 May 1616

370. John Pearson, wandering as a vagrant, was punished. He is to go to Highe Littlton, Som., where he says he was born.

2 May 1616

371. John Martyn, wandering, was punished. Assigned 4 days to go to Hampreston, Dors., where he says he was born. [Cf. no. 326]

372. Prys Williams *alias* Apprice Williams, a ballad-singer and vagrant, was punished. Assigned 5 days to go to Gold Angare, Essex.

373. Robert Osborne, wandering as a vagrant, was punished. Assigned 6 days to go to Avard, Som., where he says he lives.

12 August 1616

374. George Persevall, convicted at the last sessions for the felonious stealing of a shirt from John Watkins, had a passport to go to Don Vangan in Ireland; 1 month assigned.

Tempore Robert Norwell, mayor, 1616.

375. Peter Dove, a tinker, wandering, was punished. Assigned 20 days to go to Gresnoll, Norf., where he says he was born.

376. John Frye, wandering, was punished. Assigned 4 days to go to Bishoppes Stooke, Hants, where he was born.

28 December 1616
377. Paul Michell, vagrant, was punished. Assigned 10 days to go to Rye, Suss., where he says he was born. [Translated from Latin.]

3 February 1617
378. Elizabeth Hurste, wandering and begging, was punished. Assigned 7 days to go and be conveyed to Southampton where she says she was born.

11 October 1616
379. William Hussey, apprentice to Thomas Williams of London dwelling in Taymes Street, was found wandering. He was punished. Assigned 7 days to go to his master.

[f. 36v.] 16 October 1616
380. Anne Bevyn, widow, wandering and begging, was punished. Assigned 3 days to go or be conveyed to Lymington, Hants, where she last dwelt.

24 January 1617
381. Eleanor Clemante, daughter of William Clemante, wandering and vagrant, was punished. Assigned 4 days to go to Keyvell where she was born.

25 January 1617
382. Lucy Fletcher, wandering, was punished. Assigned 4 days to go to Meere where she was born.

10 February 1617
383. William Harris, wandering as a vagrant, was punished. Assigned 20 days in respect of his weakness to go to Sheppards Well, Kent, where he says he last lived.
384. Mary Parrye, wandering, was punished. Assigned 14 days to go to Northe Corye, Som., where she was born.

17 March 1617
385. Agnes Symons, daughter of William Symons late of Lyttleton, Som., wandering and begging, was punished. She confessed that she had wandered for the last two years. Assigned 10 days to go to Lyttleton where she says she was born. [A loose MS. note recording Agnes's punishment and that her father died two years earlier, since when she has 'wandered up and down in several shires begging', remains in the register.]
386. William Beale and Elizabeth his wife, wandering and begging, confess that they were married in Stratford uppon Aven, Warws., where they lived for the last 12 years and more. Assigned 14 days for their travel to Stratford.

28 March 1617
387. Alice Ingram, wife of John Ingram of Harbridge, Hants, petty chapman, found wandering with two children, was punished. Assigned 2 days to go to Harbridge. [Cf. no. 290]

31 March 1617
388. Anne Turner, wandering as a vagrant having a false passport, was punished. Assigned 8 days to go to Chemsford, Essex, where she says she lives.

[f. 37] 9 April 1617
389. William Norman, vagrant and wandering with a counterfeit passport, was punished. Assigned 18 days because of his lameness to go to Bedgeberye, Kent, where he says he last dwelt.

6 May 1617
390. William Urrye, wandering with a lewd woman with whom he confesses he has continued lewdly for four years, was punished. Assigned 6 days to go to Brodeassington, Glos., where he says he last dwelt. [Cf. no. 394]

20 May 1617
391. Honour Nuewater, wandering, was punished. Assigned 30 days to go to Latron in Ireland, where she says she was born.

31 May 1617
392. Elizabeth Collins and Elizabeth Harris, wandering as vagrants, were punished. Assigned 16 days to go to Chichester, Suss., where they say their dwelling is.

11 June 1617
393. John Jones, apprentice to Edward Samon of Wells, [Som.], tailor, was found wandering and punished. Assigned 3 days to go to his master.

9 October 1617
394. William Urrye, found wandering with Mary Dudlye, was punished. Assigned 6 days to go to Brode Assington, [Glos.]. [Cf. no. 390]

23 October 1617
395. Gilbert Hobbye, wandering, was punished. Assigned 2 days to go to Romesey, [Hants].

15 December 1617
396. William Morton, apprentice and servant to Henry Morton of Barbican near Long Lane End, London, is assigned 4 days to go to his master.

31 March 1618
397. Richard Barrett was found wandering and begging, sometimes saying he had lost by fire. He was punished. Assigned 3 days to go to Norton, Som., where he says his dwelling is. *He was taken vagrant in Mr. Banes's time.* [Cf. no. 222]

13 April 1618
398. Mary Marshere, spinster, wandering, was punished. Assigned 8 days to go and be conveyed to Chard, Som., where she says she was born.

[f. 37v.] 23 May 1618
399. Charles Coward, wandering as a vagrant, who had stolen certain poultry, was punished. Assigned 1 day to go to Downton where his last dwelling was.

8 August 1618

400. John Jenkins, wandering and following the court as a vagrant, was punished. Assigned 16 days to go to Feversham, Kent, where his dwelling is.
401. Henry Greene, vagrant, is assigned 40 days to go to Scarfare, Leics., where he was born.
402. Robert Guye, born at Collingborne, was taken selling small books, seeming to be distracted and wandering idly about.

4 August 1619

403. Henry Jones, Bridget his wife, and William Jones were found wandering disorderly. Henry was punished. He is assigned 6 days to go to Bristoll where they say their dwelling is. *He received punishment in 1612.* [Cf. no. 351]

11 August 1619

404. John Pike, wandering and begging, was punished. Assigned 10 days to go to Muche Hollam, Essex, where he says his dwelling is.

25 March 1620

405. Margaret Cheecke, wandering with a lewd fellow named Martin Drake, was punished. Assigned 6 days to go to Banwell, Som., where she says she was born. [Cf. no. 406. A loose MS. note of this and the two following entries remains in the register.]
406. Martin Drake, wandering as a vagrant with Margaret Cheecke, is assigned 14 days to go to Trewroe, Cornw., where he says his dwelling is. They confessed they lived together lewdly for about three years. [Cf. no. 405]

20 April 1620

407. Samson Pattizon, found wandering and drunk, was punished. Assigned 20 days to go to Lamso, [? Cornw.], where he says his dwelling is. [Cf. no. 405]

f. 38] 3 May 1620

408. Dorothy Mitchell, wandering, was punished. Assigned 3 days to go to Stanbridge, Dors., where she says her dwelling is.
409. Mary Jordayne, widow, wife of Richard Jordayne deceased, wandering, was punished. Assigned 6 days to go to Horseley, Surr., where she says her last dwelling was.

[Blank] April 1620

410. Francis Julye, wandering, begging, and a vagrant, was punished. Assigned 14 days to go to Wempham, Devon, where he says he was born.
411. Francis Parker, wandering, was punished. Assigned 10 days to go to Myniard, Som., where he was born.
412. William Eyers, wandering, was punished. Assigned [blank] days to go to Canterburye, Kent, where he says he was born.

Tempore William Raye, mayor, 1620.

8 December 1620

413. William Huntt, wandering as a vagrant, was punished. Assigned 3 days to go to Hooke, Dors., where he says his dwelling is.

Tempore Maurice Greene, mayor, 1621.

2 March 1622

414. Elizabeth Griffen, petty chapwoman, and Anne Griffen her daughter, wandering, having other idle persons accompanying them and using shifts by putting away and cozening his Majesty's subjects with counterfeit pieces or slips, were punished. Assigned 4 days to go to Farington, Berks., where they say they dwell.

26 March 1622

415. John Jerrard, vagrant, was punished. Assigned 10 days to be conveyed to St. Giles's near London to William Capgood, tailor, whose apprentice he confesses he is. [Cf. no. 416]

27 March 1622

416. Robert Hanwell, wandering with [John] Jerrard, was punished. Assigned 10 days to be conveyed to John Baninge, a brassell-grinder[1] in Teme Street, London, whose apprentice he confesses he is. [Cf. no. 415]

[f. 38v.] 5 December 1622

417. Anthony Cooper, wandering, says his last dwelling was in Buckington, [Som.].

Tempore Mr. Thomas Squibbe, mayor.

21 July 1623

418. Margaret Symes, wandering, was punished. Assigned 5 days to go to Ashweeke near Mendippe, [Som.], where she says she was born.

6 November 1623

419. John Hotkins, vagrant, confesses he is apprentice to Robert Studdocke of Froome Selwood, Som., weaver. He ran away from his master. He was punished. Passport to return to his master; 3 days assigned.

7 November 1623

420. Dorothy Burd, wife of James Burd, feltmaker. Assigned 12 days to go to Barstable, [Devon], to her husband.

Tempore Robert Jole, mayor, 1623.

6 March 1624

421. John Steddam, a vagrant and suspicious person, was punished. Assigned 12 days to go to Cullington, Devon, where he says he was born.

23 May 1624

422. Thomas Coxe, tinker, Ellen his wife, Thomas Barnes his apprentice, and two children, wandering and vagrant, were punished. Assigned 13 days to go to Gaddesden, Herts., where he was born and dwells. [Cf. no. 438]

10 April 1624

423. Philip Browne wandered with William Doggett, weaver, and William Griffen, petty chapman, for the last fortnight and they yield no account of their idleness. Browne was punished and assigned 4 days to go to Malmesburye where his dwelling is. [Cf. no. 424]

---

[1] A grinder of brazil-wood used in the production of red dye.

10 April 1624

424. William Doggett, wandering, was punished. Assigned 3 days to go to Westwood where he says he was born. [Cf. no. 423]

22 April 1624

425. John Hancock, wandering, was punished. Assigned 7 days to go to East Mowsse, Surr., where he says he was born.

5 May 1624

426. Walter Dyte, wandering and begging, was punished. Assigned 6 days to go to London where he says he was born.

[f. 39] 5 June 1624

427. Henry Horslye, wandering, begging, and abusing himself by excessive drinking, was punished. Assigned 10 days to go to Exeter where he says he was born.

22 June 1624

428. Thomas Stroude *alias* Dawbury *alias* Trowe was sent to this city by passport from Widcombe, [Som.], alleging he was born here, whereas it appears he was born in Cadburye, Som. Passport to Cadburye; 20 days assigned. [Cf. no. 436]

3 July 1624

429. John Shorte and William Pynner, wandering as vagrants, were punished. Passport to Pyddle, Worcs.; 30 days assigned.

16 July 1624

430. William Taylor, Agnes his wife, and Priscilla Greene, wandering, were punished. They are sent with two children by passport to Horsham, Suss., where they were born; 10 days assigned.

13 September 1624

431. John Pomroy, wandering as a rogue and misbehaving himself, was punished. Assigned 10 days to go to Perryn, Cornw., where he says he was born.

432. Frances Symons, wandering, confesses that she lives incontinently with William Goodman, a joiner and a lewd fellow, who impudently affirmed that they were married. She is punished and sent to Blandford, [Dors.], where she was born. Goodman is committed to prison in this city. [Cf. no. 433]

15 September 1624

433. William Goodman, joiner, wandering as a vagrant, confessed before the mayor and justices that he and Frances Symons live lewdly, not being married. He was punished. Passport to Bristoll where he says he was born. [Cf. no. 432]

6 November 1624

434. Henry Gillingham, shoemaker, and Margaret his wife, wandering, were punished. They are sent to Serne, Som. [*recte* Dors.], where he says he was born.

435. Thomas Coleman, wandering as a vagrant, was punished. He is sent to Amberlye, Suss., where he says he was born.

436. Thomas Daborne *alias* Trowe, weaver, wandering, was punished. He is sent to Reading, Berks., where he last dwelt many years. [Cf. no. 428]

[f. 39v.] *Tempore* Richard Checkford, mayor.
10 January 1625
437. William Brinckworthe, wire-drawer, wandering as a vagrant, was punished. Passport to Plymoth, Devon, where he says he was born.

4 February 1625
438. Thomas Coxe, Ellen his wife, and Mary his child under the age of 7 years, were taken begging. Passport to Gaddesden, Herts., where he says they last dwelt. [Cf. no. 422]

28 March 1625
439. Walter Warde, begging and wandering, was punished. Passport to Fisherton Anger.

5 December 1625
440. Purnell Fletcher, wandering and begging, was punished. He is sent to Hasselmere, Surr., with a little boy.

Tempore Mr. Wolstan Coward, mayor, 1625.
12 December 1625
441. Elizabeth Greene *alias* Lemster, wandering, was punished. She is sent to Upper Wallopp, Hants.

17 July 1625
442. Thomas Chamberlyn, wandering and begging, was punished. Passport to Southwarke, Surr., where he says he was born.

Tempore James Abbott, mayor.
3 March 1628
443. Peter Taylor, wandering, having unlawfully left his master, William Gerishe of Freshford, Som., weaver, was punished. Passport to return to his master.

18 April 1628
444. William Butler, wandering and begging, terming himself a glassman, having no passport, was punished. Passport to Buckland, Devon, where he says his dwelling is.

22 May 1628
445. Richard Morris and Elizabeth his wife, wandering as vagrants and he drunk, having no passport nor giving any account of their wandering, were punished. Passport to Newport Pannell, Bucks., where they say their dwelling is.

17 July 1628
446. Grace and Abraham Tuke, wandering with two small children, not giving any cause of their wandering, were punished. Passport to Froome Selwood, Som., where they say their dwelling is. *Suspected of stealing a piece of cloth from Mr. Coward; they had a new pair of shoes and confess they had no money.*

[f. 40] 6 August 1628

447. Thomas Stone, terming himself a soldier, wandering and begging, has been here and in Fisherton for four days with a counterfeit passport. He used insolent words before Mr. Mayor and Mr. Recorder, affirming that his last dwelling was in Colchester, Essex, and on further examination confesses that he does not dwell in Colchester but has friends there and desires to travel thither. He was punished. Passport to Colchester. He dares the justices and confesses that he knows neither the Lord Darcy nor any about Colchester of quality. [Cf. no. 499]

Tempore John Batt, mayor.

25 November 1628

448. John Haskins and Lerytoe his wife, wandering and begging, were punished. Passport to go with their two children to Marcham, Berks., where they say their last dwelling was.

23 February 1629

449. James Powell, wandering and begging, was punished. Passport to Wigmore, Herefs., where he last dwelt.

14 April 1629

450. Daniel Murran, an Irishman, begging. Passport to the county of Waterford in the province of Munster, Ireland.

451. John Carye, begging. Passport to Woodhaye, Hants.

16 April 1629

452. An obstinate Irishman, begging and refusing to tell his name. Passport to Bristoll and from there to Ireland.

9 May 1629

453. John Willyams, wandering and begging. Passport to Mutche Holland, Essex.

454. Thomas Miller, wandering and begging. Passport to Dartmothe, Devon.

455. Robert Yeovens, wandering. Passport to Peter Tavey, Devon.

Tempore Anthony Brickett, mayor, 1629.

7 December 1629

456. Richard Thomas, wandering. Passport to Cardycan town, Carms. [*recte* Cardig.], where he says he was born.

16 December 1629

457. Priscilla Baylye, begging, was punished. Passport to Allington where she says her dwelling is.

[f. 40v.] 22 December 1629

458. Luke Cutler, wandering and begging, was punished. Passport to Heeve near Southampton, [Hants], where he says his dwelling is.

459. David Humphrey, wandering and begging. Passport to Ruthing, Denb., Wales, where he was born and last dwelt.

19 January 1630

460. Henry Jones, wandering and begging, was punished. Passport to Hallagaia, Carms., Wales.

1 February 1630
461. Robert Newman, wandering, was punished. Passport to Downton.

3 February 1630
462. Edward Harrington, sent by passport from Marshfeild, Glos., supposing that he was born here, says that he was born in St. Giles's parish, Creplegate, London. Passport to London.

1 April 1630
463. Edward Pytman, terming himself a soldier, wandering, begging, and otherwise disordering and misdemeaning himself, pawned his writing for ale. It appears, and he confesses, that it was made in March 1629 and now it is 1630 and [the certificate] all torn. He was punished. Passport to Cattestocke, Dors., where he says his dwelling is.

10 April 1630
464. Judith Jones and Dorothy Allyn, wandering as rogues, had taken a limb of veal by unlawful means. Judith is to go to Yarnescombe, Som. [recte Devon], and Dorothy to Taunton, Som.

14 April 1630
465. Gregory Harper and Joan Martyn, who was born in Fordington near Dorchester, [Dors.], were found wandering and begging with a counterfeit passport, affirming that they are married, and were punished. They are sent to St. Mary's parish, Dover, Kent. [Cf. no. 549]

13 May 1630
466. Jenkyn Thomas, selling cups and such trifles contrary to his Majesty's proclamation and wandering with his wife, daughter, and Evan Harrye, his servant, ran away from the officers. Passport to Rackland, Mon., in Wales.

19 May 1630
467. John and Edmund Poore, begging Irishmen, were punished. Passport to be conveyed to Bristoll and thence to Ireland.
468. Elizabeth Harrison, wandering and begging with a child of 7 years, was punished. Passport to York where she says her dwelling is.

[f. 41] 2 June 1630
469. Gilbert Mawle, button-maker of London, came to this city wandering and offering wares contrary to the law.

22 September 1630
470. Roger Alderseay, Thomas Humfrey, and Margaret Aldersea, wife of Edward Aldersea, vagrant and wanderers together, were punished. Roger had a passport to Liskard, Cornw., Thomas to Decle, Kent, and Margaret to Wells, Som., where they say they live.

25 September 1630
471. Reynold Blanye, wandering and begging, was punished. Passport to St. Stephen's parish, London, where he says his last dwelling was.
472. John Brown, wandering and begging, was punished. Passport to Feske, Kent, where he says he was born.

4 October 1630
473. Thomas Beckett *alias* Berkett, wandering as a vagrant, was punished.
Passport to Skipton in Craven, Yorks., where he says his dwelling is.
474. Gilbert Gumpe, chapman, taken wandering, was punished. Passport to
Warrington, Lancs., where he says his dwelling is.
475. John and Charles Wood, wandering chapmen, were punished. Passport
to Attercliffe, Yorks., where they say they dwell.
476. Edward Kerbye, a ballad-seller, wandering, was punished. Passport to
Holborne, London, where his dwelling is.
477. William Crowche, chapman, wandering, was punished. Passport to
Brantree, Essex, where his dwelling is.
478. Edward Elder, wandering, was punished. Passport to Learpoole, Lancs.,
where he says he dwells.
479. John Ogden and Thomas Jenkins, chapmen, wandering, were punished.
Passport to St. Pulcher's, near London, where they dwell.
480. John Thomas, wandering, was punished. He is to go to West Chester,
Ches., where he says he was born.

5 October 1630
481. Constantine Adyn and Isabel his wife, wandering vagrants. Passport to
Newington, Surr., where they say their last dwelling was. He said he had
three children by his wife, which she denied.

23 December 1630
482. Thomas Warren, terming himself a soldier, wandering with a counterfeit
pass, was punished. Passport to Bristoll where he says his last dwelling was.

[f. 41v.] *Tempore* Mr. Thomas Hill, mayor, 1630.
22 November 1630
483. Alexander Awstyne, wandering and begging, was punished. Passport to
Alboroughe, Suff., where he says his last dwelling was.
484. Leonard Woolffe, wandering, was punished. Passport to Credyton,
Devon, where he says his last dwelling is.
485. John Derman, James Brenar, and Katherine Gawne *alias* Cawne,
wandering and begging, were punished. Passport to go with their children to
Bristoll, where they were landed, and thence to be transported to Waterford,
Ireland, where they say their dwelling was.

11 December 1630
486. John Greenwood, wandering, was punished. Passport to Hyndon.
487. Mary Spratt, wife of Richard Spratt of Bristoll, found begging, was
punished. Passport to Bristoll where she says she last dwelt.

24 January 1631
488. Francis Easterbrooke, wandering and begging, was punished. Passport
to Rye, Suss., where he dwelt.

15 February 1631
489. John Jones, wandering and begging. Passport to Clan Carven, Glam.,
where he last dwelt.

18 February 1631
490. John Sugge, wandering, having a passport from Yeavell, Som., dated 11 Feb. 1632, a year hence, is therefore returned back to Yeavell where he says he last dwelt.

11 March 1631
491. Christian Rose, daughter of John Rose of Downton, taken wandering and begging, was punished. Passport to Downton where she last dwelt.

14 March 1631
492. John Mell, a Dutchman, travelling through this city, fell sick for 14 days. He is sent to the Isle of Wighte to be conveyed to the Low Countries.
493. Martha Merrett and Martha Field her daughter, vagrants and wanderers, were punished. Passport to Bewlye, Hants, where they dwell.

25 March 1631
494. George son of George Masse, tailor, taken wandering and begging, was punished. Passport to Welles, Som., where he says his father dwells.

[f. 42] 5 April 1631
495. Agnes London, wandering and begging, was punished. Passport to Fisherton Anger where her dwelling is.

27 April 1631
496. Christopher son of Christopher Savidge, wandering and begging, was punished. Passport to Alderburye.

7 September 1631
497. James Groce, wandering with Anne Wooddes *alias* Buradge, affirmed that she was his wife, but on examination they confess that they were not married, that since their wandering together she has had a child which is dead, and that she is now with child. He was punished. Passport to go to Myniard, Som., where he says he was born. [Cf. no. 498]

8 September 1631
498. Anne Wooddes. Passport to Myniard, [Som.]. [Cf. no. 497]

Tempore Henry Byley, junior, mayor, 1631.
14 December 1631
499. Thomas Stone, wandering and begging, was punished. Passport to Norwich where he says he was born and last dwelt. [Cf. no. 447]

2 January 1632
500. Richard Pratt, wandering, was punished. Passport to Downton where he says he was born.

11 January 1632
501. John Luckocke, wandering, was punished. Passport to Kingeberye, Som., where he says he last dwelt.

1 February 1632
502. Katherine Bartlett, wandering and begging, was punished. Passport to Stratford upon Haven, Warws., where she says she was born and last dwelt.

15 February 1632
503. Evan ap John ap Davye, wandering and begging. Passport to Surdeon, Glam., Wales, where he last dwelt.

20 February 1632
504. William Eades and Agnes his wife, wandering and begging. Passport to Darford, Kent, where they last dwelt.
505. Thomas Jackson, wandering, was punished. Passport to St. Giles's, Oxford, where he says he was born.

16 April 1632
506. Francis Berricke, wandering and begging, was punished. Passport to Bristoll where he last dwelt. He says he landed at Portesmouthe. He abused himself in the city and John Palmer and Robert Blake, constables, [apprehended him].

[f. 42v.] 5 May 1632
507. William Gildinge, wandering and begging, was punished. Passport to be conveyed to Tottnes, Devon, where he says he was born. [Passport] made by Mr. Thomas Hill, [alderman and justice].
508. John Baylye, taken wandering and drunk, was punished. Passport to Keynton, Devon, where he says he last dwelt. Passport made by Mr. Hill.

23 May 1632
509. Alexander Pytman, wandering. Passport to Wimborne Mynster, Dors., where he last dwelt.
510. Edward Parkins, wandering and begging. Passport to Corffe Castle in the Isle of Purbecke, Dors., where he last dwelt.
511. Anthony Tolman, apprentice of Walter Davis of Bristoll, glover, wandering and begging, was punished. He is to be sent to Bristoll to his master.

8 August 1632
512. Richard Sprage, wandering and begging, was punished. Passport to Fordingbridge, Hants, where he says his dwelling is.

Tempore Mr. Bee, mayor.
10 December 1632
513. John Harvye, wandering, was punished. Passport to Bantrey, Essex.
514. Thomas Griffyn, wandering and begging, was punished. Passport to Drakesom, Merion., Wales.

4 February 1633
515. Thomas Morgayne and Thomas Pryse, wandering and begging, were punished. Passport to St. Berye, Cornw.

15 April 1633
516. A dumb boy wandering and begging, pretending he has no tongue, was punished. Passport to Trowbridge where he last dwelt.

17 August 1633
517. Mourne, late wife of John Trege of Fayre, Kilkenny, Ireland, was

found wandering with Richard Whyte, affirming that he was her husband. Richard confessed on examination that they were not married, that his counterfeit passport was written in London, and that he gave 3s. for it. She was punished. Passport to Bristoll and thence to Ireland. [Cf. no. 518]

27 August 1633
518. Richard [Whyte], wandering with Mourne [Trege], confessed he was never married to her and that the two passports were counterfeit. He was punished. Passport to Mynyard, Som., and thence to Langford, Ireland. [Cf. no 517]

[f. 43] 11 October 1633
519. John Griffyn, wandering as a vagrant, was punished. Passport to Chepstowe, Mon., Wales, where he says his last dwelling was.

14 October 1633
520. Roger son of William Ayliffe, wandering and begging, was punished. Passport to Christchurche, Hants, where he says his father dwells.

Tempore Mr. Nicholas Ellyott, mayor, 1633.
10 December 1633
521. John Jacobb, wandering and begging, was punished. Passport to Charmister, Dors., where he says he was born.

20 December 1633
522. Katherine daughter of John Morgan of Christchurche parish, Corke, Ireland, shoemaker, was found wandering and begging with a boy and a woman with a suspicious passport. On examination [it appears that] they have been various and false. Katherine landed at Padstowe, Cornw., having no land passport. Passport to Padstowe and thence to Corke. [Cf. no. 523]

23 December 1633
523. Alice Gallowhill, an Irish maid, wandering with Katherine Morgan and others, having no passport or certificate for her landing or travel, said she landed at St. Ives, Cornw. Passport to St. Ives. [Cf. no. 522]

4 February 1634
524. John Tanner and John Yerrand, a Scotsman, wandering and begging as vagrants, were apprehended by Mr. Francis Dove, constable, and punished. Tanner had a passport to Compton Chamberlyn where he says his last dwelling is, Yerrand to Southampton where he says he dwells and has a wife.

26 February 1634
525. William Wyatt, wandering and begging, was punished. Passport to Newetowne, Hants, where he says he dwells and has a house.

18 July 1634
526. Anne Jones, wandering and begging, was punished. Passport to Upper Kensome, Herefs., where she last dwelt.

23 August 1634
527. Anne Harris *alias* Gill, as she says, was found wandering with William Gill who she says was her husband; he said she is his sister. They lay together

last night at the Talbot. He afterwards said they were married at Hull; she said in London. She was punished. Passport to Kingeston upon Hull, Yorks., where she has 4 children and where she last dwelt. [Cf. no. 528]

[f. 43v.] 2 September 1634
528. William Gill was found wandering as a vagrant with a lewd woman named Anne Harris, first affirming they were brother and sister. Afterwards the one affirmed they were married at Hull, the other at London, and on further examination it is confessed they were not married and that they lived incontinently the last two months. He was punished. Passport to be sent to Leeds, Yorks., where he says he was born. [Cf. no. 527]

31 October 1634
529. Joan Ripley, wandering and begging, was punished. Passport to Gt. Tenants, Kent, where she says she was born.

30 October 1634
530. Michael Leache, wandering and begging, was punished. Passport to Lyndhurste, Hants, where he says he was born. [Cf. no. 545]

12 November 1634
531. Nicholas Dyer, wandering and begging as a vagrant, was punished. Passport to Newton Bushell, Devon, where he says he was born.

Tempore Mr. John Dove, mayor, 1634.
23 November 1634
532. Edward Taverner, wandering and begging, was punished. Passport to Finchenfeild, Essex, where he says he was born.
533. Robert Wood, wandering and begging, was punished. Passport to Halesowen, Worcs., where he says he was born.

4 March 1635
534. Thomas Jenkins, wandering and begging, was punished. Passport to Lee parish in the Forest of Deane, Glos., where he says he was born and dwelt. [Cf. no. 535]
535. Richard Davis, begging with [Thomas] Jenkins, was punished. Passport to Lee parish, [Glos.], where he was born and last dwelt. [Cf. no. 534]

5 March 1635
536. Margaret Hancocke, wandering, having a young child, was punished. Passport to Farnegam, Kent, where she was born.

28 May 1635
537. Margaret Yower, wandering and begging, was punished. Passport to Wilton where she says she dwells.

16 June 1635
538. William Speareman, begging, was punished. Passport to Beckhamsfeild, Bucks., where he last dwelt.

[f. 44] 10 August 1635
539. Thomas Crocker and Alice his wife, with a young child, wandering and begging with Thomas Phillippes, were punished. Passport to Burcleare,

Hants, near Newberye, where they say their dwelling is. [Cf. no. 540]

540. Thomas Phillippes, begging, although it appears he received sufficient relief from the treasurers for his passage, was punished. Passport to St. Edmondesburye, Suff., from where he says he was impressed. [Cf. no. 539]

3 September 1635
541. John Kempe, wandering and begging, was punished. Passport to Ipswitche, Suff., where he says he was born.

25 September 1635
542. Daniel Micarte, wandering and begging, was punished. Passport to the parish of Isle and Carye in the county of Kerry, Ireland, where he was born and last dwelt.

26 October 1635
543. Susanna Wickham, wandering and begging with three children, was punished. Passport to Spaulden, Lincs., where she says her last dwelling was. [Cf. no. 547]

544. Thomas Gittinge and Jane his wife, wandering as vagrants, not showing any ground or reason for their wandering, were punished. Passport to Hereford in Wales, where they say they last dwelt.

Tempore Maurice Aylerugge, mayor.
28 November 1635
545. Nathaniel Leache, a poor child about 9 or 10 years of age, likely to perish and die in the streets with cold, was taken begging and crying. Passport to Lyndhurste, Hants, where he says he was born. [Cf. no. 530]

27 January 1636
546. John Dykes, wandering and begging, was punished. Passport to Ashehill, Som., where he says his last dwelling was.

547. Susanna Wickham with three children came to this city with a passport to be conveyed to the place where she was born. Her passport was so torn that she could not be sent further by it. Passport to Haselberye, Som., where she says she was born. [Cf. no. 543]

548. William Jones and Jane his wife, with a young child, wandering and begging, were punished. Passport to Detford, Devon, where William said he was born.

21 July 1636
549. Gregory Harper, wandering and begging, was punished. Passport to Cleadescome, Hants, where he says he was born. [Cf. no. 465]

[f. 44v.] *Tempore* Mr. Richard Carter, mayor.
1 March 1637
550. James Pretcher, with two children under the age of 7 years, was punished. Passport to Ben Easton near Bathe, Som., where he says they were born.

10 March 1637
551. Thomas Bassett, a petty chapman, selling false and counterfeit jewels, found wandering as a vagrant, was punished. Passport to Christechurche, [Hants], where he says his dwelling is.

20 March 1637
552. Margaret wife of Thomas Fuller, wandering, had a passport dated 13 Mar. 1637 by which it was mentioned that she came from Chalke near Gravesend, Kent. In her travel she was delivered of a child in Longeparishe, Hants, and sent from there by passport to this city. Passport back to Chalke where her husband last dwelt.

8 July 1637
553. Gertrude Basse, wandering and begging, was punished. Passport to Taunton, Som., where she says she was born.

22 September 1637
554. Thomas Osborne, wandering, was punished. Passport to Taunton, Som., where he says he was born.

27 February 1638
555. Richard Flower, apprentice of John Joyner of Devizes, found wandering, confessed that he unlawfully ran away from his master. He was punished. Passport to return to his master in St. Mary's parish, Devizes.

Tempore John Banger, gent., [mayor, 1638].
556. James Frye was punished and sent to Teverton, [Devon].
557. Jasper Parker, James Douglas, and John Douglas were punished and sent away.
558. Richard Flower, William Whatley, and Robert Ellis were punished and were passed away.

[f. 45] *Tempore* Thomas Hancock, gent., mayor.
8 December 1638
559. Dorothy Hutchins, with a child, was punished. Passport to Broad Winsor near Crookhorne, Som., where she says she was born.

1663
3 February 1663
560. John Wareham of Kingsale, Ireland, mariner, vagrant with a counterfeit pass from Newcastle, was whipped. Pass to Bristoll to be transported to Ireland. [Cf. no. 561]
561. George Gibson of Kingston upon Hull, Yorks., mariner, vagrant with [John] Wareham, his name being inserted in the counterfeit pass, was whipped. Pass to Hull. [Cf. no. 560]

18 May 1664
562. Stephen Wick, mariner, vagrant, was whipped. Pass to Colport in the Forest of Dean, Glos., where he says he was born.

21 November 1664
563. John Githurst of Gloucester, labourer, a begging vagrant, was whipped. Pass to Gloucester.

13 February 1665
564. William Smith of Maydston, Kent, shoemaker, and Susanna his wife, begging vagrants, were whipped. Pass to Maydston.

[f. 45v.] 27 July 1668

565. Joyce Jones of Shrewsbury, Salop., vagrant beggar, was whipped. Pass to Shrewsbury.

566. Henry Cooke of Walton, Lancs., a begging vagrant, was whipped. Pass to Walton.

[*Blank*] January 1669

567. Richard Denton, a boy of about 12 years, a begging vagrant, was whipped. Pass to Whitchurch, Salop., where he says he was born, by warrant of Mr. Thomas Batter, J.P.

II SURVEY OF THE POOR 1625

(f. 25) The book of the view and provision for setting the poor on work within the three parishes of the city of New Salisbury begun at the Annunciation of the blessed Virgin Mary A.D. 1625 [25 Mar. 1625], the parishes being divided into several chequers and overseers, added to the legal overseers and churchwardens, appointed to look to all the chequers and divisions to see the poor do their work accordingly and to make presentment at every monthly meeting of the defaults of the workers and their work-masters, according to orders set down in the general quarter sessions held in January last for this city and in the common council of this city.

(ff. 26v.–27) ST. EDMUND'S PARISH

For the north end of Scottes Lane, the north end of Endles Street, the Beaden Row on both sides, and the north part of Church Street up to St. Edmund's church and St. Edmund's churchyard: Mr. Recorder [Henry Sherfield, recorder 1623–34], Mr. Hancocke, Mr. Ivye, [aldermen]; Mr. John Ray, Alexander Penney, William Goseney, assistants.

Masters and workfolk

John Johnson, parchment-maker: Mark Blythe (80), his wife (60), spinning.

William Mason, spinner to the market: Martha Pitt (16), in the Beden Row [alms-houses], spinning, 18*d*. to be earned.

Thomas Turner, spinner and knitter of worsted: Joan Belly (8), daughter to Austin Belly, in the Beden Row [alms-houses], knitting, to have 6*d*. weekly out of the stock; Bridget Vincent (19), daughter to Eleanor Vincent, in the Beden Row [alms-houses], spinning of worsted, 18*d*. to be earned.

Thomas Myller, weaver: John Cranch (13), son to Widow Cranch, quilling, 9*d*. to be earned and his dinner Sundays.

Philip Veryn,[1] sackcloth-maker: John Bryse (8), son to Anne Bryse, John Reade (10), son to Joan Reade, and John Stente (7), son of John Stente, to work at hempen work, and Veryn to have their work to teach them, and their friends to have 6*d*. weekly for every one till they have wages. Veryn promised to teach them within six months.

[1] Later in 1625 Veryn was appointed keeper of the workhouse and instructed to teach the Children employed there to dress and spin hemp: S.C.A., N 100, 11 Dec. 1625. He was possibly already employing children at the workhouse at the time of the survey.

Joan, the wife of John Tooker, in White Horse chequer, bonelace-maker: Anne (8), daughter of John Ricardes, bonelace-making, her mother to have 6*d.* a week allowed her for a year and her work to Tooker.

(f. 27v.) *Wholly impotent*

Margaret Swifte (99), 6*d.* weekly; Margaret Rowsell (80), 8*d.* weekly; Joan Reade (88), 8*d.* weekly; Cicely Jeffery (100), 4*d.* weekly; Mary Oram (62), 6*d.* weekly; Henry Locke (99) and Margery his wife (50), 6*d.* weekly; Thomas Blake (85), 8*d.* weekly; William Cundytt (88), 8*d.* weekly; Richard Pytt (80), 4*d.* weekly.

Impotent in part

Joan Rose (85), 4*d.* weekly; Jane Humfrey (60); Anne Clivelock (68), 6*d.* weekly; Alice Bigges (45); Alice Raph (60); William Bowden.

Apprentices

Edward Hybberd, son to Richard Hibberd; John Cranche, son to Widow Cranche; Henry Meredeth, son to Morgan Meredeth.

(ff. 29v.–30) For the Blue Boar chequer: Mr. Henry Peirson, [alderman]; Thomas Senior, Richard Carter, Thomas Turner, assistants.

Masters and workfolk

Thomas Ray, without Castle Gate, clothier: Joan (10), daughter of Hugh Ellyott and Audrey her mother, spinning, to spin 10 lb. weekly and she is to have 6*d.* weekly out of the stock.

John Butcher the musician's wife, bonelace-maker: Alice (8), daughter of the Widow Younge, bonelace-making, she [Butcher] to have the work one year and her [Alice's] mother 6*d.* weekly; Mary (6), daughter of Margaret Moodye, bonelace-making, she to have the work two years and her mother 6*d.* weekly.

(f. 30v.) *Apprentices*

John and William Sweeteapple, sons to Samuel Sweeteaple.

(ff. 32v.–33) For Mr. Swayne's chequer and Guilder Lane: Mr. Maurice Greene, [alderman]; Bennett Swayne, John Banger, John Paige, assistants.

Masters and workfolk

John Williams, weaver: Jerome Stumpe (43), weaving, to earn 3*s.* weekly.

Mr. Thomas Slye, clothier: Alice (48), his [Jerome Stumpe's] wife, spinning, 6 lb. weekly.

Philip Veryn, sackcloth-worker: Stephen Boyton (40), to work at hemp.

Mary Maylard, daughter of John Maylard, bonelace-maker: Cicely (6), daughter of Thomas Couderoy (pressed for a soldier), bonelace-making, to have 4*d.* a week for one year.

William Eaton, knitter: [*blank*] (11), daughter to William Thringe, knitting, 6*d.* weekly out of the stock for one year and Eaton to have her work.

Robert Hellis, clothier: William Browne (38) and Susanna his wife (40), carding and spinning, 8 lb. weekly.

Mr. Thomas Ray, clothier: Simon Whatleye's wife, William Whately (14), Henry Whatley (8), her sons, spinning, 13 lb.; John Harward (56) and Alice his wife (56), carding and spinning, 12 lb.; Joan (45), the wife of Stephen Boyton, carding and spinning, 5 lb.

William Summers, card-maker: Nicholas (10), son of John Harwood, card-making, 9d. to be earned.

Mr. John Tichborne, knitter: Agnes (6), daughter of John Harwood, knitting, to have 6d. weekly out of the stock for one year and her master to have the work.

(f. 33v.) [Apprentices]

Two children of William Thringe, deceased, the boy (14) fit for an apprentice, the maid (11) to be placed.

(ff. 35v.–36) For the Griffin chequer and the east side of Greencroft Street to Winchester Gate: Mr. Bartholomew Tookey, [alderman]; Thomas Slye, James Michell, William Antrum, assistants.

Masters and workfolk

Philip Veryn, sackcloth-maker: Richard Munday (28), to work at hemp.

Alice Burch, widow, [and] Priscilla Barrington, in New Street, bonelace-makers: Margaret Harelston (14), daughter of Robert Hurelston, kept by Alice Burch, bonelace-making. Alice Burch hath 12d. a week out of the church book for her, and her work is to her dame till midsummer next.

William Gardner, weaver: Katherine (38), wife of Henry White, weaver, spinning of linen, she may earn 10d. a week.

Thomas Underhill, weaver: Robert (11), son of John Hybberd, labourer, quilling, he earneth 7d. and may earn 8d. weekly.

Elizabeth, wife of Richard Brockwell, worsted-spinner: Robert (8), son of Henry Whyte, weaver, worsted-spinning, she to have his work for one year, in the meantime his father to have 6d. weekly.

William Sommers, card-maker: Robert (8), son of Henry Whyte, card-making, 9d.

(f. 36v.) *Apprentices*

William (15), son of Henry Tymbey; William Bryante's son (11), not employed.

[ff. 38v.–39] For the White Horse chequer: Mr. Byell, the elder, [alderman]; James Edmondes, Robert Belman, assistants.

Masters and workfolk

Philip Veryn, sackcloth-maker: John (10), son of John Crowche, at hemp; John (8), son of Walter Cutlipp, at hemp. The fathers to have 6d. weekly for six months and Veryn to have their work.

Thomas Hunte, in Pawle's chequer, weaver: Edward (9), son of Matthew Goddard, quilling, he hath 4d. and must earn 6d. weekly.

Maryan, wife of John Bull, in Church Street, knitter: Elizabeth (13), daughter of Matthew Godden, knitting, she hath 8d. and is to have 10d. at Our Lady Day.

John Crowch, Elizabeth his wife, and 5 children, bonelace-maker and sempster: Elizabeth (12) and Margaret (7), their daughters, bonelace-making, to have 10d. weekly.

[f. 39v.] Goodwife Hales hath 3 children and desireth 40s. to be lent her to keep them working at spinning to the market.

Goodwife Weekes hath 3 small children and desireth something weekly to relieve them.

[ff. 41v.–42] For all Castle Street within the gate: Mr. Byle, the elder, [alderman]; Henry Byle, junior, William Edmondes, John Fludd, Richard Michell, assistants.

Masters and workfolk

Robert Knighte's wife, knitter: [*blank*] (6), daughter of Christopher Benedicte, knitting, the father to have 6d. weekly and she to have the work.

Mr. Bartholomew Tookey, clothier: Christopher Benedict's wife (40), carding and spinning, 6 lb.

[f. 42v.] Jasper Dickens wanteth money to set him on work and is partly impotent.

[ff. 44v.–45] For Mr. Marshall's chequer and Thomas Pawle's chequer:[1] Mr Recorder [Henry Sherfield], Mr. Hancocke, Mr. Ivye, [aldermen]; Mr. Dove, Philip Crewe, Thomas Pawle, assistants.

Masters and workfolk

Thomas Turner, spinner and knitter of worsted: Jane (7), the daughter of John Hynton, knitting, 6d. out of the stock.

Thomas Mathewe, clothier: John (12), the son of James Greedye, spooling, to earn 14d.

John Newbye, weaver: Anthony (6), son of Mary Robertes, quilling, until he be stronger to be taught, the mother to have her allowance in the church book, 12d. weekly.

John Goddard, weaver: William (9), son of Mary Robertes, quilling, to have 9d. weekly from Goddard.

Mary Mallyard, daughter of John Mallyard, bonelace-maker: Patience (8), daughter of Mary Robertes, bonelace-making, to have 4d. weekly out of the stock for one year and then to take her for her work.

John West the bellows-maker's wife, bonelace-maker: Elizabeth (8), daughter of Joan Cosins, bonelace-making, the father to have 6d. weekly out of the stock for one year.

William Lansdall's wife at Milford, bonelace-maker: Alice (9), daughter of Giles Sylvester, bonelace-making, to have 6d. weekly out of the stock for one year.

Roger Knighte's wife, knitter: Joan (8), daughter of Joan Greedye, knitting, to have 6d. weekly and her work for one year; Joan (8), daughter of John Hynton, weaver, knitting, the father to have 6d. weekly for one year.

William Gardner, weaver: Edward (7), son of Gregory Davis, spooling.

[f. 45v.] *Impotent*

Alice Harryson (80); Widow Baker (72).

---

[1] Possibly the later 'Swanton's' and 'Gore's' chequers. George Marshall held property in 'Swanton's' in 1667: *W.A.M.* xxxvi. 421.

[ff. 47v.–48] Without Castle Gate on both sides: Mr. Norwell, Mr. Jole, [aldermen]; William Edmondes, John Fludd, assistants.

Masters and workfolk

Philip Veryn, sackcloth-maker: Christopher (10), son of Thomas Huttofte, to work at hemp, the father to have 6*d.* weekly for 6 months and Veryn to have his work.

William Gardner, weaver: Joyce Mavyon (50), spinning of linen, she may earn 2*s.* a week.

Roger Knighte's wife, knitter: Alice (8), daughter of Zachary Mylls, knitting, to have 6*d.* weekly for one year.

[f. 48v.] [*Apprentice*]

John Gale (20), to be bound to Henry Paige, pewterer, for 8 years. To have £4 lent him now and £4 more upon our next receipts.

[ff. 50v.–51] For Greenawaye's chequer:[1] Mr. William Goodridge, [alderman]; George Beach, Edward Mundey, Thomas Hunt, weaver, assistants.

Masters and workfolk

Thomas Turner, spinner and knitter of worsted: Edith Pavye (60), knitting, 12*d.*; Susan (32), wife of Thomas Harryson, knitting, 8*d.* weekly, and [to be allowed to] attend her children.

Edith Pavye, widow, spinner to market: Agnes Forsett (22), her servant, spinning, 6 lb.

Henry Sevyer's daughter, bonelace-maker: Richard (8), son of Thomas Harryson, bonelace-making, to have money for his work at midsummer next and his father to have 6*d.* weekly till then.

Mr. Bartholomew Tookey, clothier: William Lea's wife (50), 3 lb. and [to] carry coals; John Pytman's wife, 6 lb.; Katherine (35), wife of Thomas Crocher, Joan (14), and Susan (10), their daughters, carding and spinning, 18 lb.

Mr. John Tichborne, knitter: Thomas Sander's wife (40), knitting, 18*d.*

John Martyn, weaver: Edward (11), son of John Kengington, quilling, 9*d.*

John Paige, spinner to the market: John Kengington (60) and Mihill (56), his wife, spinning, 6 lb.

[f. 52v.] *Apprentice*

Thomas Harryson clothworker's son (13).

[f. 54v.] The Black Horse chequer: Mr. Lawrence Horne, Mr. Henry Person, Mr. Ambrose Prewett, [aldermen]; William Gibbes, Philip Veryn, assistants.

[*no entries*]

[f. 57v.] The Three Lions chequer: Augustin Creede, John Randell, assistants.

[*no entries*]

---

1 This chequer possibly included part of the north side of Salt Lane not covered elsewhere in the survey. It may therefore have been the later 'Parson's' chequer, where Mr. Beach, perhaps a kinsman of George Beach, one of the assistants, lived in 1667: ibid. 430.

[ff. 65v.–66] St. Thomas's Parish

For all the Oatmeal Row and the north side of Butcher Row: Mr. Godfrey, [alderman]; James Abbott, Thomas Hill, Edward Brownejohn, assistants.

Masters and workfolk

Alice George, widow, bonelace-maker: her daughters (15, 13), bonelace-making, hath allowance 4d.

[f. 66v.] *Impotent*

Widow Alshere (80), hath no allowance.

[ff. 68v.–69] For the chequer wherein Mr. Churchowse dwelleth and the south side of the Butcher Row: Mr. Squibb, [alderman]; Mr. Anthony Brickett, Humphrey Dytton, John Speringe, John Rendoll, assistants.

Masters and workfolk

William Tanner's wife, bonelace-maker: Francis Brooke (8), bonelace-making.

Richard Michell's wife, in Castle Street, bonelace-maker: Rebecca Verye (14), Anne Verye (10), bonelace-making, the eldest hath 8d. a week.

Deborah Veryn, bonelace-maker: Eleanor Foreman (16), bonelace-making, she hath 14d. a week.

[f. 69v.] *Partly impotent*

Margaret Seawell (67), widow, she wanteth allowance.

Labourers and apprentices

Henry Holton and his wife and one boy (8) and a maid (3½); John Morgan and his wife and three boys (12, 5, 3), the eldest fit to be apprentice, and a maid (8); Thomas Verye and his wife, 3 children, one boy (18) fit to be an apprentice, the other 2 maids (14, 10); Anne Pannell, widow, 6 children, 4 maids (21, 22, 17, 8) and 2 boys (13, 11), she keepeth them all at work and desireth some stock to employ them.

[ff. 72v.–73] From the Water Lane in Castle Street to St. Thomas's churchyard and so round to the Mills and Fisherton Bridge: Mr. Churchowse, [alderman]; John Vyninge, John Saunders, Henry Whitmarsh, assistants.

Masters and workfolk

Alice Swifte, widow, button-maker: Joan Swifte, James Swifte, Katherine Swifte, servants; Joan Kibbe (21), Susanna Horte (16), John Fever (14), Dorothy Cosins (11), Jane Munday (8), Francis Noble (12), apprentices, button-making, she wanteth stock to keep them at work.

Margery Clarke, spinner of thread: Katherine Clarke (11) and Margaret Clarke (8), spinning, she wanteth stock to employ them.

Thomas Edmondes, clothier: William Mare, weaving.

[f. 73v.] *Wholly impotent*

John Jorden (80), Elizabeth his wife (78), ask relief.

Partly impotent

William Clarke (74) and Margery his wife (52), wanting stock to employ 4 children; Anne Cole (80) allowed 4d.; Anne Moore (65), widow, allowed 2d.

Apprentices

Thomas Clarke (19), son of William Clark in the workhouse; Thomas

Barrett (11), John Addams (17), John Lane (12), Thomas Whyte (14), Andrew Raffe (13), Samuel Hales (10), Christopher Stevens (10), John Williams (10), John Younge (10), Alice Stevens (9), John Candye (12), John Wheeler (11), these cost 12*d.* apiece weekly out of Poplye's money. [1]

[ff. 75v.–76] For the Dolphin chequer round: Mr. Robert Banes, [alderman]; Robert White, John Tichborne, Thomas Hancocke, William Brathat, assistants.

Masters and workfolk

Mr. Thomas Ray, clothier: John Rawlyns (50), spooling, 16*d.* to be earned; Margaret Baldwyn (70), widow, spinning, 6*d.* to be earned.

Thomas Tychborne, knitter of worsted: [*blank*] Noble (50), wife of Edward Noble, knitting, 16*d.* weekly out of the stock; Elizabeth (9), daughter to [*blank*] Chitter, widow, knitting, 6*d.* weekly out of the stock.

Joan Board, bonelace-maker: Henry Coke (7), son of Henry Coke, bonelace-making, 6*d.* weekly out of the stock; Mary Phillippes *alias* Talbott (18), knitting, 16*d.* to be earned.

John Tichborne, knitter: Rachel Butcher (7), knitting, 6*d.* weekly out of the stock.

Joan Boarde, bonelace-maker: Mary (10), daughter to Francis Butcher, bonelace-making, 8*d.* to be earned.

John Willis, tailor: [*blank*] Willis, his son, at his trade, allowed 4*d.*; Willis hath three other smaller children.

Emma Westbury: three children, bonelace-making, allowed 4*d.*; Anne Luxson (9), a child, allowed 8*d.*; three children of B. Barnnes, widow, (12, 10, 6).

[f. 76v.] *Wholly impotent*

George Barrett (80), his wife (80), 8*d.* weekly; Edward Noble (80), 6*d.* weekly; Anne Peaslyn (70); Julian Robertes (65), 4*d.* weekly.

Impotent in part

Widow Balden (70), wanteth allowance; Margaret Tompson *alias* Coker (65), 3*d.* weekly.

Richard Lowe, joiner, 6 children, 3 working, 3 small, he desireth a stock; John Wayte, baker, 7 children, 3 working, 4 small, desireth a stock; Thomas Swifte, 3 small children, desireth a stock to employ himself and his wife.

Apprentices

[*blank*] Collins (17), son of Nicholas Collins; [*blank*] Sanger (16), son of Robert Sanger, but he hath a sore head.

[ff. 78v.–79] The White Bear chequer and the White Hart chequer: Mr. Thomas Ray, Mr. William Ray, [aldermen]; John Fryer, William Speringe, Thomas Edmondes, Christopher Smithe, assistants.

---

[1] The income of Joan Popley's charity from London property had been used for the workhouse stock since 1602: S.C.A., S 163 (reversed), f. 3; Ledger C, f. 237v.; *V.C.H. Wilts.* vi. 173.

Masters and workfolk
   [*no entries*]
[f. 79v.] *Wholly impotent*
   Widow Joanes (65), 9*d*. weekly; Gawen Randoll (70), 4*d*; his wife (68).
Partly impotent
   John Reade (65), 4*d*. weekly.
Apprentices
   [*blank*] Mylls, son of Robert Mylls; [*blank*] Broocke, son of Simon Brooke;
[*blank*] Pensex, son of Elizabeth Pensex; [*blank*] Brickett, son of John Brickett;
Daniel Mylborne (13), son of the girdler.

[ff. 81v.–82] From Fisherton Bridge to Crane Street, on both sides to the
Close gate, and the south side of New Street: Mr. Roger Gauntlett, [alder-
man]; William Dawlyn, William Becke, John Battyn, John Stannex, assistants.
Masters and workfolk
   John Payne's wife in Brown Street, bonelace-maker: Dorothy Edmondes
(9), in the keeping of John Watkins, a poor man, her uncle, bonelace-making,
her uncle hath 6*d*. weekly out of the church and her dame is to have 3*d*.
weekly out of the stock.
   Edith Mynterne: her three children (14, 12, 9).
[f. 82v.] *Partly impotent*
   Hector Bewster (65), 6*d*. weekly; John Beaker (70) and his wife (55),
4*d*. weekly, [and] three lame daughters (25, 16, 6); George Sanger, for a child
called John Mynterne which he keepeth, hath 8*d*. weekly; Anne Whyte
keepeth Beatrice Dickenson, a child, and hath weekly 12*d*., she desireth 20*s*.
stock.
Apprentices
   John Beaker's two sons (16, 14); Robert Hopkins's son (18).

[ff. 94v.–95] St. Martin's Parish
   The Trinity chequer: Mr. Lawrence Horne, [alderman]; Edmund Snowe,
Bartholomew Foster, Richard Lyne, Isaac Girdler, assistants.
Masters and workfolk
   Philip Veryn, sackcloth-maker: Henry Potter (14), at hemp, he earneth 8*d*.
weekly.
   Thomas Prewett's wife, knitter: John Potter (10), knitting, worketh at
home with his mother and earneth weekly 4*d*.; Eleanor Masye (14), knitting,
earneth 3*d*. weekly, her dame to have her work for one year.
   Margaret Morris (9), William Mynterne (6), Jane Plevyn (5), John Plevyn
(2), whose parents are all deceased, [receive respectively] 8*d*., 12*d*., 12*d*., 16*d*.
weekly from the parish.
[f. 95v.] *Wholly impotent*
   Chrispian Martyn (22), a cripple, 12*d*. weekly.
Impotent in part
   Flower Staples (80), 2*d*. weekly and earneth 6*d*.; Joan Masey (54), earneth
8*d*.; Annabel Sherston (72), earneth 6*d*., *dead*; [1] her husband, idle.

---

1 This and similar italicized notes are later additions in a different hand.

Mistress Talbott hath received her son's wife, great with child, likely to charge the parish. We desire she may be removed.
Apprentice
Edward Pritchett (19).

[ff. 97v.–98] The north side of Tanner Street [*now* St. Ann Street], part of Love Lane, viz. Giles Jefferye's chequer and Veriman's chequer: Mr. Richard Payne, [alderman]; John Floyde, Edward Percivall, Robert Hole, assistants.
Masters and workfolk
Lancelot Russell's wife, bonelace-maker: Eleanor Eyles (10), bonelace-making, she earneth 6*d.* weekly, *dead*; Margery Eyles, *gone*.

Joan Burde, bonelace-maker: Jane Lake (17), she earneth weekly 18*d.*; Jane Parker (14), bonelace-making, she earneth 11*d.* weekly; Anne Crosse (9), she earneth weekly 8*d.*

William Crowche, pinner: John Burte (10), pinmaking, he earneth weekly 4*d.*

Richard Lyme's wife, bonelace-maker: Bridget Burt (17), lame, bonelace-making, she earneth 22*d.* weekly.
[f. 98v.] *Wholly impotent*
Widow Acrigge
Partly impotent
Widow Eyles (45), sickly, 4*d.* weekly.
Apprentices
John Acrigge (11), *bound*; Simon Parker (12), *gone*; William Robson, an idle person.

[ff. 100v.–101] The chequer wherein Mr. Bee dwelleth:[1] Mr. Matthew Bee, [alderman]; John Hardinge, Edward Whatley, assistants.
Masters and workfolk
Lancelot Russell's wife [and] Mrs. Evered, bonelace-makers: Agnes Ruddle (9), Alice Coale (14), bonelace-making, they earn 12*d.* apiece weekly; Joan Noble (11); Mary Slatter (8).

John Evered, pinmaker: John Yeoman (11), Michael Yeoman (7), pinmaking, both earn weekly 12*d.*; Elizabeth Chambers (12).
[f. 101v.] *Wholly impotent*
William Marshall (90), 4*d.* weekly, *dead*; his wife, *dead*; John Whyte (80), 3*d.* weekly, *dead*; his wife, *dead*; Widow Androwes (80), 4*d.* weekly, *dead*; William Pettye, lame; Mary Younge (70), *dead*.

[ff. 103v.–104] The chequer wherein Mr. Burges dwelleth:[2] Mr. Richard Payne, [alderman]; Edmund Burges, Christopher Horte, George Antrum, assistants.

---

1 Possibly the later 'Rolfe's' chequer where a member of the Bee family had property in 1667: *W.A.M.* xxxvi. 426.
2 Possibly the later 'Barnard's Cross' chequer apparently not covered by the other St Martin's chequers of the survey.

Masters and workfolk

Philip Veryn, roper: William Hoskins (9), at hemp work, Veryn to have his work and his friends 6*d.* weekly out of the stock; William Wigmore (9), at hemp, Veryn to have his work till Easter and after Easter to give him 6*d.* weekly.

John Peirce, rugmaker: William Jones (9), spooling, his master to have his work and 6*d.* weekly for his diet for one year; Thomas Batchellor (9), idle now, placed with John Everat, a pinner, and his father is to have weekly out of the stock 3*d.*; Millicent Androwes (14).

Thomas Turner's four children, allowed to them weekly out of the stock 6*d.* beginning 9 July 1625.

Rowland Rose (6), son to John Rose, [works] at bonelace with Widow Ashlye, to have weekly 3*d.* beginning 9 July.

[f. 104v.] *Wholly impotent*

Widow Harryson (80), 4*d.* weekly, *gone*; Mary Puppen, a cripple, 6*d.* weekly, *dead*; Widow Stafford, sick, 16*d.* weekly, *dead*; Joan Morse, a cripple, 4*d.* weekly; Isard Little, almost blind, 4*d.* weekly; Beatrice Baker, cripple, 8*d.*; Alice Ashley (80), 4*d.* weekly; Christian Eldridge (70), 4*d.* weekly, *dead*; John Stainesmore, lame and blind, 3*d.*; Joan Leeves (70); William Batchellor (80).

Goodwife Hoskins, [who] now lieth in childbed, hath 4 children. Her husband was pressed for a soldier, [she] wanteth relief.

Apprentices

[*blank*] Hustice (12); Thomas Pyppyn (15), *bound*; Thomas Good (15), *bound*; John Tayler (17), *bound*; [*blank*] Tayler (12).

[ff. 107v.–108] From St. Martin's church to the lower end of Draggon Street [*now* Exeter Street] on the south side: Mr. Bee, Mr. Tookey, [aldermen]; Charles Jacobb, Edward Odell, William Arte *alias* Teage, Edward Russell, assistants.

Masters and workfolk

Goodwife Fortune, knitter: Sarah Sinderbury (10), knitting, to have 6*d.* weekly out of the stock and her dame 2*d.* weekly for teaching.

Elizabeth Brackston, bonelace-maker: Alice Spegge (12), bonelace-making, she earneth 10*d.* weekly.

Robert Hillis, weaver: Priscilla Barrett (12), spinning, she earneth 6*d.* and 2*d.* to be allowed her weekly out of the stock.

[f. 108v.] *Wholly impotent*

Joan Warren (80), 4*d.* weekly, *dead*; Joan Samwayes (88), 2*d.* weekly, *dead*; Mary Hunte (80), *dead*; Hugh Needle (80), 6*d.* weekly, *dead*; Mary Ingram (90); Joan Haynes (80); Francis Barrett (84), *gone*.

Partly impotent

Alice Bond (60), 3*d.* weekly; Hugh Pettye (80), his wife (68), 4*d.* weekly; Thomas Sadler (68).

Apprentice

William Candye.

III SURVEY OF THE POOR IN ST. EDMUND'S AND ST. THOMAS'S PARISHES *c.* 1635

Children	Age	Ability/Employment	Earning Weekly	Relief Weekly
[St. Edmund's Parish]				
Castle Street				
Agnes Sherland, *vidua*	90	lame in arm	6*d.*	12*d.*
Sarah Byby	50		1*s.* 8*d.*	6*d.*
Mary	16	bonelace	1*s.* 6*d.*	
Thomas	9			
Robert Miller	40	lame in his limbs		8*d.*
Joan his wife	35		12*d.*	
Rebecca	12	bonelace	4*d.*	
Robert	8	school		
John	3			
John Winter	64	cripple		6*d.*
Susan Winter	60		8*d.*	
Mary	26	bonelace	18*d.*	
Sarah	23	bonelace	10*d.*	
William Hall	52		20*d.* and his diet	8*d*
Dorothy, *uxor*	40			
Alice	14	bonelace	13*d.*	
Richard	12	learns bone		
Elizabeth	10	school		
John	8			
Dorothy	2			
Honour	2 months			
White Horse chequer				
Edward Bell	44	cripple	10*d.*	6*d.*
Joan, *uxor*	37		12*d.*	
Anne	15	bonelace	16*d.*	
Henry Senyer	62	cripple		8*d.*
Katherine, *uxor*	40		2*s.*	
Marjorie	17	bonelace	12*d.*	
Barbar[a]	9	bedridden		
Widow Smith	45		12*d.*	[12*d.* deleted]
William	14	quilling	8*d.*	4*d.*
Frances	13	bonelace	10*d.*	4*d.*
James	11	cardmaking	3*d.*	4*d.*
Scottes Lane				
Widow Bagges	75	lame in her hands	8*d.*	12*d.*
Endlesse Street				
John Rickattes	55	lame		6*d.*
Lucy, *uxor*	48		8*d.*	
Robert	7	school		
John	4			
Streete's wife	32	lame	4*d.*	6*d.*
Mr. Harwoodes chequer[1]				
Brackston, *vidua*	56	blind	10*d.*	
Thomas	10	school		

[1] Not so named in the 1625 survey but, with only a few entries, possibly identical with 'Three Lyons' chequer: see p. 69.

	Children	Age	Ability/Employment	Earning Weekly	Relief Weekly
3 Cups chequer					
Alice Plowman		14	} children at Ann Smythe's	8d.	} 2s. 6d.
William Elliott		10			
Margery Long, *vidua*		45		2s.	6d.
	Thomas	13	spool	8d.	
	Richard	9	quill	4d.	
	John	3			
3 Swans chequer					
Elizabeth Newberey, *vidua*		80	blind		1s. 4d.
Black Horse chequer					
Widow Love		80		6d.	1s. 2d.
Thomas Bollen		68		1s.	4d.
Elizabeth, *uxor*		65		1s.	
John Rowsnell [see below]					
Mr. Swayne's chequer					
Walter Danyell		81		1s.	4d.
Marjorie, *uxor*		77		6d.	
Winchester Gate					
Widow Harly		80		6d.	2d.
John Andrews		50	smith	1s.	
Margaret, his wife		40		1s.	
	Margaret	9	bonelace		
	Elizabeth	6			
	John	4			
	George	2			
Joseph Harte		60			
Mr. Swayne's chequer					
John Rowsnell		40	weak eyesight		6d.
Joan, *uxor*		37		2s. 6d.	
	Margaret	7	at the Devizes		
	Joan	4			
	Anna	1			
Widow Cacksey		75	labour done		4d.
Mr. Slyes chequer[1]					
John Nuby		46	wants work		2s.
Dinah Nuby		36			
	John	16	sick abed		
	Robert	11	sick		
	William	9	quill	6d.	
	Mary	3			
	Rebecca	1			
Hibberd Keate		45	sick		2s.
Ann, *uxor*		45	sick		6d.
	William	12	quill	8d.	
	Sarah	6			
	Joan	7			
	William	3			

[1] Possibly the later 'Vanner's' chequer where Thomas Newby was a tenant in 1667: *W.A.M.* xxxvi. 430.

	Children	Age	Ability/Employment	Earning Weekly	Relief Weekly
John Butler		40	in gaol		
Avis, *uxor*		35			1s. 6d.
	Crisse	14	bonelace	1s.	
	Nabb	9			
	Ann	7			
	Thomas	3			
Thomas Dredge		50	bedridden		
Ann, *uxor*		48		1s.	1s. 6d.
	Katherine	9	bonelace	2d.	
Milford Street					
Melior Jones		50	sometimes distracted	1s.	3d.
	Mary	10	crook-backed; bonelace	10d.	
Greencroft Street					
Anthony Stukly		31	tailor; sick		12d.
Mary, *uxor*		40	sick		
Edith Allen		30	lies in; her husband gone from her		2s.
	[blank]	3			
	[blank]	2 months			
Widow Thomas		70		1s.	4d.
William Weekes		82	lame		1s. 2d.
Pawlle's chequer 1					
Mary Brakes		29	her husband gone from her	12d.	6d.
	John	5			
	Mary	2			
Widow Pawle		70	feeble	4d.	4d.
Mr. Ellson's chequer 2					
Widow Bernester		50		1s. 6d.	8d.
	Israel	16	bonelace	12d.	
	Edward	14	wants work		
	Ann	10		2d.	
Widow Yorke		48		1s. 6d.	6d.
	William	15	spin	6d.	
	John	3			
Thomas Underhill		66	weaver	3s.	6d.
Judith, *uxor*		54	lame hand	10d.	
	Eleanor	20	bonelace	14d.	
	Elizabeth	16	spin	4d.	
	Christian	7	school		
	Henry 3	5			
Dorothy Byrd		37	her husband gone from her and she very sick	sometimes more, sometimes less	
	Margaret	2			
Thomas Randell		42	weaver	2s.	6d.
Judith, *uxor*		33		6d.	
	Thomas	11	quill	6d.	
	Anthony	4			

1 See p. 68 n.

2 Possibly the later 'Parson's' chequer where Widow York was a tenant in 1667: *W.A.M.* xxxvi. 430.

3 The existence of a fifth child is suggested by the MS. which has '5' against the children's names.

	Children	Age	Ability/Employment	Earning Weekly	Relief Weekly
Bedden Row					
Widow Cowltee		80	almost blind		5d.
Emma Browne		62	feeble	4d.	4d.
Widow Loe		68	lame	3d.	8d.
Joan Lyntch		82	labour done		6d.
Austin Belly		52	blind	10d.	10d.
Katherine, *uxor*		60		10d.	
Marian Sturges		90	blind		1s. 2d.
Katherine Dearinge		87	lame	8d.	8d.
Alice Martyn		82	deaf		6d.
Clement Lee		71		6d.	3d.
Joan Woldron		70	lame and diseased	6d.	6d.
Marjorie Locke		60	lame in her limbs	6d.	4d.
Edith Brickett		88	work done		4d.
Alice Bigges		60	lame	1½d.	4d.
Elizabeth Williames		70	blind in one eye		
Stephen Olyver		65	sight fails	6d.	3d.
John Buckett		87	sick		8d.
Ann, *uxor*		40	lame	4d.	
Ann Hibberd		53	poor	8d.	3d.
	Mary	15	bonelace	3d.	
	Honour	8			
Mary Deane		74	lame; wants more allowance	6d.	2d.
Sibyl Perry		82	very feeble		1s. 2d.
Alice Arsny		83	feeble		4d.
Kany Davis		72	feeble	8d.	4d.
William Swifte		40	glazier; idle		
Ann, *uxor*		31	miserable poor		
	William	13 ⎱ work at		
	John	4 ⎰ his trade		
	Henry	1			
Elizabeth Pitt		63	eyesight naught	8d.	4d.
Vincent, widow		70	sometimes a beggar	6d.	4d.
Edith Pavye		68	blind		4d.
Jane Phillips		58			
	Martin	12			
John Maylard		50	blind		1s.
Rachel Waterman		69			4d.
Widow Fortune		82			4d.
Agnes Dowdine		60	bedridden		1s. 2d.
Alice Andrewes		73	lame		6d.
Lucy Lake		60		6d.	3d.
Margaret Croome		90	lame		8d.
Maud Sawnders		85	feeble; wants allowance		9d.
Ann Webb		70		6d.	7d.
Joan Macy		66	feeble	4d.	6d.
	Eleanor	24	innocent; wants allowance		
[St. Thomas's Parish][1]					
Anne Cole, *vidua*		75	bedridden		1s. 2d.
Edith [Mintern][2]		63		10d.	4d.

[1] The MS. has a break here. Those named below it were all listed under St. Thomas's in a relief book of Apr. 1635: S.C.A., misc. papers, box 6, O 3.
[2] Surname supplied from relief book: ibid.

	Children	Age	Ability/Employment	Earning Weekly	Relief Weekly
Chrispian Beaker		62			6d.
William Luxell		80			6d.
uxor		75			
Henry Cooke		52			6d.
uxor		44			
	[blank]	15 ⎫		3s.	
	[blank]	12 ⎭			
Barbara Boreman		74			6d.
Anne Peasland		80			1s. 2d.
Chrispian Martin					12d.
Anne Latter					10d.
Margaret Cooke		85			16d.
Vidua Silvester		80			12d.
Anne Tither		70		6d.	6d.
Thomas Swifte		40			6d.
uxor		40			
	6 children	eldest 12 years		12d.	
Mary Hooper		60		12d.	1d.
Richard Keyes		60			6d.
uxor		36	lies in		
	4 children	young			
John Dolman		70		20d.	8d.
uxor		60			
	1 child				
Alice Elliott, vidua		76			1s. 1d.
Alexander Toby		40			12d.
	[blank]	12		12d.	
	[blank]	10			
	[blank]	11			
	[blank]	8			
Mary Keevill		60			2d.
	[blank]	4			
Elizabeth Andrewes		40	husband gone	10d.	2d.
	4 children	young			
John Alderson		80	impotent		8d.
uxor		60			
Rebecca Smith's bastard		4			6d.
Peter Toach		80			
uxor		60			
Eleanor Spratt					
Dorothy Perry		40	sick; husband gone		14d.
	[blank]	14		8d.	
	[blank]	10			
	[blank]	8			
	2 other children				
Henry Byshoppe		76	sight fails		6d.
Katherine Hewlett		60	feeble		12d.
Vidua Scriven		40			14d.
	3 children	young			
4 children					2s. 9d.
May Pride					4d.
Mr. Securis		60	impotent		2s. 6d.

Children	Age	Ability/Employment	Earning Weekly	Relief Weekly
James Simon	60			8d.
uxor	36			
[*blank*]	13			
6 other children	young			
Joan Curtis	80	impotent		4d.
husband	60			
Joan Turner	60	feeble		6d.

Persons 162. Earn weekly £3 3s. 3d.[1]

IV SURVEY OF THE POOR IN ST. MARTIN'S PARISH c. 1635

[f. 1] [*St. Martin's Street*, deleted]
Cullver Street
[*Giggine Street*, deleted]
Anthony Pagey, 3 small children; Thomas Turner, 2 small children, *alms*, 6d.;[2] Bernard Grineway and his wife; Mary Benet, one child; Alice Mowband; Henry Moore, 2 children; Joan Ashley, widow, 2 children; William [?W]ikkmoore and his wife; Thomas Wikkmore, 2 small children; Anne Cockes, widow, one small child; Emma Knightly, one small child; Giles Coofe, 3 small children; Margery Colles (Coles), 5 small children, *alms*, 12d.; John Bodman and his wife; John Fletcher, 3 small children; Arthur Elver, 1 child; Austen Knight, 2 children; Margaret Bannkes, widow, 2 small children; Isard Little, wid[?ower], *alms*, 18d.; Eleanor Accrie, widow, *alms*, 3d.; Alice Good, widow, 3 children, *alms*, 6d.; Alice Ashly, widow, *alms*, 12d.; Beatrix Baker (Baley), widow, *alms*, 12d.; Joan Mosse, widow, *alms*, 8d.

Millford Street
Thomas Battine, 3 small children; John Bruton, 2 children; John Pittman, 7 small children; Jerome Parker, 6 children; . . . [*illegible*] Davies, 6 small children; Ambrose Dowding and his wife; Bartholomew Phillipes, 4 children.

[f. 2] *Giggen Street*
Elizabeth Potter, widow, 4 children, *alms*, 14d.; Thomas Sanders, 1 child; Eleanor West, widow, *alms*, 3d.; Edward Skerie and his wife; Rebecca Carter, 4 small children, *alms*, 12d.; Thomas Pomery, 2 small children; Joseph Hibbert, 2 children; Philip Cundite, 4 children; John Atkines, 1 child; Francis Fry and his wife; Robert Spencer, 3 small children; Mary Dennis, 2 small children; John Phillips and his wife; Edith Dewe, widow; John Steavenes, 2 small children; Annice Andres, widow, 1 child; James Wilkence, 1 child; William Candy, 1 child; Richard Hibbert, 1 child;

---

[1] The totals apparently refer only to St. Edmund's parish in which 167 people earning a total of £3 5s. 3½d. are listed.

[2] The weekly sums paid to those named on ff. 1–4 and marked '*alms*' have been taken from a list of those receiving alms on f. 5. Significant variations in the spelling of surnames have been noted in brackets.

Thomas Mounsier and his wife; William Godfrie, 2 small children; Margaret Woort (Worte), widow, 1 child, *alms*, 3*d.*; Thomas Hibbert, 1 child; Henry Clifford, 3 small children; Edward Randall, 1 child; Henry Lake, 2 small children; Joan Rumsie (Rymsey), widow, *alms*, 4*d.*; Edith Hademan, widow; Widow Fenixe, 2 children; John Jones, 1 child; Richard Turner, 1 child; Thomas Graffton and his wife; [f. 3] Stephen Jerrett, 3 small children; John Crosley, 1 child; John Perry, 5 children; Thomas Goodrich, 3 children; Edward Ravener and his wife; Thomas Ravener, 2 small children; Thomas Knight, 1 small child; John Phillips, 2 small children; Thomas Whore, 3 small children; John Knowles, 2 small children; Widow Beckham, 3 small children, *alms*, 4*d.*

Ivey Street
William Okeford, 3 small children; Edward Hill, 1 child; Robert Hopkines, 1 child; Anne Addames, widow; Joan Pomery, widow, *alms*, 6*d.*; John Drayton and his wife; Miles Alexander and his wife; Richard Couletor, 1 child; Rebecca Bennet, widow; William Thorne and his wife; Thomas Burchett, 3 small children; Richard White and his wife; William Staingmore, 2 children; Sidrack Jonson, 5 children; Robert Blanchard, 1 child; John Mortimer, 5 small children; Thomas Bannes, 3 children; Mary Burdd, widow, 1 child; [f. 4] Susan Grafton, widow; Gregory Bayley, 3 children; Ann Scrudmer, widow; Joan Smith, widow; Richard Hixx, 3 small children; Justine Martine; Amble Batch, widow; Thomas Curtis, 3 children; Nicholas Yeaman, 3 children; James Clarke, 2 children; George Seawell, 1 child; Anne Cozens (Cousins), *alms*, 5*d.*; Richard Jones, 2 children; Nicholas Hulan, 1 child; John Cooke, 2 children; William Goen, 2 children; Ralph Willmut and his wife; William Pryer, 5 children; Widow Write; Widow Dennis; Thomas Abrie; Widow Wilshiere; Mistress Talbott, widow; Goodwife Minety, 3 children; Widow Busson; William Somers, 1 child; Nicholas Thomas, 2 children; John Aman and his wife; Widow Chaundler, 1 child; [Giles Trablefield, *deleted*]; Thomas Udole.

[f. 5][1] Widow Frestone, [alms], 3*d.*; Widow Hoocke; Widow Gwyer, 1 child; Elizabeth Grigge, 2 children; John Johnsune; Susan Pleare; Marmaduke Pullman; John Leagg; Edward Bishopp, 2 children; Thomas Strugnell, 5 children; William Allin, 2 children; Widow Kinge, [alms], 4*d.*; John Mathew, 5 children; Richard Hill, 3 children; Widow Godfry, 1 child; Widow Brockwell, [alms], 10*d.*; Margaret Warren; William Pettie; W ... [*illegible*] Dawline; Thomas Carter, 2 children; Richard Nash; Stephen Poole, 2 children; John Curtice, 2 children; Richard Dicksone, 3 children; Jean Porter, 3 children; Henry Teylor; Elizabeth Anderoas, 1 child.

[f. 6v.] Widow Gumblecun; John Smalle, *weaver*, 3 children; John Bandine, *hellier*, 3 children; Thomas Buck; Margaret Oxspring, 2 children, [alms], 6*d.*; Edward Harbbe; William Tibbatt, 2 children; Christopher Vinell, 2 children; John Sherland, 2 children, [alms], 2*d.*; Simeon Packer, 1 child; John Rosse, 1 child; John Thomas; John Watckines, 4 children; Widow

---

1 The following entries are in a different hand.

Stevens, 1 child; Edward Whatlie, 1 child, [alms], 12*d.*; Richard Ruddle, 3 children; Thomas Rumsy, 3 children; Mary Younge; Widow Very, 2 children, [alms], 3*d.*; Thomas Sweatman, 3 children; John Bauldin, 3 children; Widow Edds; Widow Andrwes; Andrew Sherufe; Robert Maurlowe; John Sadler, 2 children; Margaret Hyscokk; Widow Pullin, [alms], 3*d.*; Widow Vinell; Widow White, [alms], 4*d.*; John Hardin, 3 children; Widow Haines, [alms], 12*d.*; Richard Morres, 1 child; Edward Leeds, 3 children; Widow Umfry, 1 child; Philip Fry, 1 child; William Bedfurd; Thomas Leaman; Edward Dearin; John Mauncell, [alms], 8*d.*; Widow Stapples, [alms], 12*d.*; Alice Stapples; Widow Dickins; Widow Jackson, [alms], 8*d.*; Elizabeth Pryor, 1 child; Peter Supple; Widow Marchman, [alms], 4*d.*; Elias Marchman, 3 children; Ambrose Longe; John Cruch, 3 children; Widow Pettie, [alms], 16*d.*; Widow Battwell; Richard Pettie; Widow Pettie; Christopher Willmouth, 3 children; Widow Leaness, [alms], 5*d.*; Widow Buckett, [alms], 4*d.*; Katherine Williams, [alms], 2*d.*

[f. 7]

Families upon relief	34	[36 *added later; recte* 34]
Persons [on relief]	62	[*recte* 63]
[?Total families]	165	[*recte* 207]
Persons	500	[*recte* 503]

MUNICIPAL ORDERS AND PROJECTS

V A PROJECT FOR RELIEF OF THE POOR c. 1613

[f. 1] An order for the setting at work of idle wandering people and the relief of poor impotent and aged persons inhabiting within this city.

1. First, that it may please your worship [the mayor] to appoint four persons of your house in every ward, that is to say one that hath been mayor and another that is in election to be mayor and two of the 48, [1] with the help of the constables, and an officer to attend on the constable in every ward.

2. These persons being nominated and chosen and their several wards to them appointed, it shall be necessary for them to take the names of every householder, their wives, children, and family, that have not some mystery or handicraft to get their living but live only by spinning and carding, with a note how long they have remained in the city, to the intent to expel out of the city all such persons as by the statute [2] may be avoided. And for the rest to view and judge by their discretions how much wool shall be necessary for every house to serve weekly for the sustentation and maintenance of their living.

3. Secondly, to take the names in like sort of all those persons who partly may live by labour and partly have need of relief and comfort, noting likewise how much wool may serve them weekly besides the relief.

4. Thirdly, to take the names of the poor aged and impotent, registered in a book in every ward, that they who are not able to do any work at all to maintain their living, but must of necessity be relieved, may be suffered to go from door to door both within the city and the Close to gather the alms of well disposed persons. And that the said viewers do go about their circuits of their several wards every month to see that no foreigners or newcomers do not [sic] enter to inhabit within the city, neither that any person be suffered to go abroad to gather relief but those persons before appointed, who in times past had a certain badge or cognizance sewed on their coats to the end they might be known of all people.

5. Now for work to be had for the two first sorts of people before named, it may please your worship to call before you the wardens of the Companies of the Weavers, Glovers, and Parchment-makers and to cause them to bring you the names of all those that do keep looms going and put forth wool to spinning. Also to procure the names of all common spinsters that do put forth work to the end that all these or any of them (by your worship's order taken) may not put forth any of their work out of the city to be spun or

---

[1] i.e. 2 senior men from the 24 aldermen and 2 councillors from the 48 'assistants'.
[2] Presumably the 1598 vagrancy statute: 39 Eliz. I, c. 4, *Statutes of the Realm*, iv. 899–902. The law on vagrancy and settlement was ambiguous: Styles, 'Law of Settlement', *Birm. Univ. Hist. Jnl.* ix. 33–63.

woven until the city be thoroughly replenished with work sufficient for the persons before appointed. And yet not to compel any clothier, glover, parchment-maker, or spinster to find any appointed number a work but only to request them that such work as of themselves they will put forth to spinning may be preferred to the city before any foreigner.

[f. 1v.] 6. And for that the chief cause why the clothmen and others before named do put forth their wool out of the city to be spun is for that they have it more trulier done abroad than in the city, it may please your worship to direct an order that reasonable satisfaction may be made to the clothmen and others for all such losses as shall be found by the evil doing or deceit of the spinners within the city. And in what ward soever it shall please you to appoint me one of the viewers, I will be content, by the space of six months after this order following shall be taken and used, to pay of mine own proper charges for all such losses and defaults as the clothiers and others shall sustain by the spinners of that ward.

7. For the better avoiding of which losses, it may please your worship to give power and authority to the four viewers and [the] constable in their several wards to give correction and punishment for such evil demeanours and misusing upon complaint made by the clothiers and others that shall put forth work to spinning, the fault justly approved without favour or affection. For the first offence gentle admonition and warning to be given them by the said viewers of the ward. For the second offence to be taken and brought to a place of punishment for that purpose by your worships appointed and there to be whipped or otherwise punished as shall be thought meet and convenient for the offence by the discretion of the said viewers. And if they shall offend the third time then to be brought before Mr. Mayor and the justices and be punished by their discretions.

8. Now if any of these two sorts of people before named, having sufficient work and relief to them appointed and given, shall be found either within the city or the Close abegging, they may be taken by the viewer of the ward wherein they dwell and brought to the said house of punishment so appointed and there punished by the discretions of the said viewers.

9. It may please your worship to call before you the collectors for the poor with their books of collection in every parish and to view what the sums doth amount unto yearly, to see whether every man be duly assessed and do truly pay the same according to the statute, and that the said money may be disposed and distributed by the advice and discretions of the said 16 viewers with the constables in every ward upon such persons as they shall think meet and convenient.

10. Also, it may please your worship to be a mean unto my Lord Bishop and Master Dean with the rest to obtain of them the alms that is given in Our Lady Church every Sunday, amounting to £40 by the year, to be converted and disposed to the furtherance of this charitable work. [1]

---

[1] The council frequently tried to obtain part of the poor-rates raised in the Close for poor relief in the town: S.C.A., misc. papers, papers about contributions by lay inhabitants of the Close.

11. Further, it may please your worship to understand that whereas William Wotton, late deceased, hath given and caused to be delivered to the Company of the Weavers of this city the sum of £100 in money to be employed for the setting awork of the poor weavers, contrarily those persons who hath received the said money do not augment any part of their doings in clothing but rather, as I am informed, do bestow the same to such uses [f. 2] that the poor thereby is hindered, which by your worship's good order may be better looked unto for the maintenance of the poor weavers according to the good meaning of the testator.

12. Also, the worshipful Mr. William Webb gave £100 in money to the maintenance of work and avoiding of idleness in the city.

13. Also, the worshipful Mr. John Abin gave £40 in money for the relief of the poor and the avoiding of idleness.

14. Also, Mr. Lionel Tytchborne hath very charitably offered the sum of £40 in money of the goods of Henry Tyrrell to be employed to the use aforesaid. [1]

15. Also, there is in the Close of Salisbury in the hands of Mr. Colcill the sum of £40, or at the least £33 6s. 8d., of the goods of the said Henry Tirrell which by your good means may be obtained to the use aforesaid.

16. Moreover, there is yet to be brought into the hands of the said Mr. Colcill and Mr. Titchborne of the goods of the said Henry Tirrell the sum of £120, whereof I do stand bound to the dean and chapter for £60 and to be paid after 20 nobles by the year and, as I understand, Mr. Titchborne hath bonds for the other £60 to be paid after £10 by the year, which money in like sort by your worship's help will be obtained to the said use.

17. All which sums of money, being indifferently divided by your worships' [the justices'] good discretions with the consent and help of the number of the 24, will be to the clothmen and others before named no small encouragement for setting on work of the said poor people.

18. Further, the poor weavers of this city doth complain that the clothmen do keep more looms in their own houses than by the statute may be permitted which is a cause that the said poor weavers wanteth work to set their own looms going, which by your worship may be redressed according unto a statute in that behalf provided where it is expressed that no clothman may keep more than one loom going in his own house. [2]

19. Also, it is well known that Mr. Crook of Winchester doth send much wool to this city which for the most part is wrought and spun in the country, so that, this order being taken, with your worship's good help he will be entreated that the city may have the preferment thereof.

20. To conclude, as one that is very desirous to see so necessary and charitable an act to be brought in practice, I have boldly enterprised to express my simple advice herein, not thinking the same to be so perfectly

---

[1] The bequests of Wootton, Webb, Abin, and Tyrrell, dating from the mid 16th cent., were already misused by 1599: C 93/1/15; Benson and Hatcher, *Salisbury* (Hoare, *Mod. Wilts.* iv), 288, 291; Hist. MSS. Com. 55, *Var. Coll.* iv, pp. 222–3, 228.

[2] 2 & 3 Ph. & M., c. 11, *Statutes of the Realm*, iv. 286–7.

handled but that I would be very glad to give place to those that can give better counsel for the preferment hereof, which I wish and pray to God may take good effect with happy continuance and perseverance for ever, to God's glory, Amen.

VI ORDERS FOR THE POOR 1623

(f. 291)   Orders for the erection and government of the workinghouse and the election of officers thereof and for the continuance thereof, made at this common council [6 June 1623].

1. First, at this common council it is ordered that at the common council to be holden the Friday in the Whitsun week yearly there be chosen one of the justices of the peace within this city to be governor of the said house for that year following to whom the principal charge of the house and government both of the rest of the officers and of the persons there is committed, who besides his daily care for the same shall every month on a Friday in the forenoon take an account of all the other officers of such things as belong to their charge and keep a book of the foot of their account, and this governor to be assisted by the mayor and justices at any time upon request and the constables, sergeants, and beadles to be attendant on the said governor.

2. That there be also at that time one chosen to be treasurer of the said house, who shall have the charge of the goods of the said house and stocks of money and other things of the said house, and to keep a book of what is delivered to the master of the works and what is received from him of the profits of the same stocks and works and of the benevolences given for the keeping of the poor at work.

3. That there be also at that time one chosen to be master of the works of that house, who shall be answerable for the stuff received to set the poor on work and of the profits raised thereby, and to see the work well done and to punish the idlers by the surveyor and beadles under him.

4. That there be also at that time chosen one to be steward of that house, who shall take care of the diet and apparel, and to be accountable every week and to see the house and people cleanly kept by the housekeeper and laundress. And these three last officers to cast up their accounts every Friday and every month to return the same to the governor.

(f. 291v.) [5.] That at a council to be holden the Friday in the Easter week yearly auditors to be chosen and appointed to take the account of all the officers of the said workinghouse and to return the same at the common council to be holden in the Whitsun week following, when the new choice of the said officers shall be made.

[6.] That the treasurer be supplied with money as occasion of want shall be from the governor, who shall always be one of the treasurers of Popley's money or rents. [1]   And to the treasurer shall all the contribution money be

---

[1] See p. 71 n.

paid by the churchwardens and overseers of the poor of the several parishes.

[7.] That none which shall be committed to be set on work in the said house [is] to be delivered at any time during the first year unless it be at the general quarter sessions or at the common council.

Mr. Bee and Mr. Norwell, governors. At this common council Mr. Matthew Bee is elected and chosen to be master and governor of the said workinghouse for this year and one of the treasurers of Popley's rents and Mr. Robert Norwell to be the other treasurer of the same rents. And Mr. Henry Pearson, the last treasurer of the said rents, is appointed to make and yield up his account on Friday next, being the 13th day of this instant month of June, by eight of the clock in the forenoon of the same day, before Mr. Mayor, the said master or governor of the said house, and others of the 24 as will be pleased to be present at the same.

Thomas Hill, treasurer. Also Thomas Hill is appointed treasurer of the said workinghouse, John Ivye to be master of the works there, and John Stannax to be steward of the same house. [1]

William Waterman and his wife are appointed to be keepers of the said house and the woman to be laundress and nurse of the house and to be at the steward's command for the cleanly keeping and usage of those in the house.

The governor of the house to have power upon cause to remove both the keeper and laundress and to put new in their places, and to add from time to time assistants unto them in that business.

At this council it is ordered that on Wednesday next in the afternoon the overseers of the poor shall attend Mr. Mayor and the justices with the names of such in their several parishes as do beg and those of them that they shall think fit to be allowed to go to the inns to desire relief of strangers as they shall be allotted and appointed, and not otherwise; and such others as shall come not appointed to be taken up by the beadles and carried to the workhouse; and the innkeepers, finding others than are appointed to him to be at his house, to signify their names to the governor of the said house who shall send for them and cause them to be committed to the said house there to be punished; also the beadles every day to visit the inns, in the summer time at five of clock and in the winter time at six of the clock in the morning, and if they find any other there than such as are appointed at the inns to carry them to the workinghouse to be punished.

An order for providing a brewhouse. At this council it is ordered and agreed that there shall be a common brewhouse erected or provided within this city, at the charge of the chamber or city, for the good and relief of the poor of the workinghouse and other poor of the said city.

At this council Mr. Mayor, Mr. Godfrey, Mr. Bee, Mr. Banes, Mr. Gauntlett, Mr. Tookye, and Mr. Horne, [and] John Stannax, John Ivye, James Abbott, and Thomas Hill are appointed to be committees to consider

[1] On 10 Mar. 1623 Ivie, Hill, and Stannax had been appointed to survey the workhouse and report on methods of employing poor children there.

touching the provision of the said brewhouse as well of the said house, vessels, malt, wood, servants, as of all other things concerning the same and for raising of money for the provision thereof. And they are entreated to make their meetings on every Friday at eight of the clock in the forenoon to confer thereof. [1]

VII ORDERS FOR THE POOR 1626

(f. 4) *1626 Civitas Nove Sarum.* At the monthly meeting.

Orders touching the relief of the poor of the said city of New Salisbury, heretofore made and agreed upon in due form of law, and now (viz.) this second day of October in the second year of the reign of our sovereign lord King Charles of England &c. revived and confirmed and agreed to be published and made known to all the inhabitants of the said city, and to be straightly observed hereafter for the better government and relief of the said city in times to come, and for the better testimony the common seal of this city is hereunto affixed.

Whereas for the better relief of the poor people of this city many good orders have been heretofore made within the same, which not having taken so good effect as was hoped for, the mayor and council of the said city, desiring nevertheless the happy effect of the same, having called unto them all the justices of the peace within the said city and all the churchwardens and overseers of the poor of every parish within the said city and also their assistants, they all with one accord and full consent do hereby declare, publish, and make known to all the inhabitants of the said city, and the said churchwardens and overseers do hereby respectively order with the consent and allowance of the said mayor and justices of the peace, in manner and form following, (viz.):

[1.] It is declared and ordered that no persons shall have the relief of this city from the (f. 4v.) hands of the churchwardens and overseers of the poor or any of them as of the common alms unless such person shall usually frequent his or her parish church at morning and evening prayer and at sermons on the sabbath days [and holy days *deleted*], unless he or she shall be hindered by sickness or impotence of the body or other just cause. And, to the end that notice may be taken of their being at church, forms or seats are to be provided for them all together in some fit place of every parish church, and all others are to forbear the same forms and seats.

2. *Assistants.* It is declared and ordered that the assistants to the overseers of the poor shall be yearly named and chosen by the grand jury, with the allowance of the mayor and justices of the peace, at the general sessions of the peace for this city to be holden at or about Easter yearly, or at the monthly meetings if cause be.

---

[1] The first Salisbury standing committee: *V.C.H. Wilts.* vi. 107. The brewhouse was functioning by 1624: S.C.A., Ledger C, ff. 292, 294v., 297.

3. *Attend monthly meetings and present in writing.* All the churchwardens and overseers of the poor and their assistants are all to attend at the monthly meetings and there to make presentment in writing to the mayor and justices of the peace in this manner (viz.): the churchwardens and overseers of every parish [are] to make their presentments of all matters belonging to their charge over their whole parish respectively, and the assistants are to make their presentments only of the matters within their respective chequers or places allotted to their charges respectively.

4. A book is to be provided by the chamberlain of this city and kept in the council house, wherein shall be entered all the orders and directions which shall be made or given at the monthly meetings, and the same to be entered (f. 5) by the clerk of the mayor and commonalty who is to attend also at all the monthly meetings. [1]

5. All the said presentments in writing are to be filed upon a file prepared for every monthly meeting, and all the presentments of one year to be filed or bundled in one bundle at the end of every year and then laid up in the council house to be made use of as shall be requisite. [2]

6. *Begging forbidden.* It being the instant desire of all the city that all the poor people may be charitably provided for and not be enforced nor suffered to beg from door to door, which is hoped may be within a short time (if it please God) really effected, it is therefore in the meantime declared and ordered that no person that is not totally impotent and not able to work shall be suffered to beg in the streets or at any door, and that none other of such impotent persons shall be suffered to beg, but only such as shall be allowed and their names entered at some monthly meeting and have a badge of the city arms stamped in lead borne about them on their breast [are] to be tolerated for some time to beg, and that only within the parishes where they dwell.

7. *Children not to beg.* That no child be suffered to beg but that all the children of the poor that are not able to relieve them be set to sewing, (f. 5v.) knitting, bonelace-making, spinning of woollen or linen yarn, pin-making, card-making, spooling, button-making, or some other handiwork as soon as ever they be capable of instruction to learn the same, and in the meantime to be relieved by the common contribution as need shall require.

8. *Boxes at inns.* It is declared and ordered that there shall be at the charge of every parish a box for the poor with two locks and keys forthwith set up in the court or at the gate of every inn of this city to receive the alms of strangers, guests, and passengers which shall come thither, for the better receipt whereof two aged impotent poor people only shall be appointed at the monthly meetings to attend in the court or at the gate of every inn. And they at the departure of the strangers, guests, and passengers or at other fit times are to stand by the box in a quiet and still manner and to use no clamour nor other words of begging but to say thus, once or oftener if need be, in a quiet voice, 'We pray you for God's sake remember the poor', and then point to the box. And the alms to be forthwith put into the box. [Of all which boxes *deleted*]. And the ancient churchwarden of every parish is to

---

[1] See pp. 94–100.
[2] Only one file, for 1635–6, survives: see pp. 100–5.

keep one of the keys of the boxes placed at inns within his parish and the innkeeper to keep the other key, and they are not to open any of the boxes but in the presence of the innkeeper in whose house the box is placed and of all or the greatest part of the churchwardens and overseers of the poor of (f. 6) every parish, who are to enter the sum taken forth in all their books, that the ancient churchwarden of every parish who is to receive the same may be charged therewith in his account. And all the alms so collected is to go to the relief of the impotent poor and sick persons in all the parishes of this city according to [a ratable proportion of every parish as the collection of the Close was wont to be distributed, *deleted*] the necessities of the poor as shall be agreed upon and allowed at the monthly meetings, saving that all the attendants at the boxes are to have a half share more than the residue which did not attend.

9. *Brewhouse allowance to the poor, how to be employed*. It is also declared and ordered that the payment of the sum of twenty shillings, which by former order is to issue weekly out of the town brewhouse for the relief of the poor of this city, be continued and that the same shall be bestowed as hath been formerly appointed only for the maintenance and relief of the said poor children at their learning of the said work or some other until they shall be able to earn their livings thereat. And then the same allowance to cease to them and to be bestowed to like purpose upon other children which shall need it and be fit to be set to work as long as they shall so need it, and so to be continued for ever.

(f. 6v.) 10. *Employment of the brewhouse money*. It is declared and ordered that the said weekly sum of 20s. and all other sums hereafter to issue out of the said town brewhouse for the relief of the poor shall be converted and disposed of [privately *deleted*] to the like uses and for the binding of poor children apprentices and to such other good and charitable uses as shall be hereafter agreed upon. And the junior churchwarden of every parish during his junior year is to receive weekly the said sums of the governor for the time being of the said brewhouse and to pay the same accordingly for the relief and maintenance of the said poor children as aforesaid. And in those payments and receipts an equal and proportionable regard is to be had touching the poor children of every parish within this city. And the said junior churchwardens are to be accountable for the same.

11. It is declared and ordered that it shall be agreed and set down at the monthly meetings what poor children shall have such maintenance or relief and how much and how long to continue. And the junior churchwardens to have abstracts thereof made out to them by the town clerk and they to make their payments accordingly and not otherwise nor to any other. And to such purpose the governor of the town brewhouse is to attend at the monthly meetings.

(f. 7) 12. *Poor taken begging*. If any of the poor people of this city shall be taken begging (other than such as aforesaid), all the contables of this city and all the churchwardens and overseers of the poor and their assistants, calling a councillor to them, are required to cause them to be forthwith carried to the house of correction, there to be [punished *deleted*] ordered and set on work as begging and [wandering rogues *deleted*] idle persons, and not to be delivered from thence without the order of the sessions or of Mr. Mayor and one or more justices of the peace of this city or of two justices of the peace of this city at the least. And such commitment of them to be sufficient warrant to the keeper of the house of correction to receive them.

13. *Flax to be provided at the workhouse.* For the better ordering of stubborn and idle persons which shall refuse to work and labour as by the law they are required, it is declared and ordered that there be forthwith provided by the governor of the house of correction for the use of the said house one cwt. or more of flax or hemp, upon working whereof the said stubborn and idle persons are to be employed and to be corrected by the keeper of the same house if they loiter or refuse work. And they are to have the whole profit of their labour and to live thereof (f. 7v.) or by any other work, and not to have other relief unless they have it of their own. And the master or governor of the said house is to see that the wares by them made while they shall be in the house of correction be sold and the workers paid for their labour in a conscionable manner, so as the stock being preserved all the residue to go to the workers. *Master of the house of correction to give account at the sessions.* And he is likewise to have a special regard that the same house be well ordered and to give account thereof at the monthly meetings or, in default thereof, at the quarter sessions of the peace of this city if it be required.

14. It is declared and ordered that the said house of correction and the stock and orders thereof be presently viewed and considered of by Mr. Bee, Mr. Banes, Mr. Hancock, Mr. Gauntlet, Mr. Tookie, Mr. Raye, Mr. Pierson, Mr. Squibbe, and Mr. [Thomas Hill *deleted*] Ivie, Mr. John Batte, and Mr. Thomas Hill and that reformation be made by them with all expedition of whatsoever is or shall be found amiss in the same.

15. *Overseers and assistants to survey the poor weekly.* It is declared and ordered that the churchwardens and overseers of the poor and their assistants are weekly to survey all the poor within their several (f. 8) limits and to examine and see how they have laboured all the days in the week past, and at what wages, and what they have earned every day by their work, and how they have bestowed the same money. And they are to counsel and direct them how to order themselves and weekly or oftener to advise and encourage them to follow their labour, and if they want work to examine the reason thereof and to provide them work at large within the city if they can, and shall so think fit, or else to bring them to the house of correction and there to cause them to be set on work.

16. *Overseers to care for the sick poor.* It is ordered, declared, and advised that the churchwardens and overseers of the poor and their assistants do twice in every week at the least inquire within their respective charges what persons are sick within the same, and if their sickness be suspected to be infectious to acquaint the mayor therewithal with all speed that order may be taken therein as shall be fit, and if the sick persons be poor and want relief that they with all speed provide for them what shall be convenient.

17. *Overseers' accounts.* It is declared and ordered that at the accounts of the churchwardens and overseers of the poor, (which by the (f. 8v.)

law they are to make to the justices of the peace of this city at the end of their offices), all the overseers and assistants be called thereunto and be present at the same to take their exceptions thereunto if need shall be.

18. *Monthly meetings.* It is declared and ordered that the monthly meetings be hereafter duly held and kept upon the first Friday in every month and the churchwardens, overseers of the poor, and their assistants of every parish are to come into the council house in order, the first parish to come first in and so one after the other and not all at once, and the others are, for the quieter taking of their presentments, to attend until the others be received. And for the defaults both in the justices of the peace and of the churchwardens and overseers of the poor the penalties provided by the law are to be pressed, and they which make such defaults are to be enforced to pay the same.

(f. 9) A brief remembrance of some of the things which are to be presented by the churchwardens and overseers of the poor and their assistants at the monthly meetings.

[1.] *Strangers.* To present what poor people which receive any alms of this city do not usually frequent their parish churches at morning and evening prayer on the sabbath days, and also what strangers or foreigners are come to dwell in the city, when they came, and who hath taken them in.

2. *Refuse to work.* To present the names of all such as refuse to work at reasonable wages and of all the idle drunken and other disordered people within their several charges.

3· *Children.* To present what children so appointed as aforesaid to be set on work or to have relief out of the town brewhouse shall not be set to their work daily accordingly, and in whose default the same shall happen.

4. What children of the said poor children so appointed to be set on work are become able to earn their livings or part thereof, to the end that new contracts may be made with their teachers touching their work and touching the allowance out of the town brewhouse, which is thereupon either to cease or be lessened as shall be fit.

(f. 9v.) 5. *Children fit to be apprentices.* To present what poor children are ready or fit to be bound apprentices and what masters are fit to take them apprentices.

6. *Foreign apprentices.* What apprentices have been taken of foreigners' children and by whom, to the end that it may be examined whether they are justifiably taken or not, and if not that they may be displaced and their masters enforced to take the children of citizens of this city to be their apprentices.

7. *Death of poor.* To present the death or departure from this city of all such persons within [this city *deleted*] their several charges who had weekly or other maintenance or relief of the city, and when they died or departed and what maintenance they so had.

8. *Negligence of overseers.* To present the negligence, slackness, falsity, and other defaults of all the churchwardens and overseers of the poor and their assistants in their several and respective charges.

9. *Extraordinaries.* The churchwardens and overseers of the poor to present all their voluntary alms and delivery of money made in the month then ended, and to whom and upon what reasons they gave the same.

10. They are to present all other things belonging to their offices.

f. 10] [Signed] Wolstan Coward, mayor, Henry Sherfield, recorder; Thomas Eyre, Richard Godfreye, Matthew Bee, Henry Byle, senior, Robert Banes, Thomas Hancock, Roger Gauntlet, Bartholomew Tookie, Thomas Raye, Lawrence Horne, Henry Pearsone, Robert Norwell, William Goodridge, [the mark of] William Raye, Thomas Squibb, Richard Checkford, John Puxton, John Ivie, James Abbott, [aldermen]; William Marshall, John Batt, John Bowden, Michael Mackerell, Robert Tyte, Charles Jacob, George Beach, John Fryer, [the mark of] Thomas Slye, John Barrowe, John Vyning, Anthony Brickett, John Stannex, Edward Fawconer, Henry Byle, junior, Thomas Good, John Raye, Francis Clarke, Peter Banckes, John Pearson, Richard Carter, William Joyce, John Leminge, Thomas Pill, John Player, Ambrose West, Rowland Taylor, [assistants].

[f. 10v.] *St. Edmund's parish:* Maurice Aylerugge, [*blank*], churchwardens; Thomas Hooper, William Brotherton, William ... [*illegible*], overseers.

[f. 11] *St. Martin's parish:* William Windover, Edmund Snowe, churchwardens; Edward Whatly, [the mark of] Christopher Newe, John Haviland, overseers.

[f. 11v.] *St. Thomas's parish:* [the mark of] William Dowlyn, Edward Brownejohn, churchwardens; Peter Hayward, William Collis, Richard Phelpes, Robert Rutley, overseers of the poor.

POOR RELIEF

[f. 224v.]   Monthly Meeting 3 July 1635
Mr. Mayor, Mr. Abbott, and Mr. Brickett were present.
St. Thomas's Parish. Mr. Richard Payne, churchwarden, Thomas Batter and
George Legge, overseers, appeared; Mr. William Hunt, churchwarden,
Thomas Hooper and George Shergould, overseers, made default.

The said churchwarden and overseers presented that Anne Pannell, widow,
entertained Robert Scretche, a stranger coming from London, and his wife
to inhabit within this city who are ordered to give security for the discharge
of the city by bond from William Whyte, grocer, and John Barnes, joiner.

They exhibited their bill of extraordinary disbursements since the last
monthly meeting, amounting to 27s. 7½d., and there remained due to them the
preceding month 25s. 9d., being in total 53s. 4½d. Of this 42s. 9½d. was
paid them out of the tippling and profane swearing money. So now there rests
due to them 12s. 5d. [*recte* 10s. 7d.].

40s. given to Abraham Collins and his wife for taking Jane Fishe, of
tender years, apprentice, being part of Mr. Tooker's money for apprentices, [1]
which is to be repaid by the overseers at the next meeting.

They presented that Alexander Pynne, who received 10d. a week from them
for 9 weeks, is deceased.

They present that Alice Easton, widow, has entertained William Symes,
a stranger. They are to be sent for and questioned.

Mr. Edward Edmondes paid 5s., which he levied by warrant on the goods of
George Batter, for being drunk on Tuesday 2 June 1635. Of this 2s. 6d.
was given to Mr. Edmondes towards providing apparel for Edith Goffe.
St. Edmund's Parish. Mr. Thomas Mathewe, churchwarden, Mr. Gardner,
Ambrose Smythe, and John Fishelake, overseers, appeared; Francis Dove,
churchwarden, and John Gilbert, overseer, made default.

Received from the churchwarden 10s. 5d. which was received at the
church doors in the basins. Of this 10s. was paid to them for their extraordinary disbursements since the last meeting as appears by their bill of
particulars. The 5d. given to Mr. Gardner to be accounted for.

They present that Robert Sutton, a hostler, being a stranger, is become
an inhabitant. It is ordered that he be sent unto and questioned.
St. Martin's Parish. Christopher Newe and Christopher Batt, churchwardens,
made default; Samuel Bell and Christopher Jupe, overseers, appeared;
Richard Chamblayne and Thomas Randes, overseers, made default.

---

[1] Given by Bartholomew Tooker (Tookie) and William Marshal in 1624: Benson and
Hatcher, *Salisbury* (Hoare, *Mod. Wilts.* iv), 333.

The overseers exhibited their bill of extraordinary disbursements since the last meeting and it appears they laid out in relieving Henry Pressye, deceased, in the time of his sickness, 12s. 7d. They are to be allowed the money at the next meeting.

Thomas Gower, being drunk and convicted for swearing 4 [oaths] in St. Thomas's parish on 30 July 1635, has forfeited 9s. to the use of the poor of that parish which William Phettiplace, glazier, has promised to pay at 6d. a week.

William Smythe, innholder, paid 10s. on 31 July 1635 for permitting Ambrose Whyte and Andrew Reade *alias* Bucke to sit and remain drinking and tippling in his house contrary to the statute.

[f. 225]   Monthly Meeting 14 August 1635

Mr. Mayor, Mr. Recorder, Mr. Bee, Mr. Abbott, Mr. Brickett, Mr. Hill were present.

St. Thomas's Parish. Mr. William Huntt and Mr. Richard Payne, churchwardens, George Shergall, Thomas Hooper, and George Legge, overseers, appeared.

The churchwardens' and overseers' receipts from the boxes:[1] of Mr. Collis 30s.; Thomas Rawlinges 13d.; Mr. Lawrence 17s. 1d.; Philip Seynior 12d.; Mr. William Raye 5d.; Mistress Fryer's 2s. 7d. Total: 52s. 2d.

They exhibited their bill of extraordinary disbursements since the last monthly meeting, amounting to 40s. 6d. There remained due to them on their last monthly bill 12s. 5d. Paid them now the said box money, 52s. 2d., and 9d. of drunken money formerly received, in all 52s. 11d.

The overseers must pay the 40s. taken out of Mr. Tooker's money for an apprentice.

Mr. Huntt, the churchwarden, received at the choir door at the communion in St. Thomas's church 8s. 6d. Received from Thomas Rawlinges 4s., part of 10s. due for tippling. For one profane oath sworn by a stranger, 12d. Total: 13s. 6d. Of this 9s. was allowed to Mr. Huntt which he disbursed in extraordinaries. So remains in stock 4s. 6d. which is put with the tippling money.

St. Edmund's Parish. Mr. Thomas Mathewe *alias* Kynton and Francis Dove, churchwardens, John Gilbert and John Fishlake, overseers, appeared.

The churchwardens and overseers received 21s. 9d. from the basins, which is given back to Mr. Mathewe towards their extraordinary disbursements.

St. Martin's Parish. Christopher Newe, Christopher Batt, churchwardens, Samuel Bell, Christopher Jupe, Richard Chamberlayne, and Thomas Randes, overseers, appeared.

They exhibited their bill of extraordinary disbursements since the last meeting, amounting to 12s. 2d. There remained due to them last month 12s. 7d. and they disbursed for the relief of Cole's wife and five children (her husband being gone from her) 12d. a week for six weeks, 6s. All this is paid them: 30s. 9d.

1 The boxes at inns: see pp. 89–90.

Mr. Bee received from a stranger of Winchester, being drunk on 14 July, 2s. 6d. From [blank] Seywell, shoemaker, for a profane oath, 12d. From Christian Yeoman for a profane oath, 12d. From William Riche, turner, for being drunk, 2s. Total: 6s. 6d.

Paid out of the tippling money to the churchwardens and overseers for all their extraordinary disbursements 30s. 9d. Paid to Samuel Bell what was left of the tippling money for providing clothes for Deverell's child which is kept at Sherland's 2s.

Received 7 Oct. 1635 from Geoffrey Hudles by order of sessions to be given to George Shergall for the use of the poor 4s.

Monthly Meeting 7 September 1635

The churchwardens and overseers of all the parishes appeared and were ordered to finish their accounts with Mr. Brickett and thereupon discharged.

Mr. Shergall is charged with the receipt of 5s. at the sessions on 5 Oct. 1635 from fines for drunkenness. He accounted for the same at the monthly meeting held 12 Oct.

[f. 225v.] Monthly Meeting 12 October 1635

St. Thomas's Parish. Mr. William Huntt, churchwarden, and George Shergall, overseer, appeared.

They charge themselves with the following receipts: the money at Mistress Fryer's box 5½d.; at Mistress Lawrence's 5s. 4½d.; at William Raye's 6d.; at Thomas Rawlinges's 3d.; at John Perrye's nothing; at Collis's 17s. 10d. Total: 24s. 5d.

Mr Huntt received at the communion 3s. 9d., and he paid 6s. in full payment of the 10s. which he undertook for Thomas Rawlinges for suffering persons to tipple in his house contrary to the statute. Total: 9s. 9d.

George Shergall received from Thomas Southe, presented at the sessions for selling ale without licence, 20s.

They pray allowance for money disbursed since their last account, as appears by their bills of particulars, £3 11s. 11d. The tippling money formerly received and more which was received from Wigge and Hudles at the last sessions was paid to them, £3 3s. 2d. So remains due to them 8s. 9d.

St. Edmund's Parish. Thomas Mathewe *alias* Keynton, churchwarden, Thomas Gardner, John Gilbert, Ambrose Smythe, and John Fishlake, overseers, appeared.

They charged themselves with the following receipts: at the church door in money 12s. 6d.; from the boxes at George Bedburye's 19s. 8d.; at Mr. Wyatt's 3s. 8d.; at Mr. Barrowe's 5s. 4d.; at Mr. Batter's 8d.; more received at the church door 6 Sept. 7s. 8d. Total: 49s. 6d.

They pray allowance for their several bills of extraordinary disbursements since 3 July last by reason of divers sick persons who have been visited with extraordinary sicknesses in Greencroft Street: £5 12s. 6d.

The money formerly brought [on 14 Aug.] and that received by them at the church door and from the boxes was paid to them, £3 11s. 3d. So there remains due to them the 5*d*. allowed them which was in Mr. Gardner's hand and 40*s*. 10*d*.

St. Martin's Parish. Christopher Newe, churchwarden, Samuel Bell, Thomas Randes, and Christopher Jupe, overseers of the poor, appeared.

At this meeting the widow Reynoldes, presented for suffering Thomas Waller to tipple contrary to the statute, paid 3*s*. 4*d*. and in regard of her poverty the rest is remitted; Simon Haylocke for the like offence paid 3*s*. 4*d*. and in regard of his poverty is also remitted; John Pennye for the like offence paid 16*d*. These presentments were at midsummer sessions last. Also Mr. Bee paid 2*s*. which he received of a stranger for two profane oaths; Thomas Holton for one profane oath, 12*d*.; William Riche, turner, for one profane oath, 12*d*.; Thomas Jarvis's wife for one profane oath, 12*d*. Total 13*s*.

They pray allowance and payment for their several disbursements for the relief of the poor of that parish for the two last months past amounting to 22*s*. 7*d*. The money formerly received paid to them, 13*s*. So rests due to them 9*s*. 7*d*.

[f. 226]   Monthly Meeting 2 November 1635

St. Thomas's Parish. Mr. William Huntt, churchwarden, Thomas Hooper, George Shergall, and George Legge, overseers, appeared.

They charge themselves with the receipts following: from Mistress Lawrence's box 2*s*.; Mistress Fryer's box 7*d*.; at church after the communion 3*s*. 10*d*. Total: 6*s*. 5*d*.

Received from John Perrye, innholder, for suffering Richard Easton and others to tipple in his house unlawfully 10*s*. From young Banckes, butcher, for uttering and selling bull's beef in the market, the bull not baited,[1] 3*s*. From William Modge, musician, for a profane oath upon the testimony of John Weste and others, 12*d*. From George Shergall, which he received from William Smythe, innholder, for suffering tipplers in his house unlawfully (presented at the sessions), 5*s*. Total: 25*s*. 5*d*.

They pray allowance as follows: the remainder of the last monthly account, 8*s*. 9*d*., and their extraordinary disbursements since the last monthly meeting, 25*s*. 4*d*., in all 34*s*. 3*d*. [*recte* 34*s*. 1*d*.]. Paid to them 16*s*. 8*d*. formerly received [*recte* 25*s*. 5*d*.]. So rests due to them 8*s*. 8*d*.

They paid the 40*s*. taken from Mr. Tooker's apprentice money which was lent them towards the placing of Fishe's child.

St. Edmund's Parish. Mr. Thomas Mathewe, churchwarden, Mr. Thomas Gardner, Ambrose Smythe, John Gilbert, and John Fishlocke, overseers, appeared.

They charge themselves with money received at the church door 8*s*.; from Bedburye box 4*s*. 2*d*. Total: 12*s*. 2*d*.

They pray allowance for money laid out in extraordinaries, as appears by the particulars, 43*s*. 4*d*. There remains due to them from last month

---

[1] The baiting of bulls was supposed to improve their meat: *Agrarian Hist. of Eng. and Wales* 1500–1640, ed. J. Thirsk, 481; C. H. Haskins, *Ancient Trade Guilds and Companies of Salisbury*, 282.

40*s*. 10*d*. Mr. Gardner was paid the money formerly received, 12*s*. 2*d*. So rests due to him 28*s*. 8*d*., and to the other collectors 43*s*. 4*d*., in all £3 12*s*.

St. Martin's Parish. Christopher Batt, churchwarden, Samuel Bell and Thomas Randes, overseers, appeared.

The extraordinaries disbursed since the last month 12*s*. There remained due to them last month 9*s*. 7*d*. So due to them in all 21*s*. 7*d*.

They present Mistress Elizabeth Vaughan for entertaining [*blank*] Widnall who lately came from the Devizes to inhabit in this city.

[f. 226v.]   Monthly Meeting 7 December 1635
St. Thomas's Parish

The churchwardens and overseers being present charge themselves with receipt of the communion money 21*d*. Their extraordinary disbursements this month £3 1*s*. 2*d*. Due to them last month 8*s*. 8*d*. Deducting 21*d*. there remains due to them £3 8*s*. 5*d*. [*recte* £3 8*s*. 1*d*.] which was paid 6 Dec. 1635.

St. Edmund's Parish

The churchwardens and overseers being present charge themselves with the receipts for this month from the basin at the church door 8*s*. 6*d*.; from the box at Mr. Bedburye's 1*s*. 5*d*. Their extraordinary disbursements this month £4 7*s*. 5*d*. Due to them at the last monthly meeting £3 12*s*. Deducting 9*s*. 11*d*., which is now paid to John Fishelake, there remains due to them £7 9*s*. 6*d*.

They present that Giles Silvester has entertained one Barnes who married his daughter and lately came from Laverstocke and lives with Silvester. They are to be sent for and ordered to remove.

St. Martin's Parish

The churchwardens and overseers being present exhibited their extraordinary disbursements for the last month 29*s*. 3*d*. Due to them at the last monthly account 21*s*. 7*d*. So rests due to them 50*s*. 10*d*.

So remains due in all to the overseers of the three parishes £13 8*s*. 9*d*. which is paid 11 Dec. 1635.

7 Dec. 1635, Katherine Eaton, widow, and Thomas Southe, grocer, have undertaken and promised to pay 6*d*. every week towards the relief of George Eaton, son of the said Katherine, being an idle and disorderly boy, as long as the said George shall remain in the workhouse within the city.

11 Dec. 1635, the sum of £13 8*s*. 9*d*. was taken out of the Chest and paid to the overseers of the three parishes and it is agreed and ordered that the same shall be repaid again. [1]

[f. 227] The division of the city whereby a certain part of the city is limited to the persons hereunder written to take the care and oversight within their divisions as heretofore has been appointed, [2] first that the poor be relieved, that all idle persons be set on work, vagabonds and rogues punished, and

---

[1] There is no evidence that the sum was repaid. Deficits at the end of 1636 were met by loans from the mayor and aldermen and then by an 'extraordinary' tax on top of the normal poor-rate. In 1641 the poor-rate was revised to take account of rising expenditure: S.C.A., S 162, ff. 231, 232, 246.

[2] Cf. pp. 65–74.

[they are] to consider of alehouse-keepers who are fit to be continued and who are to be suppressed, and [to look] for inmates, under-tenants, and strangers; by Mr. Mayor, Mr. Recorder, and other his Majesty's justices of the peace within the same city, 9 Dec. 1635.

Mr. Abbott: from the Cheese Cross, all Castle Street on the west side and the east to Scots Lane, the north side of Scots Lane, Endles Street, Bedden Row to St. Edmund's church and churchyard. Mr. Ambrose Weste, John Fludd, Henry Byley, junior, assistants; Richard Whyte, constable; John Gilbert, gent., overseer.

Mr. Maurice Greene: the Dolphin chequer, the Oatmeal Row, the Lyons chequer, Mr. Gauntlette's chequer, the Butcher Row, the Fisher Row, the Antelope chequer. Mr. Humphrey Ditton, Christopher Brathatt, John Beache, ironmonger, assistants; William Whyte, constable.

Mr. Wolstan Coward: the south side of New Street to the Close gate, from the Close gate all Crane Street, the west side of High Street to Fisherton Bridge and so to the Cheese Cross. Thomas Hooper, John Batten, Nicholas Snowe, assistants; Godfrey Spickernell, constable.

Mr. Thomas Hancocke, senior: the Blue Boar chequer, the White Horse chequer, Mr. Sherfeild's chequer, the Three Swans chequer. Mr. Thomas Lawes, Mr. Francis Dove, Robert Belman, assistants; Thomas Griste, constable.

Mr. Anthony Brickett: Greencroft Street from Sir Giles Estcourte's up to Mr. Payne's, upon the outskirts. Mr. John Payne, Edmund Snowe, Simon Rolffe, assistants; John Butcher, constable.

Mr. John Ivye: the Three Cups chequer, Thomas Pawle's chequer, the Griffin chequer, Mr. Elson's chequer. John Barrowe, junior, Cuthbert Creede, William Erlye, assistants; Ambrose Smythe, constable [Thomas Maye, constable *deleted*].

Mr. Matthew Bee: the White Hart chequer, Mr. Bee's chequer, John Trewman's chequer, from St. Martin's church to the almshouses in Dragon [*now* Exeter] Street. Mr. John Windover, George Antram, Christopher Jupe, Robert Hole, Christopher Humfrey, John Trewman, assistants; Thomas Maye, constable.

[f. 227v.] Mr. John Batt [Mr. James Abbott *deleted*]: the Trinity chequer, the Black Horse chequer, Mr. Swayne's chequer, Mr. Burges's chequer. [Mr. Edward Edmondes *deleted*] Isaac Girdler, Christopher Newe, William Symes [Mr. Christopher Batt, senior *deleted*], Thomas Blake, assistants; [Robert Freind, constable *deleted*] John Trewman, constable.

All these assistants within their several divisions are to observe these particulars following:

1. To take weekly notice of all newcomers and inmates and to give information to the alderman of that division.
2. To examine every house within their division what persons are there, how many children, of what ages, and how they are employed to get their living, and to present the names of such as are fit to be placed apprentices.[1]

---

[1] Possibly the origin of the *c.* 1635 censuses of the poor: see pp. 75–82.

3. To take care that none wander up and down begging, and if any do to present their names to the alderman of that division.

4. To take care that such as are able to work do keep themselves to work, and to see that those impotent persons which cannot work may have fit relief to prevent their wandering abroad.

IX OVERSEERS' PAPERS 1635-6

1. Good friends, we are here desired in the behalf of [a] good painful and honest widow, our neighbour, who hath been a great painstaker in teaching of young children here amongst us and very religious and careful in breeding and edifying her own children, having nothing left but what she hath and doth get by her fingers' ends for maintenance of herself and children. Now she having match[ed] one of her daughters with a lewd idle fellow and of a loose life and conversation, the which she is informed that he is gone and left her [daughter] desolate of comfort and relief so that she is likely to perish (if she should not take some compassion over her), or that you like good devoted and pious parishioners shall take some care and commiseration of her and her children now being in some distress (as she hath informed her mother), who is so tender over her and her poor grandchildren that, though she be very old and decaying of her painstaking, she so religiously respects them forth of her motherly love that she is content to take them home here to her, although she be so in age that she needs a comforter herself; but [she] will suffer in her old age and bear some part of her [daughter's] misery and poverty though she suffer herself. Now her humble request is that we here her neighbours and parishioners would be suitors to you the churchwardens and overseers of the parish to move the parishioners and neighbours to commiserate her [daughter's] wants and poverty and bestow some relief on her and her children towards the carriage home hither to her mother, as also somewhat towards the keeping of that child which was born with you, . . . [*document torn*]. Not doubting of your charitableness herein (we take our leaves), being ready to hasten and effect any such like occasion moved to us by you, if the like now were or shall be any time afterwards desired. So we rest your loving friends, [signed] Widow Manninge, . . . [*two names illegible*], Richard Edmonds, Richard St . . . [*torn*], overseers. Weybridge, 12 Dec. 1634.

2. The collectors of St. Martin's have laid out in extraordinaries since the last monthly meeting to this 4 May: paid for a shroud for Cole's nurse child, died 26 Apr. 1635, 1s. 6d.; to Cooke's wife being sick 6d.; to Grigg's wife being sick 2s.; to the Widow Beckham lying in 2s.; to Lemmon's wife 1s.; to the Widow Banckes 4d.; to the Widow Acrie 4d. The sum is 7s. 8d. Paid this bill 3 June 1635.

3. Extraordinaries, 3 June 1635. Paid to Pressly being sick 1s.; to the Widow Beckham 1s.; to Grigge's wife 1s.; to Lemmon's wife 1s.; to the Widow Acrie 1s. The sum is 7s.

4. St. Thomas's parish, 2 June 1635, the box money. Received out of Mr Collice's box 19*s*. 6*d*.; at John Perrye's 0; at Thomas Rawllinges's 11*d*.; at Mr. Fryer's 1*s*. 7*d*.; at Mr. Senior's 7*d*.; at Mr. William Raye's 1*d*. Total: £1 2*s*. 8*d*.

5. To the right worshipful Mr. Mayor and the rest of his Majesty's justices of this city of New Salisbury, the humble petition of Thomas Bolwine of this city, weaver. Whereas your petitioner hath lived of long time together with his wife, being both very aged in so much that they are not able by their labour to relieve themselves in any sort, in tender consideration whereof they humbly craveth your worships to be pleased to take such order with the churchwardens and overseers of the poor of the parish of St. Edmund's, where they live, that they may have some relief out of the said parish for their better relief, what your worships shall think [fit], and your petitioners according to their bounden [duties] shall for ever pray for your worships' happiness.

6. St. Edmund's parish, 3 July 1635. The churchwardens and overseers do present that Robert Sutton, an ostler at the Cornish Chough being a stranger and foreigner, is become an inhabitant in Winchester Street in the land of Britford. Signed, Thomas Kynton, Thomas Gardiner, John Fishlake.

7. St. Thomas's parish, 3 July 1635, the presentment of the overseers, [signed] Thomas Batter, George Legge. The Widow Pannell has taken a house upon the ditch and entertains her son-in-law, Robert Screach, new come from London. William Symes at the Widow Eastman's in New Street [is] entertained, being a stranger.

8. I was in hope to have been with you this morning but God will not have it so. I am given to understand of one William Sims who is lodged in New Street at the Widow Easton's: his conversation is not well thought of. If he may be voided the town, let be done. A stranger I hear he is. The Lord direct you. Your friend, B. Tookie. [1]

9. 13 Aug. 1635, St. Thomas's parish, the churchwardens' bill. Received at communions 8*s*. 6*d*.; of Mr. Hill for one that swore an oath 12*d*.; from Thomas Rawlines at 12*d*. a week for 4 weeks for some drinking in his house, being part of 10*s*., 4*s*. Total: 13*s*. 6*d*. Laid out for the carrying away of George Gifford's wife and 2 children 5*s*.; to a strange woman which was delivered of a child at Sebole's house 2*s*.; for washing of her clothes 2*s*. Total: 9*s*.

10. St. Thomas's parish, 13 Aug. 1635, an account of such sums of money as have been disbursed extraordinarily by the collectors since 4 July 1635.
    6 July: to Agnes Cromes for attending Anne Cole 9*d*.; to John Allderson being sick 1*s*.; to George Bellsheare's wife 4*d*.; to John Allderson 1*s*.; to Agnes Cromes for attending Anne Cole 9*d*.
    13 July: to John Allderson 2*s*.; to Peter Tracie's wife 4*d*.; to Anne Tyther 2*s*.; to Agnes Cromes for attending Anne Cole 9*d*.

---

[1] A Salisbury alderman: cf. pp. 87, 94.

20 July: to Jane Curtes 4*d.*; to George Bellsheare's wife 6*d.*; to John Allderson 2*s.*; to Margaret Willborne by Mr. Bee's order 1*s.*

25 July: to Agnes Cromes for attending Anne Cole 9*d.*; to John Rogers towards the apparelling of Henry Cooke *alias* Tomson whom he hath taken an apprentice 10*s.*

27 July: to Jane Curtes 4*d.*; to George Belshear 6*d.*; to John Allderson 2*s.*; to Anne Tyther 2*s.*; to Agnes Cromes for attending Anne Cole 9*d.*; to Anne Peasland 1*s.* 6*d.*

3 Aug.: to Jane Curtes 4*d.*; to George Bellsheare 6*d.*; to Anne Tythei 2*s.*; to John Allderson 2*s.*; to Agnes [Cromes for attending] Anne Cole 9*d.* [*Entries for 10 Aug. torn away.*]

11. Received from Mr. Bayley of Norton, 9 Aug.: for swearing 5*s.*, for being drunk 5*s.*, total 10*s.* Received out of the boxes in St. Thomas's parish, 13 Aug. 1635: at Mr. Collice's £1 10*s.* besides 2*s.* 9*d.* Mr. Collice disposed of in his house; at John Perrie's 0; at Thomas Rawlens's 1*s.* 1*d.*; at Mistress Larrance's 17*s.* 1*d.*; at Philip Senior's 1*s.*; at Mr. William Raye's 5*d.*; at Mistress Fryer's 2*s.* 7*d.* Total: £2 12*s.* 2*d.*

12. St. Edmund's parish, 14 Aug. 1635. Received at the church door in the basins: 5 July 3*s.*; 12 July [*blank*]; 19 July 4*s.* 7*d.*; 25 July 2*s.* 8*d.*; 2 Aug. 5*s.* 6*d.*; 9 Aug. 6*s.*; sum is 21*s.* 9*d.* This money resteth in Mr. Mathewe's hands towards the extraordinaries the overseers have laid out.

13. Collectors of St. Martin's, 14 Aug. 1635. Extraordinaries laid forth by me Samuel Bell, collector of the parish of St. Martin's, since 3 July 1635 unto this 14 Aug. 1635: paid to Frye's wife being sick 1*s.*; more to Frye's wife being sick 6*d.*; to Beatrice Baker being sick 6*d.*; to Alice White being sick 8*d.*; to Flower Staples being sick 6*d.*; to Frye's wife more being sick 6*d.*; to Flower Staples more being sick 6*d.*; to Rose his child being sick 6*d.*; to Alice White more being sick 6*d.*; to Frie's wife more being sick 6*d.*; to Widow Worte and her daughter being both sick 1*s.*; to Flower Staples more being sick 6*d.*; to Alice White more being sick 6*d.*; to Alice White more being sick 6*d.*; to the woman for attending Widow Worte and her daughter 1*s.*; to Widow Worte more being sick 6*d.*; to Goodwife Pomery being sick 6*d.*; to Widow Worte more being sick 6*d.*; to Widow Worte more being sick 1*s.* Total: 12*s.* 2*d.*

14. St. Martin's, 14 Aug. Laid out to Goody Coale in money: 5 July 1635 12*d.*; 12 July 12*d.*; 19 July 12*d.*; 26 July 12*d.*; 2 Aug. 12*d.*; 9 Aug. 12*d.*

15. Collectors of St. Martin's, 14 Aug. Extraordinaries laid forth by us Samuel Bell and Christopher Jupe, collectors of the parish of St. Martin's, since 3 June 1635 unto this 3 July 1635 as follows: for one shirt for Henry Pressy 2*s.* 6*d.*; for 3 ells of canvas for Henry Pressy 2*s.* 9*d.*; for making clean of Pressy's lodging 1*s.*; for a drinking cup and for brown thread for Pressy 2*d.*; to four men which carried Pressy to church 1*s.* 4*d.*; for one knitch of straw for Pressy 4*d.*; to two women which attended Pressy 1*s.* 6*d.*; for the digging of the grave for Pressy 6*d.*; to Knight's wife being sick 2*s.* 6*d.* Total: 12*s.* 7*d.*

16. Collectors of St. Martin's. Extraordinaries laid forth by us Samuel Bell and Christopher Jupe, overseers of the parish of St. Martin's, since 14 Aug. 1635 unto this 7 Sept. 1635 as follows: paid to the Widow Worte being sick 1s.; to the Widow Buckett being sick 6d.; to the Widow Worte more being sick 1s.; to Grigge's wife being sick 1s.; to the Widow Worte more being sick 1s.; to the Widow Worte more being sick 1s.; to Lemone's wife being sick 1s.; to the Widow Beckham 1s.; to Cole's wife for her month's pay 4s.; to Goodwife Playre 1s.; to the Widow Worte more being sick 6d. Total: 13s.

17. St. Thomas's parish, an account of all such sums of money that hath been disbursed extraordinarily since 14 Aug. 1635.

Paid Agnes Cromes for attending Anne Cole 9d.; to Anne Peasland 1s. 6d.

17 Aug.: to Jane Curtes 4d.; to George Belshere 6d.; to Anne Tyther 2s.; to John Allderson 2s.; to Anne Peasland 1s. 6d.; to Agnes Cromes for attending Anne Cole 9d.

24 Aug.: to George Bellsher 6d.; to Jane Curtes 4d.; to John Allderson 2s.; to William Robbartes 1s.; to Anne Peasland 1s. 6d.; to Widow Turner 6d.; to William Robartes 1s.; to Agnes Cromes for attending Anne Cole 9d.

1 Sept.: to George Bellsher 6d.; to John Allderson 2s.; to Jane Curtes 4d.; to William Robbartes 1s.; to Anne Tyther 2s.; to William Robbartes [1s.]; to Anne Peasland [1s. 6d.]; to Agnes Cromes for [attending Anne Cole] 9d.

[*Entries for 7, 14, 21 Sept. torn away.*]

28 Sept.: to George Bellsher 6d.; to Jane Curtes 4d.; to John Allderson 2s.; to William Robbardes 2s.; to Anne Tyther 2s.; to Agnes Cromes for attending Anne Cole 9d.; to Widow Turner 6d.; to Anne Peasland 1s. 6d.

5 Oct.: to Jane Curtes 4d.; to George Belsher 6d.; to William Robbartes 2s.; to John Allderson 2s.; to Roger Clarke 2s.; to Goodwife Longman 1s.; to Peter Tracie's wife 6d.; to Agnes Cromes for attending Anne Cole 9d.; to Widow Turner 6d.; to Anne Peasland 1s. 6d.

Total: £3 11s. 11d. [Receipts:] £1 13s. 5d. Rests: £1 18s. 6d.

18. St. Edmund's, 7 Sept. 1635, an account of such money as hath been disbursed in extraordinaries since 3 July 1635.

12 July: to Goody Allen 6d.; for salve for Benester's children 2s.; for clothes for Whitehorne 2s.

15 July: to Edward Bell 4d.; to Dorothy Bird 1d.; to Goody Allen 3d.; to Goody Godder 2d.; to Goody Allen 6d.; to Goody Dearinge 1d.

20 July: to Goody Allen 6d.; to Goody Saunders 6d.

27 July: to Goody Allen 6d.

2 Aug.: to Saunders 6d.; to Richard Swayne 6d.; to Goody Newby 1s.

3 Aug.: to Swayne 9d.; to Goody Streete 3d.; to Thomas Halles 4d.; to Goody Williams 4d.; to Goody Dearinge 1d.; to Goody Vincent 1d.; to Emma Browne 1d.; to Allen's wife 8d.; to Goody Rickatts 4d.

[*Remainder of document torn.*]

19. 7 Mar. 1636, monies extraordinary for the poor of St. Thomas's parish.
1 Feb. 1636: paid Goodwife Alderson 2s.; Widow Easton [for] one of
Perie's children 1s. 4d.; Goodwife Ellmes [for] one of Perie's children 1s. 2d.;
for tending Widow Sprat 1s.; Mistress Alice Elliot 1s.; Widow Bremble
[for] one of Perie's children 1s. 4d.; old Widow Swift 9d.; Edward Lane 1s.;
Widow Spratt 1s.; George Belshere 6d.; for tending Widow Coale 9d.;
William Clark 8d.; Goodwife Tracie 4d.; for washing Goodwife Perie's
clothes 1s. 6d.; for tending Goodwife Perry 2s.; Goodwife Allexander
[for] one of Perie's children 1s. Total: 17s. 4d.
8 Feb. 1636: paid Goodwife Alderson 2s.; Widow Easton [for] one of
Perie's children 1s. 4d.; Goodwife Ellmes [for] one of Perie's children 1s. 2d.;
Widow Bremble for one of Perie's children 1s. 4d; Mistress Alice Elliot 1s.;
old Widow Swift 8d.; Widow Tither 4d.; Widow Brikett 4d.; Edward Lane
1s.; Widow Sprat 1s.; for tending Widow Coale 9d.; William Clarke 6d.;
Goodman Hart 6d.; George B[elshere] 4d.; for tending . . . [torn] 1s.;
Goody A[lexander for one of Perie's] children 1s. Total: 14s. 3d.
15 Feb. 1636: paid Goody Alderson 2s.; Goody Easton [for one of Perie's
child]ren 1s. 4d.; Goody Bremble 1s. 4d.; old Widow Swift 6d.; Goodwife
Ellmes for one of Perie's children 1s. 2d.; Mistress Elliot 1s.; Goody
Sanger 6d.; Goody Bricket 4d.; Goodman Cookny 6d.; for tending
Widow Sprat 1s.; Timothy Hibard's wife 8d.; for tending Widow Coale
9d.; Widow Sprat 1s.; William Clark 6d.; Goodman Hart 6d.; Goodwife
Allexander for one of Perie's children 1s.; George Belshere 4d. Total:
14s. 5d.
22 Feb. 1636: paid Goody Alderson 2s.; Mistress Elliot 1s.; Widow Tither
4d.; Widow Eason for one of Perie's children 1s. 4d.; Widow Bremble for
one of Perie's children 1s. 4d.; Goody Ellmes for one of Perie's children
1s. 4d.; old Widow Swift 6d.; Jeboll for charges of Goody Perie's burial
1s. 6d.; for tending Goodwife Sprat 1s.; Widow Briket 3d.; for tending
Widow Cole 9d.; Widow Sprat 8d.; Anthony Turnam 1s.; George
Belshere 4d.; Goody Clare 1s.; Goody Ellexander for one of Perye's
children 1s. Total: 15s. 2d. [recte 15s. 4d.]

20. Blue Boar chequer, 4 Mar. 1636.[1] We present Richard, son of Thomas
York, age 15 years, fit to be an apprentice; Robert Sutton a non-comer
[to church] in Chipper Lane; Joan Mitchell, widow, 1 son, age 14 years, makes
bonelace, and a daughter, 11 years, makes bonelace; George Mills, 1 son, 12
years, fit to be apprentice.
White Horse chequer. We present Sarah, daughter to Thomas Carter, age
18 years, makes bonelace; Widow Smith, 3 children, ages 13, 14, 10, the boy
of 14 years to be put to be apprentice.
Bedden Row. Widow Pitt, 1 daughter, 20 years old, works with Mr. Stevens;
Widow Hibbord, 2 daughters, age 15, 9, makes bonelace; Joan Phillups, 1
son, 9 years; Widow Coles, 1 daughter, 18 years, makes bonelace; Widow
Avery keeps a sister's daughter, 16 years old, makes bonelace.

[1] Cf. the poor listed in the c. 1635 census: see pp. 75, 78.

21. St. Edmund's parish, basin money delivered 4 Apr. 1636. Received 15 Mar. 3s.; 10 Mar. 3s. 2d.; 27 Mar. 7s.

22. From the north side of Fisherton Bridge up all Castle Street and so to the college.[1] At Thomas Brigmore's, the old Goody Sivier wanting relief; at Thomas Goden's, Mistress Wadhames; at the Widow Currior's, Richard Wootton; at Henry Langly's, John Winter want[ing] relief; at Thomas Sutten's house, the widow Fortune and her daughter, John Creech and his wife, Richard Michell and wife, William Hall and six small children wanting relief; at the Widow Bybee's, Barbara Cuper and 2 children wanting relief; at John Francis's, Robert . . . [torn] and his wife and 3 children wanting relief; at Goody Tiper's, Thomas Deverell and his wife; at Thomas Hapgood's, Christopher Benat and three children want relief. John Reckat and three children in relief, and Margaret Street want[s] relief, and Jane Eliot and three children to be placed. Nicholas Creed and 4 children wanting relief.

X WORKHOUSE ACCOUNTS 1627–30

[f. 156v.] 14 Mar. 1628. The account of Mr. Thomas Raye and John Frye, the master and governor of the workhouse in the city of New Salisbury, before the right worshipful Mr. James Abbott, mayor, Mr. Godfrey, Mr. Byle, Mr. Baines, Mr. Marshall.

The said accountant charges himself with the remainder of last year's account 14s.; he charges himself with part of the rents of Popley's lands,[2] received from Mr. Dawes, £30. Total receipt: £30 14s.

Whereof he prays allowance for beer for the poor this year £5; delivered to John Fryer for victuals for the poor £4; paid to Edmund Stevens for two years' rent for part of his house employed with the workhouse 40s.; delivered to John Pearson 40s.; paid Mr. Abbott for linen as appears by the last account and for a shroud 22s. 1d.; paid Mr. Nicholas Ellyott for frieze as appears by the last account 17s. 4d.; for the relief of the poor 4 and 11 Nov. [1627] 4s.; to Waterman for two weeks which was due in Mr. Gauntlette's year 15s.; for Ewsle's and Lane's children 4s.; for straw and other charge 3s. 8d.; paid Waterman for the commons of the poor for 3 weeks, 18 Nov., 22s. 6d.; paid 25 Nov. 6s. 6d.; paid 2 Dec. 5s. 6d.; paid for two weeks 11s.; for curing a boy's head 8d.; for 8 weeks' diet 54s.; paid 17 Feb. and for 6 weeks after, at the rate of 6s. 6d. a week, 45s. 6d.; paid 19 May for 7 weeks 52s. 6d.; for burying a boy 8d.; for a petticoat and waistcoat and making thereof 8s. 8d.; for cloth for 5 jerkins 13s., and breeches 13s., the making thereof and buttons 7s., 5 ells of canvas 4s. 2d., 6 pairs of stockings and points 6s. 6d., 6 pairs of shoes 3s., 46s. [recte 46s. 8d.]; paid the clerk for writing and entering the last account 5s. Total allowances: £29 0s. 3d. [recte £29 5s. 3d.].

So remains: 28s. 9d. which is delivered unto Mr. Henry Pearson, the next master and governor of the house. Also delivered to Mr. Pearson one

---

1 Cf. the poor listed in the c. 1635 census: see p. 75.
2 See pp. 11, 86.

obligation of John Ellyotte's for the payment of 40s. and an inventory of the goods of the workhouse.

[f. 157] A rental of the lands late Popley's in Bassingshawe, London, made 9 Dec. 1629.

The quarter's rent due at the feast of St. Michael the Archangel, 1629, £15 11s. 8d.

Mr. Richard Welbye £5 6s. 3d.; John Rylye £12 6s. 8d.; Randoll Claxton £8; John Badger £6; Anne Badger, two tenements, one late Rawlinge's, the other late Richardson's, £5; Mistress Cicely Pettitt, late Mr. Cannon's, £4; Mr. Churche, late Edwarde's and since Dorothy Shawe's, £3; Hanna Gifford, late Edginton's now Wharton's, £3; Widow Nibleye £4; John Shawe 40s.; Widow Harrison 6s. 8d.; Henry Mansell, late Kurbye's, £4.

The whole year's rent is £57. The rents to be received every Michaelmas and every 25 Mar. are £15 11s. 8d. The rents to be received every Midsummer and Christmas £12 18s. 4d. The half-year's rent is £28 10s.

[f. 157v.] 1628. The account of Mr. Henry Pearson and John Vyninge, master and governor of the workhouse in the city of New Salisbury, from 14 Mar. 1628 to [blank] Dec. 1630, made and taken [blank] Dec. 1630 before the right worshipful Thomas Hill, mayor of the city of New Salisbury, Matthew Bee, Bartholomew Tookye, and John Ivye, gent.

The charge: the remainder of the last account taken 14 Mar. 1628 28s. 9d.; received from Mr. Dawes, receiver and collector of the rents of lands in Bassingshawe, London, late Popley's, as parcel of the said rents, 2 May 1628 £13; received more 7 Aug. £15; received more 23 Dec. £15; more from Mr. Dawes £5. Total receipts: £49 8s. 9d.

Allowances: paid to Waterman, the keeper of the poor and workfolks in the house, 4 Apr. 1628 7s.; more 8 Apr. 7s., 17 Apr. 7s., 23 Apr. 7s., 21s.; paid Mr. Abbott 2 May for canvas to make shirts for the poor children 26s. 6d.; paid Waterman 2 May 7s., 6 May 7s., 10 May 7s., 21s.; paid Waterman his quarter's wages 25s.; paid Waterman 13 May 7s., 21 May 7s., 26 May 7s., 21s.; paid 26 May for making six shirts and 9 bands 2s. 6d.; paid Waterman 28 May 7s.; paid 31 May to Peasland for 9 pairs of shoes 14s. 10d.; paid Waterman 7 June 7s., 12 June 7s., 19 June 7s., 21s.; paid for two burdens of straw 12d.; 26 June to Waterman 5s. 6d., 2 July 5s. 6d., 11s.; more by Mr. Mayor's appointment 4s.; paid 8 July 9s., 15 July 9s., 18s.; 15 July Waterman's quarter's wages 25s.; paid Waterman 21 July 9s., 28 July 9s., 7 Aug. 9s., 14 Aug. 9s., 19 Aug. 9s., 27 Aug. 9s., 54s.; paid Waterman for 36 lb. hemp 8s., more 2 Sept. 8s., 16s.; given Widow Parsons 6d.; paid 12 Sept. 8s., 17 Sept. 8s., 24 Sept. 8s., 24s.; [f. 158] paid Lanyle, the cobbler, for mending 9 pairs of shoes 4s. 6d.; paid Waterman 2 Oct. 9s., 7 Oct. 7s., 16s.; paid Waterman the same day for his wages 25s.; paid 14 Oct. 7s., 23 Oct. 7s., 14s.; paid Edmund Stevens for the rent of part of his house 20s.; paid 30 Oct. 6s., 4 Nov. 6s., 11 Nov. 6s., 18 Nov. 7s., 25 Nov. 7s., 2 Dec. 7s., 39s.; paid Edmund Stevens 22 June 1629 for his rent 20s.; paid 23 Sept. the Widow Parsons and three children 12d., 1 Oct. 12d., 9 Oct. 12d., 14 Oct. 12d.,

23 Oct. 12*d*., and the Widow Lynche at two several times 12*d*., 6*s*.; paid for the boy which was put apprentice to Elizabeth Williamson, widow, for a pair of stockings 12*d*., for three yards of frieze 4*s*. 6*d*., for making his hose and doublet 2*s*., 7*s*. 6*d*.; paid Mr. Aylerugge for 4 yards of frieze to make Cole's apparel 7*s*., and for the making thereof 2*s*. 6*d*., 9*s*. 6*d*.; paid Mr. Vyninge 13 Dec. for 9 yards of frieze 12*s*., and Mr. Abbott for 5 ells of canvas for lining 5*s*., and for the making thereof 2*s*. 6*d*., 19*s*. 6*d*.; Mr. Abbott delivered 9 yards of frieze and the account paid for the making 2*s*. 8*d*.; paid 16 Dec. 1629 to Mr. Vyninge for 11 yards of frieze for 3 poor people 13*s*., for two ells of canvas 2*s*. 2*d*., for making apparel 2*s*., for 3 pairs of stockings 3*s*. 3*d*., for two pairs of shoes for children 2*s*. 6*d*., one pair of shoes for Dorothy Cooper 2*s*., and for her two smocks, one other little shirt, and a little smock 9*s*., 33*s*. 11*d*.; for Mowdye's child for two smocks and two pairs of shoes 5*s*. 2*d*.; for three yards of frieze 3*s*. 8*d*., and for the making 6*d*., 4*s*. 2*d*.; paid 6 Mar. for two burdens of straw 12*d*.; paid to Anthony Perrye 17, 18, 19 Mar. 1630 for 92 ft. of board 9*s*. 2*d*., for 73 ft. of timber 6*s*. 8*d*., for five days work 5*s*. 3*d*., one form to hold the work 18*d*., for nails 18*d*., for the carriage of two packs of hemp from Shaftesbury to Salisbury, 7 Apr., 3*s*. 6*d*., 27*s*. 7*d*.; paid 10 Apr. 1630 for the mending of old Tornes 5*s*. 6*d*., and paid Belshere 15 Apr. for mending a chimney 3*s*. 6*d*., 9*s*.; paid for two pairs of cards 2*s*., to the sexton of St. Thomas's for making a grave and a bier for the burial of Pride's daughter [8*d*.], 2*s*. 8*d*.; paid 17 June for 4 bundles of Roddes earth and the hellier's work 3*s*. 4*d*.; more to Mr. John Ivye 5 Dec. 1628 £20; more to Mr. Brickett 6*s*. 8*d*. Total allowances: £49 3*s*. 8*d*. [*recte* £49 17*s*. 6*d*.]

So rests in Mr. Pearson's hand: 5*s*. 9*d*. [*recte* 8*s*. 9*d*. *deficit*].

[f. 158v.] Mr. Ivye 1627. The account of Mr. John Ivye in the sickness year,[1] part of 1627 and [1628 *deleted*] 1629.

He charges himself that he received from Mr. Pearson's part of Popley's rents, as it appeareth in Mr. Pearson's account, £20; he received from Philip Dawes £5.

Allowances: for relief and setting poor children to work.

St. Edmund's parish: one child of Elizabeth Michell's at 6*d*. a week for two years 52*s*.; Mary Robertes's child, 6*d*. a week for two years, 52*s*.; two children of Grace Banister, 12*d*. a week for 2 years, £5 4*s*.; Richard Holloway and Grace Holloway, 2*s*. a week for 2 years, £10 8*s*.; one child of Widow Smythe, 6*d*. for 2 years, 52*s*.; one child of Widow Newman's, 6*d*. for 2 years, 52*s*.; one child of Giles Silvester's, 6*d*. for 2 years, 52*s*.; one child of Widow Slade's, 6*d*. for 2 years, 52*s*.; one child of Widow Weekes, 4*d*. for 2 years, 34*s*. 8*d*.; one child of Widow Hibberde's, 6*d*. for 2 years, 52*s*.; two children of Widow Jones, 12*d*. for 2 years, £5 4*s*.; William Browne, a child, 6*d*. for 2 years, 52*s*.; John Hynton, a child, 4*d*. for 2 years, 34*s*. 8*d*.; one child of Widow Bybye's, 6*d*. for 2 years, 52*s*.; one child of Widow Hole, 6*d*. for 2 years, 52*s*.; Widow Parsons's three children, 18*d*. for 2 years, £7 16*s*. Total: £58 1*s*. 4*d*.

St. Thomas's parish: one child of John Beekes, 6*d*. for 2 years, 52*s*.; one child

---

[1] 1627: see pp. 7, 117–28.

of Widow Mynterne's, 6d. for 2 years, 52s.; one child of Widow George, 6d. for 2 years, 52s.; one child of Wilmotte's, 6d. for 2 years, 52s.; one child of Christopher Martin's, 6d. for 2 years, 52s.; John Barnes's 2 children, 12d. for 2 years, £5 4s.; Widow Stokes's two children, 12d. for 2 years, £5 4s.; James Symons's three children, 18d. for two years, £7 16s. Total: £31 4s.

[f. 159] St. Martin's parish: William Gillett, a child at Buckette's, 8d. a week for 2 years, £3 9s. 4d.; Widow Eyles's 2 children, at 12d. for 2 years, £5 4s.; Spegge's child at Wigmor's, 6d. for 2 years, 52s.; Elizabeth Potter's 2 children, 12d. for 2 years, £5 4s.; Elizabeth Chambers's one child, 6d. for 2 years, 52s.; Thomas Turner's child, 6d. for 2 years, 52s.; John Androwes's child, 4d. for 2 years, 34s. 8d.; Christopher Farder's child, 6d. for 2 years, 52s.; Widow Banckes's child, 6d. for 2 years, 52s.; Dorothy Hoskins's child, 6d. for 2 years, 52s.; Pytte's child at Hamell's, 6d. for 2 years, 52s.; John Humfrey's child, 6d. for 2 years, 52s. Total: £36 8s.

Mr. Ivye disbursed in the years 1627, 1629, 1630, 1631 as follows: to Waterman for the diet of the poor there for 20 weeks £3 9s. 6d.; for 20 barrels of beer 33s. 4d.; paid Bun for Alice Graunte's diet for 4 weeks 2s. 8d.; for the poor in the workhouse at 10s. a week for 25 weeks £12 10s.; paid Snowe for 10 bushels of lime 4s.; paid Townesend for work, laths, tiles, and nails about the workhouse 23s. 6d.; paid in this three last years at 5s. 2d. a week for diet of the poor in the house £40 6s. Total: £59 9s. Total allowances: £185 2s. 4d. [1]

[f. 159v.] The account of Mr. James Abbott, 1627 and 1628.

He charges himself that he received of Philip Dawes, 15 Dec. 1627, from the rents of Popley's lands £15.

Allowances: money paid to Waterman for diet for the poor for two weeks, 19 and 26 Nov., at 10s. a week 20s.; paid for three weeks at 9s. a week 27s.; paid more for one week 8s.; more for one week 7s. 6d.; for 11 weeks at 7s. a week, ended 26 Mar. 1628, £3 17s.; paid for 5½ ells of cloth to line the children's breeches 5s.; for six shirts 9s. 2d.; paid the tailor for making apparel 7s.; for making their shirts and one ell of cloth 23d.; for 11 pairs of shoes 3s. 7d.; paid Waterman for 1½ year's wages £7 10s.; paid Mr. Tookye for [blank] pair of stockings 14s.; paid for drink at the brewhouse for the poor of the workhouse 32s. 8d. Total allowances: £18 2s. 10d.

---

[1] It is not clear how expenditure was met, apart from £25 from Popley's rents, but those rents, which should have yielded £57 a year, were not wholly accounted for 1627–30 and were possibly used for Ivie's extra disbursements.

APPENDIX

A DECLARATION

Written by John Ivie, the elder, of the city of New Salisbury in the county of Wilts., and one of the aldermen. Where he hath done his true and faithful service for above forty years for the good of the poor and the inhabitants thereof. But now so it is that not only the mayor but myself with many other justices have been most falsely and unjustly abused by the overseers and some of the churchwardens, with others that should have had more wit, as these ensuing lines will declare much of it, but not the half.

London, printed for the author, 1661.

(Sig. A2)   To the Reader

These lines here written I pray read, without respect to the matter or author, not pouring upon one point until you understand the whole, and then you shall be able to judge in the fear of God the whole intent of the matter and writer, who hath hereafter declared in the presence of God he had never in his heart any other thought by this work but to advance God's glory and to settle a livelihood for the comfortable living of poor souls whereby God may be glorified and our city comforted, and many poor souls having ten years been enforced (sig. A2v.) to beg their bread or starve, which had been at this time again prevented had it not been for the ungodly men hereafter written of.

The measures in most markets do very much wrong poor and rich.

J.I.

(p. 1) A Declaration written by John Ivie, the elder, of the city of New Salisbury in the county of Wilts., and one of the aldermen.

Mr. Christopher Batt, then mayor,[1] Mr. William Eyres, minister of St. Thomas's parish, Henry Eyres, esquire, and James Heely, gent., late in the evening sent for me about the poor. I went to them, who told me that they had been in serious discourse all that evening about the poor, that were much increased and ran about abegging to the dishonour of God and good government. They then desired me to assist them in some way to order the poor. I told them I was now grown old and could not tell how to travail in such a business for my sight did much fail me. I said, 'What is it you desire to have my assistance in, or what is it you desire to have done?' Who replied, 'We do desire to have the storehouse to be set up again, for we have heard that in that time of the storehouse there were no beggars in the city.' I told them I did fear our government was now so divided and our church officers so unruly that I thought it impossible to set up so good a work. I told them in

---
[1] Batt was mayor 1658–9.

short, and am able to make it appear, it is possible by that way to relieve six score poor souls better than they can any other way four score; besides by that order you shall not have one beggar in the city. 'Oh!' said the recorder, 'I wish I could see it so ordered once more.' I told him that I had not only seen it so, but had ordered it so [for] ten years in the city without any trouble to the then governors. [1]

But now they pressed sore upon me once more to undertake it, and they would provide a sufficient stock. I told them I could not with comfort do it but, if they would provide an (p. 2) honest man that would receive the money of the collectors and buy in provision, I would make no doubt in one month to make him understand the order of the whole work as well as myself. Whereupon they pitched on Mr. George Leg, one of the city [council], to be the man to undertake the work and within three weeks they would make an order in sessions, which was accordingly done. But then was not time to buy provision, but [we] must stay until Easter for to buy in some materials and provide an house for the work, which was done.

But, before the time came, I heard of a great combination of the overseers against the work in hand, whereupon I persuaded the mayor to call a council to consult together about the work then begun. At that council it was ordered that the work should go on according to the order of sessions with a full consent. Yet I did perceive that there was one old herb [2] that I thought would spoil the whole pot of pottage. Therefore I entreated the mayor that he would warn a meeting of the justices and I would provide something to put to them for the better settling of the work. I saw there was one that was able to do more wrong among the rude overseers than all the rest could pacify again. So when all the board of justices set their hands to the order he would not but pretended as if he were willing but did do wickedly.

The churchwardens and overseers, as soon as they were chosen, began to rebel against the mayor and justices in such a rude manner that I believe in no civil government was ever the like seen, to the great scorn and contempt of justice. Whereupon the mayor required them to be civil and told them if they would not come and do their office he would bind them to the sessions. They answered they would not be bound for him. He told them he would send them to the gaol. Then was their *mittimus* made. The mayor told them, rather than they should go to the gaol, he would take their own recognizance. Then they jeered at the mayor and thought he had been afraid of them. So being sent to the gaol they remained there about ten days; and when they had gotten advice to sue the mayor and justices then desired to be bailed upon their own recognizance, which was granted. At our assizes the right honourable the Lord Chief Justice Foster and Judge Tyrrel heard of their baseness in the assizes. I pray God (p. 3) to work for his glory in it and for the true good of justice in this unjust contention. [3]

---

1 Ivie supervised the storehouse 1628–32 and 1637–40 (see below). He was asked to revive it in 1649 and in Sept. 1658: S.C.A., Ledger D, ff. 42v.–43v., 107v.
2 Possibly Maurice Greene, a J.P. of royalist sympathies, an old antagonist of Ivie, and a brewer: see p. 130 and n.
3 See pp. 14, 133.

It is desired I should set down some rules how the profit doth arise to the poor by the storehouses. I will prove it to be as followeth. First, for the bread they spend [i.e. consume] weekly, they save above 5s. in every 20s., and thus it will appear it riseth. First I go and buy one quarter of wheat in the market and it costs now, as the price is, 6s. 6d. the bushel, which is £2 12s. the quarter. The baker hath for baking and grinding 6s. the quarter; then he bakes it at £2 18s. the quarter. I buy of the same wheat and it costs £2 12s. the quarter; I will use the poor well, I will take nothing for baking and grinding, and yet where the baker goeth on the assize-book 6s. for his charges in every quarter, I say I will go back upon the assize-book and bate 4s. on every quarter of [the price] that the wheat did cost. So by this rule it doth appear that the storehouse doth bake cheaper in every quarter 10s. than the baker doth. Yet every loaf shall be more in weight than the baker's loaf is by 6 oz. in every penny loaf. This is another rule to try [the case] further: the wheat [being] at £2 12s. the quarter I buy in the market a market quarter; out of this market quarter I take six bushels and three pecks, which makes a baker's quarter according to the standard; for baking it he hath 6s.; then I begin to look back [to see] what is left and there I find one bushel and one peck remaining, which cost 8s. 1½d., and then is gotten in every quarter in the baking and grinding 2s., which is in every hundred quarters £10. Besides I find in over-measure upon my book above nine bushels to the quarter in three hundred bushels baking is at least saved, by heap measure above 4 lb. [1]

Now to show you how the profit doth arise to be 5s., 6s., or 8s. in every hundred of cheese, [which] is spent by the poor weekly, [it] will appear thus. There be in the city of inns, alehouses, and hucksters above 150 that do daily serve the poor in their victuals. These hucksters for the most part of them do go to the market two or three times a week to buy the cheese which they sell to the poor. They come to a market (p. 4) cheeseman where they see fair broad thin cheese to cut out in broad pennyworths to the poor. These hucksters do ask the cheeseman the price of a cheese; it may be he asketh 10d. or 12d. for the cheese but, however, he will have more by 2d. in the cheese than he would [if he were to] sell in the hundred together. Then these hucksters having bought one or two cheeses together, and too dear by 2d. apiece, they go home and the best of them do mark out to the poor at 3d. in each shilling profit, to the great wrong of the poor.

The order of the storehouse is, when a market is at a stand, [for the officer] to go forth and cheapen, and he is known to buy great store if he like the market. And after he have bought some many will say, 'Sir, I pray you buy of me four or five hundred; it is as good as any you have bought.' Then I tell them, 'Try the most of your market; if you cannot sell as you would, come to me; if you will be reasonable I will buy it all for the use of the poor.' They have come to me after sunset and entreated me to buy. I have

---

[1] In Ivie's first calculation the saving depended on excluding production costs from the price of bread and apparently making a loss on the original market price of the wheat, in his second on surpluses produced by different stages and standards of measurement. In later examples economies depended on bulk-buying.

then bought by candlelight above £20 worth at a cheaper rate than I could have the same cheese in the morning, by 4s., 5s., or 6s. in every hundred. By this way you may plainly see that the poor hath their cheese at least 6s. in the pound from the storehouse cheaper than they can provide for themselves.

And for their butter there is more to be gotten in that, if care be taken to pot it in the summer, there may well be saved 6s. in the pound and some years a great deal more.

Now for the profit to them in their beer, by this order I will make it appear that in one sort of their beer, which we call ten-groat beer, they gain but 4s. in the pound. In this sort of beer we pay as much for it as the alehouse doth and in a barrel I find 72 quarts of beer. This barrel doth cost 3s. 4d.; 60 of these quarts do make 40 thurndels, [1] which is sold to the poor for 3s. 4d., which is the price the barrel cost the alewife. There is left when the barrel is paid for 12 quarts; these 12 quarts makes as before eight thurndels, which is sold by the alewife for 8d. So the alewife gets in six barrels 4s., and there is saved to the poor but 4s. in that (p. 5) strong beer. Now for the other sort of beer that is such as is commonly used by the inhabitants of the city, and all sorts of men do pay 2s. 6d. for a barrel of it, which is more profit in the pound to the alehouse than the former strong beer is. And this [following] way the storehouse did take formerly until the unjust overseers did refuse to do their office for the poor as they ought to have done. I will make it appear [that] the poor did save in that sort of beer 10s. in every 20s. that was laid out for all the poor in the city that they did weekly spend. Thus I make it appear.

I go to a brewer and tell him, 'Sir, I have an occasion to use much beer this year (if you please furnish me) for the poor's use; I will pay you weekly.' This he is willing to do. Then I tell him I will give him for the best beer 3s. 4d. the barrel, which is the full price that all men pay, and in it as before is gotten but 4s. in 20s. 'And for your half-crown beer,' [I say], 'I will give you but 2s. for the barrel.' Then for the good of the poor the brewer and I do so agree, and by this sort of beer is saved to the poor in laying out every 20s. weekly 10s. And thus it doth appear.

The alehouse and all other men do pay for eight barrels of half-crown beer 20s.; and for 20s. I buy ten barrels. So by laying in of that store I save two barrels in ten, which is 5s. Then this do I know, by the alewives' measure (if by mistake [they] should fill their pot), they will and do gain by sale of eight barrels of beer above 6s. in the sale thereof. Now reckon the 5s. saved in the buying and 6s. which the alewife gains, [it] will appear to be gotten in the pound full 11s. to the poor in every 20s. weekly spent.

Now if you desire to know what is saved to the poor in their firing, I tell you. Formerly when I first kept the storehouse I did buy at the wood, when the sales were, some two or three acres of wood for the poor and had it made up into very large faggots to serve them at a penny apiece; but they were worth a farthing apiece more. Then the poor would fetch them with

---

[1] A thirdendeal pot held ⅓ gallon.

their money or [the] tokens that they should have bought their victuals from the storehouse for themselves and children [with], [1] and would (p. 6) carry these faggots to the alehouse and there would sell them for 3d. profit in twelve faggots. Yet the servant that did serve out these faggots to the poor (whose name was James Summers) did very much wrong the poor in taking away much of the best wood, and did thereby cozen the poor, and was for his pains set in the pillory.

I had much to do to stop the current of their selling of the faggots until I made another sort of tokens that should buy nothing but faggots, and by that means they had so many faggots as they could spend without selling [any].

Now for this last setting up of the storehouse, which was at Easter last was two years, [2] I was not able to travel to the wood. But I spake with one Mr. Robert Good, that was then and yet is woodward to the right honourable the earl of Pembroke, to entreat him to set out for our poor 200 lug of copse wood and to set a price upon it, as it was well worth, which he very justly did and got it felled and made into faggots and got carts to bring them to our storehouse. And they were according to our order something heavier than the hucksters' faggots were. Yet there was a huckster that was an overseer of the poor that did very wickedly abuse the work, and said they were the worst faggots in the city, and so did draw off the poor from the storehouse to himself and others. Whereupon I sent to his house, and at least to ten hucksters more, and bought two or three faggots apiece at each house, and took good witness what was done; and so we went to weights and did not find any of all the hucksters' faggots to be full the weight of the poor's faggots but wanted 1 or 2½ lb. in every two faggots, which was not to be spoken of. Yet it was enough to prove them base in their report.

Now because the poor should not use deceit to fetch the faggots from the storehouse and sell them, as formerly they had done, I gave order to the woodman to have the faggots made but a small matter bigger than the hucksters'. But in these lines following you shall understand that the woodward, for the wood carriage and other charges, had of me £10 8s. Yet though they were a little heavier than the hucksters', there came home from the wood, as by the book it doth appear, [3] (p. 7) so many hundred [faggots] as did pay all the charge at a penny apiece. And there was left for the poor to have amongst them in the winter for nothing 650 faggots, which would have cost £2 14s. 2d. By this £10 laying out there is above 5s. in the pound gotten to the poor.

Now for to set this work on foot. First, you must have an honest man that is of some power to be the governor of that [store]house and all the poor. And between the mayor and the justices and [the] master of the house there must be articles drawn and sealed between them or else the work cannot stand for one year. This must the covenant be: that at Easter when you view your poor you shall appoint them their allowance, what they shall have weekly from the

---

1 For the token system see pp. 10–11.
2 i.e. 1659.
3 Probably the storehouse account bk.: S.C.A., Y 216. The accounts are not detailed enough to test Ivie's assertion.

storehouse, and see that the poor may have their money paid weekly or monthly to the master of the storehouse, so he will be enabled to buy their provision the better cheap for the poor souls, that he may pay them their allowance the better weekly. Which he may very well do, and allow them fifteen pence for a shilling. But if there be not articles drawn, whereby the master of the house may refuse to take in any poor body but at Easter or to receive any ticket from the mayor or any of the justices to allow any poor body 6*d.*, 8*d.*, or 12*d.* a week until further order, I say if he be not freed from this charge the stock will be spent in the first year. For many of the justices will be very charitable to the chewrers [1] or others upon the storehouse stock until all be spent.

Neither should the master be compelled to take in any more poor into the storehouse than be delivered him at Easter. For then, be it never so many, he will be able to relieve them and yet increase their stock, and to relieve any of them upon extraordinaries if they fall sick, and be able to bind the children of them poor apprentices, and not to expect any further relief from any of their stock.

But if you will compel the master to take in all such as these men before written, and all [whom] the charitable overseers will bring in without restraint, they will put in so many that shall spend your whole stock twice in one year. For there be in the three parishes (p. 8) six churchwardens and twelve overseers, besides their eighteen wives, which most or all of them have children, and to each of them belong chewrers, which commonly are their good dames', who will make their good masters to set them on the book to receive if it be but 8*d.*, 10*d.*, or 12*d.* weekly [or else] she will not come and make the fire in the morning nor wash the child no longer. Then the master, to please his wife Nannekin, he comes at the next monthly meeting and presents the name of his chewrer to be very sick, and it may be she hath a child, and he will tell you unless she have allowance she will starve. Then saith the justice, 'Set her down until next meeting.' 'What will you I shall set down for her weekly?' Answer is made, 'Eight pence.' 'Indeed,' saith this charitable collector, 'it is too little for she must have one to help her.' 'Then,' saith the justice, 'make it twelve pence.' One stands by and saith, 'I wonder where you will have all these additions?' The overseer then answers, 'Pray Sir, be you not against the poor. We hope to raise it well enough.'

And when these charitable overseers have pleased their mistresses, then the next or second monthly meeting they will be on the mayor and justices for money to supply their chewrers. Now there is no way found to have money out of the storehouse stock, which is too little already. 'Then,' say they, 'we must needs have three or four months' rate upon the city extraordinary.' [By] which [means] by their unjust course they do most years find sixteen, or eighteen, or twenty months in one year, to the grief of the inhabitants. [2]

Now I think one of the greatest causes of this wrong is that there is no

---

[1] i.e. 'chorers', charwomen or persons doing odd jobs of housework.
[2] e.g. in 1636 an extraordinary rate was raised on top of the normal poor-rate: S.C.A., S 162, [f. 232].

law to swear an overseer or churchwarden to be just in their office for the good of the city and poor.

At Easter the new officers are chosen and they are desired to go to the old collectors and to see their books and to bring in the names of the inhabitants to be rated to pay the poor. The day is set for them to bring in their books and the day before that to give [a] meeting to view the poor and to see what is fit to allow of each of them. The day is come; they bring in their book rated. If the mayor say, 'We should have a hand in this rate as well as you', they say, 'We have the power and we have done it. (p. 9) If you please to sign our book, we will collect the money and pay the poor. If not, pay them yourselves.' Which they have of late done to the great trouble of the mayor and justices. Now we know that the law doth allow all inhabitants to be rated that are ratable. I presented to the overseers of St. Edmund's parish unrated of able housekeepers 350, in St. Thomas's parish of able inhabitants unrated 224, and in St. Martin's parish of able housekeepers unrated 94. All these are in number unrated 668 housekeepers. Some of these were since rated and some paid 6d., 4d., or 2d. weekly. Some of these housekeepers the overseers would not rate afterward. When they saw we presented the names of this great number then they took into their book some three or four in a parish that did afterwards pay, as before is written. Yet they left out unrated, and will not rate them, the number of six hundred, fifty, and odd which I can show the names of. And rather than they will be compelled to reform this error, or to procure sureties to answer their contempt, they will go to gaol and lie there eight or ten days (yet we offered to take their own recognizance).

The reason of this is for not rating of the better sort of the inhabitants. Yet they did take some money of them but brought it not in upon any account, which for two reasons I think they would not do if they were sworn officers. The first reason is that they will not return their names because they will dispose of the money, where they list, upon themselves or others. The second reason is because these men be rich and will not be found upon the poor's book, because then they should be made pay to all rates and payments which they thereby avoid. I can prove that there be dead two of these men within this year and [a] half which were never rated and left behind them about £3,000 in money, having no charge.

If this be not the way for overseers to help such deceit to go hoodwinked I know not what is. I wish the state of the land would make some law to order them. Put any statute to them, they will waive it, and as I said before rather go to gaol than submit (p. 10) to justice or the law, as many of them have of late done, and lately have said [so] both to the then mayor and justices, and carried their business so as that they would be sure to overthrow them. For they were gracious with the bailiff of the court and, when they had taken away all the counsel in the city with the chief attorneys, then knowing there was no counsel to plead for us (all other counsel were at the term), they warned the mayor that then was and three other justices, that committed them, to the bishop's court and there had so ordered the matter that within two hours they did impanel a stout jury that did the work.

I am persuaded, had we ten of the best counsel that were to be had and they but one attorney and their cause as bad as may be, the jury would have found for the plaintiff. There was found all the court very ready, the bailiff and all the pole-catchers were very nimble. For in two hours the court was called, the jury sworn, the trial past and judgment given, and execution granted and served in the time aforesaid by five of the bishop's bailiffs, who came upon me basely in my house and served their execution and had of me £10, who then reported that some of the plaintiffs did give them order to arrest me with the greatest disgrace they could. [1] I think it stands upon justice to look to it for my glass is almost run out, having been in this city and parish almost three score and ten years and by the mercy of God I have been a member of this corporation above fifty years, [2] where I have seen justice in his due course and the government so ordered that it hath had the praise of our most gracious king at council board in the hearing of that right honourable judge, Sir Robert Hyde, then our worthy recorder, but in his unhappy absence by reason of the late wicked war. [3]

Whereby we have such a mighty increase of lewd persons and unruly poor that our government is at a stand, and I cannot hope to see God's glory advanced amongst us in this poor city whilst I live. For our poor do swarm about the city, Close, and country and [with] no restraint, whereby bastardy is much increased to the great grief of the inhabitants who complain of their great charge to maintain that which doth so much dishonour (p. 11) God. [Neither] the overseers nor but few of the constables do take care to suppress it.

But had the last work gone on, I mean the storehouse that was so barbarously abused and unjustly put down, these overseers, had they not done it that year, they should not have had one beggar in the city, nor none to want, nor no additional month made use of to grieve the inhabitants, nor none of any rank over-rated; but all should be as in former time set to work and their children bound apprentices, which hath been formerly done, and [there should be] take[n] off all the beggars from the inns that are like sometimes to pull travellers of any rank from their horses every morning to the great scandal of our government.

It pleased God to put it into my mind to give travellers some content; thus I began. I caused fourteen iron boxes to be made with lock and key and fixed them in the yards of fourteen of the chiefest inns. The gentry and other travellers, when they saw what course was taken for the relief of the poor and none at the inns to trouble them, they did give freely to the boxes which was every month opened and notice taken of every box what was given therein. And some years we have had above £20 in them all. We have had a ten-shilling piece of gold in one box and store of other money, and at

[1] See p. 14. No record of the bishop's city court survives for the period.
[2] Councillor 1616, alderman 1623: S.C.A., Ledger C, ff. 156, 195.
[3] Ivie's view of Hyde had been very different before the Restoration. He had taken a leading part in the royalist recorder's removal from office during the Civil War: P. Slack, 'An Election to the Short Parliament', *Bull. Inst. Hist. Res.* xlvi. 108–14.

another inn in their box a five-shilling piece with other money of their charity that gave it to the great relief of the poor that then were. [1]

I thought to have done the like again now but all the charge would have been upon my loss for all the poor and overseers were against it in a mad way. But as yet it is not God's time to do any good in this city.

It is not full two years before these boxes were set up, it pleased God then to give power to men to lay the office of mayor upon me, that was neither worthy nor ready for such an employment. [2] It pleased God [that] for the first part of the year all things went well until after Christmas was spent. But after Candlemas was past the Lord sent upon us a very sore and grievous plague. And as many persons of the city that had any friends in the country that would receive them into part of their houses or barns did fly as if it were out of an house on fire; insomuch (p. 12) they did load forth of goods and wares above three score carts a day until all of any ability were gone, and this in four days.

And then there was none left to assist me and comfort the poor in so great a misery, neither recorder, justice, churchwarden, or overseers in all the city, nor high constable, but only two of the petty constables that had no friend to receive them in the country. [3] Wherefore I got them to stay with me and they did prove to me a great comfort both by night and by day; and I did give them ten shillings apiece by the week. And by the power of the Lord Chief Baron Tanfield and Baron Denham [4] and by their order [it was possible] to command those constables to come home or else to pay that twenty shillings weekly to their partners that remained in the city, being constrained to do their work. They are yet both living, by name Christopher Brathat and John Pinhorne, which were to me as sent from God both night and day to carry out the infected persons to the pesthouses and to help order the unruly bearers and a multitude of rude people, which was like both night and day to ruinate the whole city. But God being merciful unto us did put into my heart to rule so great a multitude. I had sent away my wife and maid; I had then my chief sergeant in my house and one man and an old servant maid that had been with me many years. We did all make a vow and promise together that whosoever it pleased God to visit of us the other[s] should be faithful to him.

Then after the first week the poor and all the inhabitants were in a sad condition by reason there were none left to give an alms. I had then only about four score and odd pounds in my house, which was but a poor help for such a multitude being then in a very low condition, and [we] were afraid we should be starved or [the multitude] break out into the country. I then sent unto the Lord Gorge, Sir Walter Vaughan, and other justices of the country to

1 See pp. 89–90, 95–8.

2 Ivie was elected mayor 2 Nov. 1626: S.C.A., Ledger C, f. 331v.

3 The flight of the city governors is exaggerated but between Apr. 1627 and Jan. 1628 only one council meeting was held and only 17 councillors, a third of the normal number, were present: ibid. f. 335v.

4 The assize judges. There are no records of assize orders for this period but what appears to be a draft of the order referred to here is in the mayor's correspondence: S.C.A., N 101, doc. 15.

raise a contribution according to the law, which they did with all speed. [1] But I saw, before that pay could come in, many of us might be starved. Wherefore I sent to one Mr. Limming of Laverstock near the city to send me one quarter of wheat and a quarter of barley ready ground for the poor, to be done with speed, he having a mill of his own to do it, which was accordingly sent. I presently sent for a baker. Which being mixed (p. 13) together was forthwith made into bread, and in the morning I did dispose of it to the church poor; and [I] did set our town brewers to make half-crown beer for that use, and I would pay for it when money came in. I sent also to many farmers for abundance of wheat to feed so many people.

For had I stayed until the county had furnished us with money many a hundred might have been starved. For before our money came in to supply us I was engaged for above £300 worth of wheat, and there were come upon relief three thousand poor people wanting but twenty-seven souls; and we did then bake, as the account will show, for a time twenty-seven quarters of wheat weekly, and [consume] three load of butter and cheese weekly and sixteen hogsheads of beer weekly. And then I had built a pesthouse and provided three storehouses in the three parishes to serve the poor their victuals, each upon his day, so upon every fourth day. The whole city was paid and all the infected houses likewise.

Yet the rude people were out of order weekly and gave out they were two hundred strong and would have better allowance. Then in the evening came to my house their captain to speak with me, whose name was Richard Coulter. I saw him coming; I stood at my door to receive him and was provided for him. Being come he began to swear beastly and said, 'Do you think we will be starved? Our allowance is too short for us. We will see what the runaways have left behind them in their houses.' I replied, 'You will not search my house, will you?' He answered me that 'Yours would serve me a great while.' I had then with me my whole show of goldsmith's ware which one of these base fellows might have carried at his back. My thought [was that] this fellow did so deliver himself as I thought he would presently have had it. Whereupon I presently fell upon him and took him; my sergeant and my man came forth and laid hands on him but would not let him go till he was delivered to the gaol, where he was kept ten weeks.

And then I presently sent to all the honest men in the city a private word that if they did hear any drum beat in the city, either at my house or at the council house, they should come to assist me; for in the council house there were two drums of the trained bands. I had one [sent] to my (p. 14) house if need were. The third day after one George Giffard, a drummer to Sir Walter Vaughan's band, went in a morning timely to Fisherton Mills and there beat up his drum about three of the clock, and upon a sudden I had about my house many hundreds to help me. I hearing the noise leaped out of my bed and seeing many honest men asked, 'What's the matter?' They answered, 'You best know, for we heard your drum and are come to assist

---

[1] The county justices agreed to levy a rate of £50 a week for the infected in Salisbury but payments were always in arrears: W.R.O., Q. Sess. min. bk. 1626–31, Trin., Mich. 1627, Hil. 1628.

you,' which rejoiced me very much. And said I, 'I will be with you presently.'
I put on my gown and ran down and unhung the drum and beat the head of
him, and then opened the door and my house and backside was presently full.
So we drank freely and I gave them hearty thanks and so we parted.

After that it pleased God to strike a fear in the courage of the baser sort
of people and it held well for three days. Then came to me one of the constables and told me, 'Sir, we shall be spoiled in the night for we shall have no
more watch this year. For there are gotten together two and thirty men with
bills and halberds and [they] tell me they will not watch unless they may have
six pence the night and eight pence the day for watching.' I asked the constable,
'Where are these men?' He replied they were at Senior's door over
against the council house. I asked him who was the chief speaker amongst
them, who told me Thomas Johnson, the cobbler, was their speaker. And
when I turned at the corner, being near them, I ran in amongst them crying,
'I require you all in the king's name to assist me to take this traitor.' And
then I caught Johnson and pulled him out from his fellows and did not loose
my hand from him until I had housed him in the gaol. Then I went, God assist-
ing me, and sat in the court where the assizes is kept, and caused all the people
to keep silence, and commanded the sergeant to make proclamation that
everyone that was warned to watch that night for his own house, according to
the custom of the city, to come and do his duty upon pain of imprisonment.

The first which was called to watch was one William Painter, a hellier,
who answered, 'I will not watch unless I have pay', as above is said. I leaped
off the bench and seized on him, requiring help, and dragged him to the
gaol stairs where he took hold of one of the posts and did roar and beg for
pardon, and (p. 15) would watch. But I refused to accept him a while until
all the rest said, 'We will all watch.' Then I called him again and he was
sworn and did watch. And I told all the rest that [those that] were warned
for themselves should watch for themselves; and if the watch were not four
and twenty then to take any other houses in the same row that were shut up by
any that were gone into the country [and] to appoint a man to watch for that
house, and to come to me in the morning and I would pay him for his watch.
And so [I] did for all that were wanting. And so by God's mercy we had a
good watch all the year after.

Besides this I had a sad hand with the bearers for I could get at first but
three and two to carry the first corpse to the grave, who was Giles Capon.
They would have of me four shillings apiece; then they bore the corpse to the
grave. And to house them was much to do. In the churchyard were two
tenements which I put both into one house. The two tenants were put into
one part thereof and the three bearers were put into the other. As soon
as I was come home, one of the neighbours told me that Mr. Robert Belman
had pulled her out of her house because she was wife to one of the bearers.
Presently this Belman came to me and I asked him why he had thrown
that poor woman out of doors and her goods. He told me that she should not
be there for her husband would come to her in the night, and so he with his
wife and family should be infected with the plague. I required him to take
in this poor woman and help her in with her goods again; 'If not, give me

your answer.' He replied, 'I will not.' 'Then will I make you lie in the gaol.' Presently I fell upon him and took hold of him. Then he said he would give bail, but I would not take it, but said, 'As soon as you are in the gaol I will break up the door and put the poor woman into her own possession again.' By this time he was half way to the gaol. Then came many of his friends and entreated for him. So at last the woman was in her house again.

Before this was scarce ended the bearers were come to my house. I said, 'What is the matter?' Now they told me Mr. Slie, a clothier, had brought a great company to the house they were in and fell upon the house and swore that if they would not come out they would beat down the house upon (p. 16) them. So they craved leave to pass quietly without hurt. So they presently came to me. I was in a maze what to do with them. It was upon the sabbath day after candle light. So then I bethought myself that I had caused three tenements in Bugmore Lane to be ready for to remove any sick people into them until we had built a pesthouse. There I put them in peaceably that evening, and thereby was a victualling house; I gave them something for their supper.

And by that time [that] I was come home and supped these bearers were with me again. I said, 'How now?' They answered, 'Oh! Master, we shall be killed; carry us whither you will. For Justice Bee [1] brought upon us above five hundred people, and have vowed our death, and have torn the tiles very much, and hath thrown in much cold water and scalding water upon us.' I said unto the bearers, 'Be courageous. I will house you there before I sleep or in my house. Stay a while.' So I made ready and took my staff and walked down to the same houses again, and before we were espied, being late in the night. They were no sooner in but the crew came together again. I had some honest men then about me with weapons. We had not stayed long but their captain, Mr. Bee, was come and required the bearers to be gone. I told him they should lodge there. His reply was, 'They shall not', and [he] thrust me. 'If you do thrust me again, Sir, I will pitch your nose in the channel, or you mine.' The chiefest rebel amongst them was one Lancelot Russel, a tanner. Seeing Mr. Bee and myself so contending [he] drew his sword, and had not God in mercy prevented his thrust by the hand of Mr. John Pierson, one of the high constables, he had run me through. Then I said to the officer, 'Make proclamation to still the noise four times. "O yeas!" say after me, "the mayor doth straitly charge men and all manner of people in the king's Majesty's name, that hath not to do here, by the command of the mayor presently to depart upon pain of imprisonment." '

I began first with Mr. Bee, 'Sir, will you be gone? I require you to your house.' 'Me, Sir?' 'Yea, Sir. You maintain a most horrid rout and riot upon me. Wherefore I say once more be gone, or else as sure as I live I will set you by the heels.' Then in great choler away he went and all the rest vanished away. Then came one Mistress Good that dwelt in Mr. Bee's Friars and she

---

[1] Matthew Bee, an alderman and J. P. and a former supporter of new schemes for poor relief (see pp. 9, 87), owned part of the former Franciscan friary at the end of Bugmore Lane where the pesthouse was set up. Ivie also described the riot in a letter to Sherfield 30 Apr. 1627: Hants R.O., J. L. Jervoise, Herriard Coll. 44M69/S6/XXXVII. 29.

began to treat (p. 17) and scold. I commanded her to her house. She would not. Whereupon I delivered her to the constable to carry her to the cage, who was going with her. Then came a great many women who hanged about her crying and entreating for her. I released her. Then she and all her troop were gone. Thereby was an alehouse where was one Thomas Ravener standing, more troublesome than any man, with many maids and boys in his company, mocking and jeering. I heard him say, 'Mr. Mayor is in a chase. I care not if I give him two pots.' So I kept on my walk, as I did before, and every turn I got some ground nearer to my promised two pots. And when I was come within a start I had my man Ravener by the collar and asked him where I should drink the two pots he promised me. I called the constable and other help and told him I did not like the ale at that end of the city; we would go and drink at the middle thereof. So I brought him to the gaol and kept him there nine or ten weeks until I had good bail to appear at the next sessions, where he was well whipped.

This night being past, I had peace a long time until the bearers were in rebellion. They came to the council house and would speak with me. One Mr. Windover came and told me there were four gentlemen at the stairs' foot would speak with me. I desired him to entreat them to come up; he told me they would not. I went down and there I found my four bearers, each of them with a good hedge stake in his hand. I said, 'What make you here?' They replied with oaths [that] they would have better allowance; they would not live with four shillings a week apiece. I stepped down by them and said, 'You shall', and looked about for stones in the street and put them into the skirt of my gown until it was full, and called to men and boys to fling stones at them as I did. They did the like. The bearers gathered stones and threw them again at me but it was God's will that I should hit one of them on the head. Then the stones came so fast upon them that they began to run. I with all my company followed them until I had housed them. I caused one Nicholas Perry to go to my house with speed and fetch me a musket that had a fire-lock, that was then charged with a brace of bullets. And when he came, the bearers being then in their cabin, (p. 18) I told them, 'You dally with me but I am in earnest with you. Will you let go the sheep that you have taken from Robert Tipper, the butcher, that had bought them at Amesbury fair and gave fifteen shillings?' They answered, 'We will not.' 'Then betake yourselves to your prayers. You shall all die.'

My man shot at the cabin and tore the boards but missed, for so it was ordered. I called to the man to charge again, which was done. Then they saw no hope of life; they fell down and begged favour and let go the sheep and promised they would be civil. If I would give each of them a shirt and give them a bible, they would deserve it and have no more but their ordinary allowance. So I promised I would presently send them a bible and, the next money I received, I would buy shirts for them, which was accordingly done. Three days after one desired me to walk to the churchyard where I should see good sport with the searching woman and the bearers. I came to a place where I could see and hear them, and when I came I found the four bearers, each of them having on their shoulders a thurndel pot of ale, and the woman had on her head a thurndel pot of ale. These five were dancing amongst the graves singing, 'Hie for more shoulder-work!' in a fearful manner. And when they saw me they ran away. Shortly after one of them died, which put me to much care for another, for then the plague did much increase and in that summer died nine bearers.

The next careful chore was to suppress the alehouses, which were above four score, licensed and not. The time was come to renew their licences in April. I warned them all in and to bring their licences with them. So I received them all in one morning and told them when I had leisure I would send for them again. And then [I] sent for all those that sold without licence and gave them a charge not to sell at their peril until they and the rest were licensed, which for fear of the gaol they did not. Then I sent to all the brewers, to each alike, to certify them that there was no alehouse in the city upon licence; therefore [they must] look to the law. As soon as the alehouses saw I would not give them licence they desired time to sell off that they had. I denied and said, 'What time would you have? I will give you but one week.' Some said, 'I shall not sell all in three months.' 'Then (p. 19) let the brewer have it to serve his other customers; for I will not suffer the city to be undone for to maintain the Devil's school in so many houses. I know you will complain to the brewers; I will not hinder you. But if I find any of you to take in any drink to sell I will in the first place take it from you and give it to the poor; and when you have any occasion for relief you shall not have any.'

Upon this strict order I had suppressed near one hundred sellers of drink. By this course I did gain the ill will of thousands of good and bad people. First they that began to rail were the brewers, or the most part of them, the bakers in general, all the hucksters were mad, cooks, and most of the innkeepers, all the drunkards, whoremasters, and lewd fellows, with their allies. It will easily appear that there is not so few as three thousand did seek my ruin. Yet my comfort is my merciful God and all good men do take part in my behalf against this great unjust rude rabble, which I pray God give into the hearts of them which have power to make laws that such a rude number may be ordered, or else it will be worse.

Here is in this city about three parishes and in those three parishes above fifty inns and alehouses at least four score. When I first suppressed the alehouses, at my first being in the place of the mayor, I then, as before is written, put down above four score. Yet there was one John Chappel that would not submit to order of justice but made me answer to my face that he would not give off the selling of drink, having a licence (though out of date, yet he would make it good), and so went on his way. He was a man that did lodge journeymen weavers, but at that time [they] were gone out of the city upon Thursday morning into one of the suburbs called Fisherton. The Saturday morning following one John Williams, a weaver, came to me and would have of me a warrant to fetch home his journeymen from Fisherton. I told him I would grant no such warrant; it was out of my liberty. I wished him to let them alone; they would do more hurt than good here. The same John Williams came to me very sad on the Monday morning and told me, 'Sir, I was with you for a warrant on Saturday, but those four men came home at night and fell to drinking all night, and by prayer-time the next day in the afternoon they had (p. 20) drunk up all that was in the house.' So they agreed to go to one Mr. Payne's, an ale-brewer, and buy one cowl of ale, the price 3s. 4d., which they did, and brought it home to this Chappel's house, where their lodging was, and set the cowl upon the table, and set another empty cowl by, and made a vow that they would, before they left, drink all that was in one and put their urine in the other, which they did with speed.

Their workmaster Williams heard of their being there, went to them, and did reason with his men, and told them they would undo him for he should lose his workmasters for want of that cloth that should have been at home to have been sent to London this week. One of them said, 'We will be with you at work by three of the clock next morning.' One of them went to bed; the other would fain have slept there right, but at last he went to bed. In the morning light he came that first went to bed and did knock very earnestly to come in. His master came to the window and said to him, 'What's the matter [that] you are in that posture?'

'I pray, Sir, let me in for my fellow is dead.'

'How came you forth? Be the folks up?'

'No, Sir. I beat down a pane of the wall and so came out.'

The Monday night following this fellow died, and by the Thursday morning about four of the clock were all that were in the house buried; the four journeymen, the master, John Chappel, his wife and maid were all dead in three days and few hours after their great drinking.

It pleased God to give me power to suppress all saving that one house; then the God of power did suppress that house in his own judgement. There was near the like judgement upon one Stout, a tailor. The tailors would have kept their accustomed feast for those of their company that were left in the city but I would not suffer it. But this Stout and five more would keep a feast, but that same week they were all dead of the plague save one.

In this time before-written, our markets being gone from us to Wilton, the artificers did want supply of corn for their use and would have had some of my store. But I could not spare it, but told them I should have a load in the morning; if they would have it, they should, at the price I had it. They were very thankful. That day I caused the two beadles to make clean a study of (p. 21) a friend's that I had the key of and shut it there. Then the neighbours came in. The wheat cost 4s. 6d. the bushel. 'If you will give one penny in a bushel to the measurers of the market and the two beadles that must measure it for you I say you shall have it.' This way did I buy for the poor tradesmen above £300 worth of wheat. Then a great number of my back friends said I had bought it for [?from] the shopkeepers' abundance of wheat by chalk measure and sold it to the poor neighbours by Brown's cut or statute measure, which is less than the measure I bought it by one bushel and one peck or more in every quarter. But they did not know the wrong I sustained in it, as afterward it did appear.

As soon as the plague was almost past, by God's mercy, my year was over and a good part of my successor's. Then the recorder [1] was come home and there was no use of a sessions all that year following. To the next mayor I kept up the storehouse. But at the next sessions holden I thought to have some ease, having been in that grievous trouble two years and knowing that the custom was that a man being out of the office of the mayoralty should not be chosen again into the commission of the peace, not until his time came, which might not be under seven or eight years, until by the death of some of the ancient justices turn came.

But when the time of the sessions was come and all the ancient sat in the council house, they sent to me and proposed to me a question and said, 'You have done your country good service, for which we are all beholding to God and you.' I thanked them for their good opinion of me, and I hope it will prove so, notwithstanding some wickedness is put upon me.

'Sir,' said the recorder, 'we have so good an opinion of you that we must needs make further use of you and must desire you to take one office more upon you, or else we are run aground.'

'Sir, I shall be ready to do the city any service upon good terms, if you please to enable me.'

The recorder replied, 'God's time is come, and we have need of one to sit with us and to be in commission with us.'

'Gentlemen, I am sorry I cannot gratify your desire. I do thank you for your good opinion of me, if it be real. I believe that I can show you such reasons that I hope you will excuse me and do me right, if you all knew; (p. 22) for that place is not for me, there being before me seven or eight which are more ancient in place.'

The recorder said, 'We will dispense with that.'

'I pray you excuse me. I will not say I will not. But I tell you I cannot, for reasons best known to myself.'

They pressed me very sore, and told me they would inform the Lord Chief Justice of me and compel me to serve. I told them it was not in my lord's power to alter our charter. The recorder said it was, but did hope I would not put them to it.

Then I told them, 'I am in the mouths of many men rendered very base and if I come in among you my adversaries will say he is gotten into the number of the justices for protection. Therefore I would stay longer to free myself of their aspersions.'

The recorder said, 'Sir, all this will not bring us out of our resolution.'

'Sir, if you will needs lay that office upon me, I beseech you all do it not until the sessions be past, for I intend to indict four men that have abused me, which, if any part be proved, I am not worthy to sit upon the bench.'

'Sir, what is it you would have?'

'I say, Sir, if you please to send for those four men, by name Mr. Thomas Lord, an attorney, and Arnold Gardyner, baker, with two other bakers more.'

The next morning these unjust men did appear to their indictment, which was that they had reported that I had bought for the poor neighbours above

1 Henry Sherfield, recorder 1623–34; see also p. 9.

twenty load of wheat of chalk measure and sold it again by Brown's cut or the statute measure, which is less by one bushel and one peck in the quarter. Then the three men were called into the court to bring the measures they sold it by, which were just measure of nine bushels to the quarter. There were in court men that had bought of it all the year and said they had always as good measure as they did ever buy. The three men that sold it, with divers that bought it, being all upon their oaths, the recorder did call to the three men that sold out the wheat to the townspeople, 'You are upon your oaths; what had you over in every load by measure?'

'We were to have a penny profit in every bushel, but we did measure it out by these two measures and when the load was all measured out we had very little more than an half-penny, for most of them would catch from us a blessing, as they called it, which was half our profit. And this upon our oaths is the truth.'

'All this while,' said the recorder, 'you say nothing how much you allowed Mr. Ivie for the (p. 23) little measure he sold.'

'We do not know of any he sold, nor of one load sold by him, but that we received and sold.'

'What did you allow Mr. Ivie for the use of his house that you made use of?'

'Sure, nothing. Neither do we know upon the oath we have taken of any profit he had any way.'

'How much do you think he sold by that order?'

'We think at least two hundred and fifty bushels for no profit, or ever had.'

'Now you that stand there indicted, what think you of yourselves that have so wronged this man that ventures his life to do you all the good that ever he could?'

When I thought my chore was settled a base woman, the widow Biby,[1] being in her cabin at the pesthouse, desiring to do the Devil's work, set the pesthouse on fire in the window side, and presently it was burnt down, where there were in it eighty-seven poor souls. I ran to it and found all the poor sitting in the field upon the bare earth in a miserable condition, many of them almost naked and one of them quite naked until two or three of the poor women that came out of the city did take off their own clothes off their backs to cover her. I gave order they should all go home to their own houses again, which was a grievous sight to look on. But with all speed we built another house, and with much trouble had them out again, and but few of them died. So once more the Lord was pleased to settle that chore.

In that time there was one Bull, a wood-cleaver, and two of his children [who] were all three sick of the plague and speechless. I was told of it by the attender of their house. I went to the door of the house to talk with his wife.

I asked her, 'How do you all? How is it with you, your husband, and your children?'

---

1 For Sarah Biby see p. 75.

She said, 'My husband and two of my children cannot speak to me, and [I] looks for a good hour.'

'I pray take it not amiss; I must in the night remove you all to the pest-house. Therefore provide what you will have carried with you.'

She railed on me very sorely. Yet late in the night I came to have them all out, but she would not open the door, but in a rude manner did scold at me, and asked me whether I came of a woman or a beast that I should do so bloody an act upon poor people in their condition. I bid the bearers break open the door but they would not or could not. Whereupon I sent my man home for my iron bar. Yet she would not open (p. 24) her door. I gave the bearers order to strike in the bar between the durns [door-posts] and the door and at the second stroke the door flew open. Then two of them went in and came out again immediately and told me their lives were as precious to them as mine to me; they would not go in again; the house was so hot they were not able to stay there. For the smell of the house, with the heat of the infection, was so grievous they were not able to endure it. I told them, 'You must and shall endure it.' I had then with me my two petty constables, my sergeant, and my man, and from the pesthouse two able men to bear the barrow. Those two men with the four bearers did carry these three speechless people to the pesthouse, but the bearers stood to their word: they would not go in again. So we placed ourselves above and below them, for if need were we had good weapons. But we did so beat them with stones that they were forced to go into the house for shelter. It was a close house and but one little door to the street and a little window. So they brought out the sick and whole and carried them into the fields to the pesthouse, and they were all there in two rooms. And then God so ordered for them through his mercy that they all came home again in health, to my comfort.

As I find my notes I write them down, as you may find before written. The overseers give out that the poor and sick are tied up to take their allowance in the storehouse victuals, which is false. For when the payday was, if I were abroad myself, I left money with my kinswoman, twenty or forty shillings, to change all the tokens the poor did bring in, which by my account doth appear, for want of better government, that they did change above half of their allowance into money for to please the overseers and churchwardens.

Yet one of the churchwardens, one Thomas Bosley, came a witness for an overseer, John Harrison, at the last assizes holden in the city before the right honourable the Lord Chief Justice Foster and Judge Tyrrel[1] and there did take his oath before the jury that the poor were tied up to take their victuals of the storehouse sick or well. For, as he said upon his oath, there was a man sick of a fever that could not have anything to succour him but the storehouse victual, which is very false and a (p. 25) great scandal to government. Unless he can make it appear that it was so he is not a fit man to be a witness in a court of justice.

At the time aforesaid the mayor of this city understood that the poor did change so many of their tokens [and] met with me and told me, 'Sir,

[1] See pp. 14, 133.

you do not well to change so many of the storehouse tokens. I understand they spend their money at the alehouse as basely as ever they did.' I told Mr. Mayor, 'Unless you will order your collectors I must do what pleaseth them. Yet if I am in the way but few drunkards will come to change their tokens, for they know I have something to say to them for changing their tokens, whereby they starve their children.'

Another way they had to rail at the [storehouse] beer, and said if they had their money they could go to Mr. Payne, an ale-brewer, and to Mr. Greene, a beer-brewer, and then they could have for a penny of English money a gallon of new ale out of the keene, [1] and then putting a little balm to it [it] would continue fresh until they had drunk it all out. [I replied,] 'I desire you should have all your beer and victuals the best way. I pray you have patience until the next payday; I will think upon some way to satisfy you. Now you have three quarts for a penny; I perceive by your words that you can have four quarts for a penny.' Then said some of them, 'This three quarts is better than five quarts of the washing of the brewers' grains.' Another answered, 'I have lived in this city above thirty years but I could never have from the alehouse above two quarts of the same half-crown beer for a penny, and here we have three quarts for a penny.' 'But,' saith another, 'if I fetch a pennyworth, before I drink it, it is dead.' 'I do not so,' saith another, 'for I go for my pennyworth three times and have my quart pot full of fresh beer at every time, for there is none bad, as it is commonly at the alehouse, for theirs is longer a-drawing.'

Before the next payday I went to Mr. Payne, the ale-brewer, and told him, 'Sir, the poor doth desire to have of your penny-a-gallon drink; I pray, if it please you, when they come, to take their tokens for it, and when you please to have them changed I will give you money for your tokens again.' He said he would do it and so did Mr. Greene promise to do also. Then the next payday I told the poor it was ordered, 'If you go to Mr. Payne's or Mr. Greene's you shall have penny gallon ale or beer for (p. 26) your tokens.' Some of them were very sad for they thought they should have money to buy it where they would. Mr. Payne in eight weeks did take of his great customers one penny and Mr. Greene did take in seventeen weeks seven pence. Then were all their customers ashamed. All these passages must not be spoken against in these times.

In the time of the plague, when I was first mayor, in our greatest affliction there came a young man running to me with his blood about his ears. I asked him, 'What's the matter?' He said, 'Oh! Sir, our town is taken by a great many of soldiers; they have hurt me and have rifled our shop and are yet in our house.' I took my staff in my hand and with such help as I had ran to them in Katharine Street, there being of them thirty-three persons; and by that time [that] I got to them I had above thirty halberds come to my assistance. And being come near them thirty of them began to march away; only three of them stood at the Lamb door, as it were facing of us. One of them was a tall black-haired man. His fore-top of hair did reach over his head and a large

[1] Perhaps 'cane', meaning pipe.

lock on his shoulder knit up with a bow knot; the other two had long locks but not knit up. I took the gallant by the sleeve and demanded, 'Sir, what are you?' He replied, 'A man.' I said, 'I doubt it.' 'Why do you doubt it?' 'Because you behave yourself like a beast and a thief.' He swears high upon the Welsh tongue. I pulled him and said, 'Come you along', and bade the constables bring the rest. Then he spat the same Welsh again. I understood his meaning to be, 'Whither will you lead me?' My answer was, 'Whither please me.'

By this time we were come to the council house door, where I had caused the stocks to be formerly set. I bid the beadle open the stocks. I said to him, if he pleased, he might ease himself, but he strove until he was weary. I caused him to be so ordered that I put him to his own choice whether he would put in his head or his leg, for one must and shall be put in one. At last his understanding was come to him; his leg was in. The other two seeing this done were very quiet. Then I demanded of them which way their conductor was gone for quarter this night. They said, 'Four mile off at a place called Downton.' I had the name of their leader and their names also. After which I went up and wrote (p. 27) their pass and then caused them to be taken forth and brought into the audit house. Then I caused the constable to bring up the chief man to me, and read the pass to him. 'Sir, you are for shedding of blood and taking away of goods and robbing an house adjudged to go to the post and be well whipped.' Then he swore strongly and when his hands were tied to the post he sprung out his heels and paid the beadle before he had paid him. I saw his great unruliness out at the window. I called to the beadle and told him the madness of the man was in his hair (I meant his great long lock). But the beadle thought I had meant all his hair, for when he had cut off that lock he did reach together the fore-top and whipped it off too, and caught hold of his poll and docked him to show that he was a strayer and taken in an infected and much afflicted city. They were marked all alike that their conductor might know them, and by them to know their fellows that fled from us, and take a special care to keep them all together for some time to see what God would do with them. Otherwise it may fall out that they may overthrow the king's design whether they were to march to the Isle of Ree, as they said. [1] In this be you careful.

After the plague, the fifth of December 1628, at a sessions then holden, I was entreated to continue the storehouse until the city were a little better settled. The charge of the storehouse for all the city for that year, 1628, was £308 17s. In the year 1630 the charge was £248 3s. 1d. In the year 1631 the charge was £187 5s. In the year 1632 the charge was £175 19s. 7d. The charge of this last four years is £920 4s. 8d. Here is abated of the first charge at the beginning of the storehouse, when it was £308 17s., and it is now for all the year but £175 19s. 7d. So it doth appear that there is abated in these last four years £315 3s. 4d.

---

[1] Buckingham's expedition to the Isle of Rhe left in June 1627. For troop movements around Salisbury late in 1626 see S.C.A., N 101, doc. 13, 36, 38, 75, 80.

(p. 28) In the year 1633 I put off the storehouse to Mr. Hill and Mr. Bricket, and the yearly charge was that year £175 19s. 7d. The next year, 1634, they raised it to £258 3s. 4d. In the year 1635 they brought the charge to £295 0s. 4d. In the year 1636 they brought the charge up to £395 10s. Which in the whole charge for the four years last past amounted to the sum of £1039 13s. 3d. In the first four years the charge was abated £315 3s. 4d. The next four years, in Mr. Hill and Mr. Bricket's time, [it] was raised £119 8s. 7d.[1]

This may not be ascribed at all to the fault of the governors of the storehouse but to most of all the overseers of the poor. For the justices would give their chewrers or other neighbours tickets to the masters of the storehouse for to deliver them 8d., 10d., or 12d. a week till further order, which was a great abuse and wasting the stock by the pressing on of the poor by the overseers and churchwardens, by which means they increased the charge, as before is seen, above £100.

In the year 1628 I received then in stock of the then mayor the sum of £100. And when at the four years' end I delivered up the stock to Mr. Hill and Mr. Bricket in money and chaffer it came to above £200. And in the time of their four years they had spent all the stock except £27. And the poor very much abroad abegging again and neglected their work.

And in the year 1637, at a general sessions for the city, I was over entreated to keep the storehouse once again. I had delivered to me in stock £27. So I went on and kept it three years and a half, in which time there was not one beggar seen, either in the Close or city. At that time the storehouse was let down by the great trouble that was raised by some innkeepers (p. 29) and alehouses, bakers and hucksters and brewers, and all the loose unruly rabble.[2]

Now in the year 1659 there was a sessions holden at Twelfth-tide. It was then ordered in regard of the great increase of the poor, Mr. Christopher Batt being then mayor, that Mr. George Legge, an alderman of the city, should be master of the storehouse for one year, and Mr. Ivy was entreated to be his assistant to bring him acquainted with the order of the storehouse, which I did undertake at the next common council for the city. Mr. Legge being not there, Mr. Mayor caused to be delivered to me twenty-seven pounds odd monies to buy provision for the poor.[3] It was no sooner begun but the Fathers of the Poor, for so they call themselves, began to storm madly and would not allow of anything that the mayor and justices did do, but did in as much scorn as ever I saw abuse both the mayor and justices. But the mayor was very willing for the good of the poor to set forward so good a work. [He] did warn the common council of the city to inform them what a siding there was by the

---

[1] The arithmetic in this paragraph is incorrect. The 'charge' of the storehouse was the total amount spent on the ordinary weekly relief of the poor, apart from 'extraordinaries' noted in the accounts (see pp. 94–8). The figures are from notes in Ivie's hand in the storehouse bk.: S.C.A., Y 216, ff. 188v., 196v.–198v. The accounts in the book do not correspond exactly to these figures (see above, p. 13).

[2] The storehouse, having proved uneconomic as well as controversial, was abolished in July 1640.

[3] S.C.A., Ledger D, f. 113.

overseers, alehouses, hucksters, and victuallers [and] that he would entreat their advice in the work. They did with one consent agree to have the work go on. Yet I did know there was one Judas amongst them that would not be wanting to do his worst, as he had not long before done, to the wrong of the city in their government and the poor souls to the value of above a thousand pounds, all which I am able to make appear. The like wrong was set on foot of late by the then mayor for, as soon as he did understand the way that the old mayor and council of the city and the sessions had with great care begun to settle a course for to order the poor, as before is written, [he acted as follows.][1]

As soon as he was elected he fell into familiarity with the church officers, that did so much contest with the old mayor, that he told me himself that if he were once sworn he would comply with the overseers, which he was wanting to do in his way to the great scorn of all his brethren, in the work which they had with great care and charge begun. Whereupon the company of justices did leave him to see what he would do with that rude company of overseers. But, as soon as they saw the justices did begin to leave him, they fell (p. 30) upon him worse than they did upon us and sued him and recovered from him at least £10, which is easily done in the city. For I do believe, had an honest man as just a cause as ever came in court, we have such strong men in juries that will carry it for the plaintiff if they go and talk with them while they are drinking two pots, and the verdict shall go how they will have it.

I have formerly written something of the overseers for not rating of the inhabitants that are ratable. I have here before written of many hundreds unrated. If there be any man that will not believe that in such a city there should be so foul an abuse suffered I am able to show the names of the housekeepers and the streets they dwell in. It is not above three years since I did, for the mayor and for the use of the collectors, in each parish make four books, that is in the three parishes twelve books, which was for every collector a book, that did show to each of them his ward and the names of them which they should with the mayor and justices' consent make [subject to] rates. Upon which they utterly refused and said they would go their own way. The books are all to be seen. These twelve books above mentioned were for every collector one. I first wrote them into one book, but severally, to be always in the hands of the mayor, and three more to be in my own hands so long as I did order for the storehouse. Mr. Mayor's twelve books were to lie always in the council house for himself and all the justices to search and see what foul abuses was acted by the overseers, which indeed was too foul.

Besides these books there was written [others] for the overseers, each of them to have one to show him his ward and every man that did pay and what his pay was; and every man's rate was set down weekly, some 6d., some 4d., some 10d., the next door one rated to pay a farthing a month, another to

---

[1] The new mayor, elected Sept. 1659, was Thomas Abbott. The 'Judas' was possibly the 'old herb' (see p. 110), perhaps Maurice Greene who succeeded Abbott as mayor for the year 1660-1 against Ivie's candidate and supervised the Restoration in the city: Ledger D, ff. 120v., 123.

pay two farthings a month, another one penny a month; of the great pay-masters they should collect weekly, and of the monthly men either monthly or once in two, three, or four months. Thus they were set down upon the books where they did dwell that it was no labour for them to collect. For one man shall sooner collect his ward by three parts than if they were all together because one makes the other idle, and [they] do invent such ways as never was seen in any well ordered government. (p. 31) For in their books they do invent such ways for their preambles and crossways to be found that but few can find [for] them, but with long search, the man that is looked for. By this way they have a very good shift to leave out of their books whomso-ever they will. I have both their book and above forty of my own to be seen.

I wish there were a good committee to view these books whereby a good order may be made to settle the government in this distracted city. I would not think my pains too much to come to London to wait upon some power to set us right. I make no doubt but God would bless their labours which should be bestowed upon so good a work. Yet it is short of what I have seen in this city. For God doth know I have desired to see the poor live without begging. It is forty years since I was overseer. I had then little knowledge in government but to bring my book blank to the mayor and justices, desiring them to rate our book, and we would look on and assist them. And if any were over-rated in our judgement we would go to the mayor; and if there were no reason to the contrary the party was abated. By this means we had that respect that did belong to us.

But now it is otherwise, as before is written. For now a collector that hath not been two years out of his apprenticeship is so well skilled that he will order a whole court of justice. I think it were good, as before is written, to swear them to be faithful in their office and to serve therein two years apiece as other officers do. It will be a hard matter for our overseers to be brought to it for they are chosen but for one year. There are four of them and as soon as they do enter upon their office they divide themselves into two companies, and the cunningest couple will take the first half-year to discharge the office for six months (their time doth always begin at Easter). And against winter the other two overseers do enter, not skilled in their office, neither collecting nor ordering the poor, then presently they run behind in arrears for money for want of skill and help of their partners.

Then they come with open mouth to the mayor and tell him, 'Sir, we must needs have a double rate for three or four months; we cannot tell what to do else.' This great fault is by dividing themselves, and in taking of an ill course in their collection, and for that they will not rate all that be ratable; (p. 32) for this is their answer, 'Such men are poor enough already.' But I know it is the way to make them richer to be rated and themselves to be the better ordered and ready for to do good. For, as before is written, if they be rated and so if any foreigner come to settle here, that may be chargeable to us, these men being rated will never leave complaining until they have gotten them removed. This is a good way to avoid a great charge that doth light upon us.

'Now,' saith another, 'what relief is this to the poor men that be rated?'

I say their relief will rise in this order. We have every year given by well disposed gentlemen some considerable sums of money to be given to poor housekeepers and such as have a charge of children. Some sums that are given are £20 or more or less. Our order is as soon as that money is come in the mayor sends for all the church officers, and when they come in there is brave sport in the dividing of it, and then they give it very unworthily; and when another sum comes in it is as ill disposed of. And in my opinion this is a way to dispose of a good part of it more to God's glory than ever it was done. For upon the receipt of this money there should be inquiry made where is most need, that the honest working poor may have it, and there bestowed, which may be done to the glory of God and (as I think) pleasing to the donor.

If you ask me, 'Where would you have it bestowed?', I tell you where. Look upon your collection book and where you find men stands there rated to pay one farthing a month, another two farthings, another three farthings, another four farthings a month, sure these be poor and honest people for the most part and worthy to receive the donors' money. There may you find housekeepers good store to receive it. And if this order were observed you have many of these hundreds before written that would desire to be rated upon the book, that were never rated. Neither should you have so much of good donors' money pissed against the wall by drunken lewd fellows as now it is for want of good order, which I pray God to put into the hearts of higher powers to make laws to establish this, or as much of it as by better judgements is thought fit to be made use of.

Further I must declare of the foulest abuse that ever was (p. 33) committed in any civil government by an overseer of the poor. I will not write anything of his abuse to the then mayor and justices in the council house. But for his behaviour against the work that then was afoot concerning the storehouse: there came a poor woman to the servant of the storehouse and told him, 'I would have for my weekly allowance a ten-penny loaf and the rest in cheese.' The servant replied, 'I have but two ten-penny loaves left, and they were baked four days since.' She said, 'I will have that to choose.' So she went away well pleased. Eight days after she came again with a piece of that loaf very mouldy and did ask the baker what course she might take with her mouldy bread. Many in the bakehouse said, 'I have sprinkled it with water and set it into the oven, and it hath done it good.' 'I will try that,' said the poor woman, and went into the backside and put it under the pump until it was very moist, then cast it into the oven until the batch was drawn, then took it out, the which showed it me, which threw it into her pigs' draught.

One of the overseers that set her to work, I verily believe, came into the house where it was thrown into the pigs' draught, and took it out and made it dry, and took great pains with it in carrying of it about most streets in the city and to most of the gentry in the Close of Salisbury. When the market was at the highest he carried the same bread through the same with a kind of proclamation, and showed it to many thousands together thinking to strengthen his party thereby. Then he came to the storehouse and showed it unto me in a rude manner, and would have me taste it, and offered to put some in my mouth, for which cause he was indicted. And the witnesses being his friends, with the jury, would not find the bill, which hath ever since emboldened that party to a greater height of insolency and pride against civil government.

About twelve years since I was unfortunately drawn into the office of mayor once again.[1] And as before is written I did find the alehouses much increased. At that time of the year they were wont to renew their licences. I took them all into my hands and would not grant any licences that year. Whereupon one of the chief brewers asked me what the poor should do for (p. 34) drink. I told him I had provided for them. 'I have sent for above twenty of the innkeepers who have promised me the poor shall have their chaffer, both for bread and beer and faggots, at better rates than the alehouses can serve them.' The brewer replied, 'Let any innkeepers serve drink out of doors, I will make him pay dear for it.' But [he] did not dare to do it. About two months after I was riding out of the city and over-rode one Mr. Spander who is there yet living.

He said to me, 'Mr. Mayor, you have undone our excise.'

'What are you?'

'I am clerk to the committee.'[2]

I told him, 'I meddled not with your committee.'

'I am sure,' said he, 'since you put down the alehouses we excise 18 or 20 quarters of malt weekly less than we did before the alehouses were down.'

I told him I thought he did mistake. His answer was, 'I can show my book for it and will swear it.' I told him I did doubt he did not understand how many quarters it was in one year. 'Yes,' said he, 'I know it to be above a thousand', as indeed it is. In these times if these thousand quarters were spent by the poor in bread I hope the prices of wheat would not rise so fast. Look to it that can reform it.

The assizes were held at Salisbury 29 July 1661 by the right honourable judges Sir Robert Foster, knight, Lord Chief Justice, and Judge Tyrell. The overseers of the poor brought a *nisi prius* against the mayor and justices, as false an action as ever was brought before the face of any court. But they were sure of freedom by their jury and did no doubt know what verdict the jury would bring in. Wherefore they did provide to come to hear the verdict, I believe, above 600 persons to wait for to hear the verdict given for the plaintiff and then to give a most shameful shout. I never heard a more uncivil noise at any bear- or bull-baiting, which did much disturb the worthy judges. But in Westminster, in the honourable Court of the Common Pleas, it was discoursed of more soberly and justly.[3]

(p. 35)   Postscript

This is my last request to any that have power to make orders for good government for the poor, especially in Salisbury where I know the want of it.

1 Sept. 1647: S.C.A., Ledger D, f. 31.
2 Probably the 'committee' of excise sub-commissioners for Wilts.
3 See pp. 14, 126. The case would have come before Common Pleas when the assize jury's findings were submitted to the court at Westminster for judgment.

In the first place at Easter choose four collectors for to serve two years apiece, and two for to go out free every year and two to come in that must serve two years apiece. And those four men to have each of them one ward apiece to look to, as now it stands divided, if either of these do want the help of a constable or of one of his partners to strain or to persuade the party to pay, without taking any distress. If those overseers be not sworn to serve in their office, as other officers are, all is to no purpose, and [it is necessary] to enjoin them to observe such by-laws as are to be made in sessions for the good of the poor, which are now grown numerous and necessitous, which may be easily holpen if men would do their duty to God and their country.

Wheat being now at 10s. the bushel with us in Salisbury, I am able to make it appear for want of true execution of the law and a true order and size in measures that the poor souls be deceived in a quarter of wheat at least 15s. in the measure only, besides other wrong these poor souls do suffer in, as before is to be seen in this book.

I pray God to give zeal and power to mend it.

J.I.

INDEX

Places other than major towns that are not stated in the index to be in another county or described as *unidentified* are to be understood to be in Wiltshire, including those described as *unspecified* without the addition of a county name. The county in which a place outside Wiltshire lies is given after the name where it appears in its alphabetical position, and not elsewhere.

References are to page-numbers. The index does not indicate when a name or subject occurs more than once on a page.

WILTSHIRE RECORD SOCIETY
(As at 1 August 1975)

PRIVATE MEMBERS

ANDERSON, D. M., 64 Winsley Road, Bradford-on-Avon

APPLEGATE, Miss Jean M., 55 Holbrook Lane, Trowbridge

ARCHER, P. J., Cotswold View, 9 Station Road, Highworth

AVERY, Mrs. Susan, 21 High Street, Downton

BADENI, The Countess, Norton Manor, Malmesbury

BAKER, M., 73 Easton Royal, Pewsey

BEATTIE, Prof. J. M., Dept. of History, University of Toronto 5, Ont., Canada

BERRETT, A. M., 65 Mandeville Road, Southgate, London N.14

BIDDULPH, G. M. R., c/o Personnel Records British Council, 65 Davies Street, London W.1

BIRLEY, N. P., D.S.O., M.C., Hyde Leaze, Hyde Lane, Marlborough

BLAKE, T. N., 16 West Hill Road, London S.W.18

BLUNT, C. E., O.B.E., F.B.A., Ramsbury Hill, Ramsbury, Marlborough

BONNEY, Mrs. H. M., Flint Cottage, Netton, Salisbury

BOULTER, E. J., The School House, 34 West Street, Wilton

BRICE, G. R., Branchways, Willett Way, Petts Wood, Kent

BRIGGS, M., Glebe Cottage, Middle Woodford, Salisbury

BROOKE-LITTLE, J. P., M.V.O., Richmond Herald of Arms, College of Arms, Queen Victoria Street, London E.C.4.

BROWN, W. E., The Firs, Beckhampton, Marlborough

BRYE, The Comtesse de, Boyton Manor, Warminster

BUCKERIDGE, J. M., 104 Beacon Road, Loughborough, Leics.

BURGE, S. F. M., The Old Rectory, Huish, Marlborough

BURNETT BROWN, Miss Janet M., Lacock Abbey, Chippenham

BUXTON, E. J. M., Cole Park, Malmesbury

CALLEY, Sir Henry, D.S.O., D.F.C., D.L., Overtown House, Wroughton, Swindon

CANNING, Capt. J. B., 51212 Wall, Spokane, Wash., 99204, U.S.A.

CAREW-HUNT, Miss P. H., Cowleaze, Edington, Westbury

CARTER, Miss N. M. G., Gatehouse, Cricklade

CLANCHY, M. T., Dept. of History, The University, Glasgow W.2.

CLARK, J. W., Manor Farm, Etchilhampton, Devizes

CODRINGTON, Miss N. E., Wroughton House, Swindon

COLLINS, W. Greville, Luckington Manor, Chippenham

COOMBES-LEWIS, R. J., 18 Bishopthorpe Road, London S.E.26

COX, Miss P. M., 6 Silverbeech Avenue, Liverpool

CRITTALL, Miss Elizabeth, 16 Downside Crescent, London N.W.3

CROWLEY, D. A., 333 Cranbrook Road, Ilford, Essex

CUFFE-ADAMS, E. J., Merryfield, St. George's Road, Bickley, Bromley, Kent

DANIELS, C. G., 81 Goffenton Drive, Oldbury Court, Fishponds, Bristol

D'ARCY, J. N., Monkswell Cottage, Edington, Westbury

DAWNAY, Capt. O. P., Wexcombe House, Marlborough

DEDMAN, The Rev. S. C., The Rectory, Great Wishford, Salisbury

DIBBEN, A. A., 222 King Street, Hammersmith, London W.6

DOYLE, Leslie, Cheviot, Clay Lane, Wythenshawe, Manchester 23

DYETT, B. T., 72 Douglas Avenue, Exmouth, Devon

DYKE, P. J., 35 Buckleigh Avenue, Merton Park, London S.W.20

EGAN, T. M., Vale Cottage, Stert, Devizes

ELKINS, T. W., 42 Brookhouse Road, Cove, Farnborough, Hants

ELRINGTON, C. R., Institute of Historical Research, University of London, Senate House, London W.C.1

FLOWER-ELLIS, J. G. K., Skogshogskolan, S104 05, Stockholm 50, Sweden

FORBES, Miss K. G., Bury House, Codford, Warminster

FOY, J. D., 28 Penn Lea Road, Bath, Som.

FRY, Mrs. P. M., 18 Pulteney Street, Bath, Som.

FULLER, Major Sir Gerard, Bt., Neston Park, Corsham

GHEY, J. G., 1 Sandell Court, The Parkway, Bassett, Southampton

GIBBON, The Rev. Canon Geoffrey, 1 North Grove, London N.6

GIBBONS, M. E., 11 Fleetwood Close, Neston, Corsham

GIMSON, H. M., Grey Wethers, Stanton St. Bernard, Marlborough

GODDARD, Mrs. G. H., The Boot, Scholard's Lane, Ramsbury, Marlborough

GOUGH, Miss P., Senior Common Room, Shenstone New College, Burcot Lane, Bromsgrove, Worcs.

GOULD, C. P., 1200 Old Mill Road, San Marino, Calif., 91108, U.S.A.

HALL, G. D. G., President, Corpus Christi College, Oxford

HALLWORTH, Frederick, Northcote, Westbury Road, Bratton, Westbury

HAMILTON, Capt. R., West Dean, Salisbury

HARFIELD, Maj. A. G., Royal Brunei Malay Regiment, Berakes Camp, State of Brunei, B.F.P.O. 605

HARFIELD, Mrs. A. G., Royal Brunei Malay Regiment, Berakes Camp, State of Brunei, B.F.P.O. 605

HATCHWELL, R. C., The Old Rectory, Little Somerford, Chippenham

HAWKINS, M. J., 121 High Street, Lewes, Sussex

HAYMAN, The Rev. P. E. C., The Vicarage, Rogate, Petersfield, Hants

HEMBRY, Mrs. P. M., 24 Thorncliffe, Lansdown Road, Cheltenham

HILLMAN, R. B., 38 Parliament Street, Chippenham

HOARE, H. P. R., Gasper House, Stourton, Warminster

HOBBS, Miss N., 140 Western Road, Sompting, Lancing, Sussex

HOPE, Robert, 25 Hengistbury Road, Bournemouth

HUMPHREYS, Cdr. L. A., R.N. (Rtd.), Elm Lodge, Biddestone, Chippenham

HURSTFIELD, Prof. Joel, D.Lit., 7 Glenilla Road, London N.W.3

IMREDY, Mrs. D. M., 2132 Yew Street, Vancouver, B.C., Canada

JACKSON, R. H., 17 Queens Road, Tisbury, Salisbury

JENNER, D. A., 98 Prince's Avenue, London, N.W.5

JONES, The Rev. Kingsley C., Wollaston Vicarage, Middletown, Welshpool, Mont.

KEATINGE, The Lady, Teffont, Salisbury

KEMPSON, E. G. H., Sun Cottage, Hyde Lane, Marlborough

KINROSS, J. S., Leigh's Green House, Corsley

KITCHING, Mrs. W. M., Willow Cottage, Pitton, Salisbury

KOMATSU, Prof. Y., Institute of European Economic History, Waseda University, Tokyo 160, Japan

LANSDOWN, M. J., 53 Clarendon Road, Trowbridge

LAURENCE, Miss Anne, 37 Denning Road, London, N.W.5

LAURENCE, G. F., 1 Monks Orchard, Petersfield, Hants

LEMMON, Miss C., 7 Chapel Rise, Atworth, Melksham

LEVER, R. E., Reads Close, Teffont Magna, Salisbury

LITTLE, J. E., The Pantiles, Chapel Lane, Uffington, Berks.

LONDON, Miss V. C. M., Underholt, Westwood Road, Bidston, Birkenhead

McCULLOUGH, Prof. Edward, Sir George Williams University, 1435 Drummond Street, Montreal 25, Que., Canada

McGOWAN, B., 108 Dixon Street, Swindon

MACKECHNIE-JARVIS, C., 9 The Close, Salisbury

MACKINTOSH, Duncan, C.B.E., Woodfolds, Oaksey, Malmesbury

MADDEN, I. B., Rosslea, 15 Belvedere Street, Epsom, Auckland 3, N.Z.

MANN, Miss J. de L., D.Litt., The Cottage, Bowerhill, Melksham

MARGADALE, The Lord, T. D., Fonthill House, Tisbury

MERRYWEATHER, A., Frithwood Cottage, Bussage, Stroud, Glos.

MILLBOURN, Sir Eric, C.M.G., Conkwell Grange, Limpley Stoke, Bath, Som.

MITTON, A. W. D., The Dungeon, 239 Earl's Court Road, London S.W.5

MOODY, G. C., Montrose, Shaftesbury Road, Wilton, Salisbury

MOORE, I. G., Raycroft, Lacock, Chippenham

MORRIS, Miss Bronwen, 9 Cleveland Gardens, Trowbridge

MORRISON, The Hon. Charles, M.P., Fyfield Manor, Marlborough

MOULTON, A. E., The Hall, Bradford-on-Avon

NAN KIVELL, R. de C., 20 Cork Street, London W.1

NEATE, E. G., 19 The Park, Carshalton, Surrey

NEWALL, R. S., Avon Cottage, Lower Woodford, Salisbury

NORTHAMPTON, Emma, Marchioness of, O.B.E., The Curatage, Horningsham, Warminster

O'GRADY, Miss C., 49 Oxford Street, Ramsbury, Marlborough

OSBORNE, Major Robert, 3 Royal Tank Regiment, B.F.P.O. 38

PAFFORD, J. H. P., D.Lit., Hillside, Allington Park, Bridport, Dorset

PASKIN, Lady, Wishford, Salisbury

PERRY, S. H., 117 London Road, Kettering, Northants.

PHILLIMORE, Miss M. G., 18 Queens Street, Worthing, Sussex

PONTING, K. G., Becketts House, Edington, Westbury

POTHECARY, S. G., 41 Australian Avenue, Salisbury

PUGH, Prof. R. B., D.Lit., 67 Southwood Park, London N.6

RAMSAY, G. D., 15 Charlbury Road, Oxford

RANCE, H. F., Butler's Court, Beaconsfield, Bucks.

RATHBONE, M. G., Craigleith, Snarlton Lane, Melksham Forest

RAYBOULD, Miss Frances, 20 Radnor Road, Salisbury

REEVES, Miss Marjorie E., F.B.A., 38 Norham Road, Oxford

REYNOLDS, A., The White House, Riverfield Road, Staines, Middlesex

ROGERS, K. H., Silverthorne House, East Town, West Ashton, Trowbridge

ROOKE, Mrs. R. E. P., Old Rectory, Little Langford, Salisbury

ROOKE, Miss S. F., Old Rectory, Little Langford, Salisbury

ROSS, Harry, Leighton Villa, Wellhead Lane, Westbury

ROWE, Mrs. H. M., 85 Charnhill Drive, Mangotsfield, Bristol

RUNDLE, Miss Penelope, 46 St. Andrews Road, Bemerton, Salisbury

SANDELL, R. E., Hillside, 64 Devizes Road, Potterne

SANDQUIST, Prof. T. A., Dept. of History, University of Toronto 5, Ont., Canada

SANGER, Mrs. J., 46 Woodside Road, Salisbury

SAVERNAKE ESTATE, Savernake Forest, Marlborough

SAWYER, L. F. T., 51 Sandridge Road, Melksham

SHADBOLT, Mrs. L. G., Birkhall House, High Kelling, Holt, Norfolk

SHEWRING, D. G., 4 Clifton Street, Treorchy, Rhondda, Glam.

SKINNER, M., 19 Cheyne Court, London S.W.3

SMITH, R. G., 142 Peabody Estate, London N.17

SOMERSET, The Duke of, D. L., Bradley House, Maiden Bradley, Warminster

STEELE, Mrs. N. D., Milestones, Hatchet Close, Hale, Fordingbridge, Hants

STEVENSON, Miss J. H., Institute of Historical Research, University of London, Senate House, London W.C.1

STEWART, Miss K. P., Moxham Villa, 57 Lower Road, Bemerton, Salisbury

STILLMAN, G. H., Unit 8, 10 East Street, Maylands 6051, West Australia

STRATTON, J. M., Manor House Farm, Stockton, Warminster

STYLES, Philip, 21 Castle Lane, Warwick

TAYLOR, C. C., Royal Commission on Historical Monuments (England), 13 West End, Whittlesford, Cambridge

TOMLINSON, Sir Stanley, Flat 6, 24 Buckland Crescent, London S.W.1

TURNER, I. D., Warrendene, 222 Nottingham Road, Mansfield, Notts.

TURNER, Miss M., 4 Elm Grove Road, Salisbury

TWINE, S. W., Park Fold, 6 St. John's Way, Charlton, Malmesbury

VERNON, Miss T. E., Dyer's Leaze, Lacock, Chippenham

WARNEFORD, I. P., 18 Woodhall Park Mount, Stanningley, Pudsey, Yorks.

WATKINS, W. T., Carn Ingli, 16 Westbury Road, Warminster

WEINSTOCK, Sir Arnold, Bowden Park, Lacock, Chippenham

WILLAN, Group Capt. F. A., D.L., Bridges, Teffont, Salisbury

WILLIAMS, N. J., 57 Rotherwick Road, Hampstead Garden Suburb, London N.W.11

WILTSHIRE, D. C. S., 17 Macaulay Buildings, Bath, Som.

WILTSHIRE, Julian M., 7 Lalor Street, S.W.1

WOODHEAD, Miss Barbara, 47 High Street, Ramsbury

WORTHINGTON, B. S., Vale Lodge, Colnbrook, Bucks.

YOUNG, C. L. R., 25 Staveley Road, Chiswick, London W.4

UNITED KINGDOM INSTITUTIONS

Aberdeen. King's College Library
Aberystwyth. National Library of Wales
   ,,   University College General Library
Allington (S. Wilts.). Bourne Valley Historical Society
Bangor. University College of North Wales
Bath. General Reference Library
Birmingham. Central Public Library
   ,,   University Library
Bridgwater. Somerset County Library
Brighton. University of Sussex Library, Falmer
Bristol. City of Bristol Library
   ,,   University Library

Cambridge. University Library
Canterbury. University of Kent Library
Coventry. University of Warwick Library
Devizes. Wiltshire Archaeological and Natural History Society
Dorchester. County of Dorset Library
Edinburgh. National Library of Scotland
   ,,   University Library
Exeter. University Library
Glasgow. University Library
Gloucester. Bristol and Gloucestershire Archaeological Society
Hull. University Library
Leeds. University Library
Leicester. University Library
Liverpool. University Library

London. British Library
„ College of Arms
„ Guildhall Library
„ Inner Temple Library
„ Institute of Historical Research
„ London Library
„ Public Record Office
„ Royal Historical Society
„ Society of Antiquaries
„ Society of Genealogists
„ University of London Library
„ Westminster Public Library
Manchester. Rylands University Library
Marlborough. Adderley Library, Marl-
borough College
Norwich. University of East Anglia
Library
Nottingham. University Library
Oxford. Bodleian Library
„ Exeter College Library
„ New College Library
Reading. Central Library
„ University Library
St. Andrews. University Library

Salisbury. History Dept., College of Sarum
St. Michael
„ Diocesan Record Office
„ The Museum
„ New Sarum Public Library
„ Royal Commission on Historical
Monuments (ngland), Manor
Road
„ Salisbury & South Wilts. College
of Further Education
Sheffield. University Library
Southampton. University Library
Swansea. University College of Swansea
Library
Swindon. Thamesdown Public Library
„ Swindon College Library
Taunton. Somerset Archaeological and
Natural History Society
Trowbridge. Wiltshire County Library
„ Wiltshire Record Office,
County Hall
„ The Wiltshire Times
York. University of York Library,
Heslington

INSTITUTIONS OVERSEAS

AUSTRALIA

Adelaide. Barr Smith Library, University
of Adelaide
Canberra. National Library of Australia
Melbourne. Baillieu Library, University of
Melbourne
„ Victoria State Library
St. Lucia, Brisbane. Main Library, Univer-
sity of Queensland
Sydney. Fisher Library, University of
Sydney

CANADA

Downsview, Ont. Scott Library, York
University
Kingston, Ont. Queen's University
London, Ont. Lawson Memorial Library,
University of Western Ontario
Montreal, Que. Sir George Williams Uni-
versity Library
Peterborough, Ont. Thomas J. Bata
Library, Trent University
Toronto, Ont. University of Toronto
Library
Ottawa, Ont. Carleton University Library
St. John's, Newf. Memorial University of
Newfoundland Library
Vancouver, B.C. Main Library, University
of British Columbia

Victoria, B.C. McPherson Library, University of Victoria

DENMARK

Copenhagen. The Royal Library

GERMANY

Göttingen. Niedersächsische Staats- und
Universitätsbibliothek

REPUBLIC OF IRELAND

Dublin. National Library of Ireland
„ Trinity College Library

JAPAN

Osaka. Institute of Economic History
Kansai University
Sendai. Institute of Economic History
Tohoku University

NEW ZEALAND

Wellington. National Library of New
Zealand

Upsala. Kungl. Universitetets Bibliotek (Royal University Library)

Ann Arbor, Mich. General Library, University of Michigan

Athens, Ga. University Libraries, University of Georgia

Atlanta, Ga. The Robert W. Woodruff Library for Advanced Studies, Emory University

Baltimore, Md. Peabody Institute of the City of Baltimore

Bloomington, Ind. Indiana University Library

Boston, Mass. Public Library of the City of Boston

„   „   New England Historic Genealogical Society

Boulder, Colo. University of Colorado Libraries

Cambridge, Mass. Harvard Law School Library

„   „   Harvard College Library

Chicago, Ill. University of Chicago Library

„   „   Newberry Library

Cleveland, Ohio. Public Library

De Kalb, Ill. Northern University of Illinois, Swen Franklin Parson Library

East Lansing, Mich. Michigan State University Library

Eugene, Oreg. University of Oregon Library

Evanston, Ill. Garrett-Seabury Western Theological Libraries

Fort Wayne, Ind. Public Library of Fort Wayne and Allen County

Hattiesburg, Miss. University of Southern Mississippi Library

Haverford, Pa. Haverford College Library

Iowa City, Iowa. State University of Iowa Library

Ithaca, N.Y. Cornell University Library

Las Cruces, N. Mex. New Mexico State University Library

Los Angeles,Calif. Public Library of Los Angeles

„   „   „   University Research Library, University of California

Minneapolis, Ma. Dept. of History, Minnesota University

Newark, Del. University of Delaware Library

New Brunswick, N.J. Rutgers State University Library

New Haven, Conn.   Yale University Library

New York, N.Y. Columbia University of the City of New York

„   „   „   Public Library, City of New York

Notre Dame, Ind. Notre Dame University Memorial Library

Philadelphia, Pa. Pennsylvania University Library

Princeton, N.J.   Princeton University Library

Salt Lake City, Utah. Genealogical Society of the Church of Latter Day Saints

San Marino, Calif. Henry E. Huntingdon Library

Santa Barbara, Calif. University of California Library

Stanford, Calif.   Stanford University Library

Urbana, Ill. University of Illinois Library

Washington, D.C.   Library of Congress

„   „   Folger   Shakespeare Library

Winston-Salem, N.C. Wake Forest University Library

LIST OF PUBLICATIONS

The Wiltshire Record Society was founded in 1937, as the Records Branch of the Wiltshire Archaeological and Natural History Society, to promote the publication of the documentary sources for the history of Wiltshire. The annual subscription is £4 50p. In return, a member receives a volume each year. Prospective members should apply to Mrs. N. D. Steele, Milestones, Hatchet Close, Hale, Fordingbridge, Hants. Many more members are needed.

The following volumes have been published. Price to members £4 50p and to non-members £7, postage extra. Available from the Hon. Treasurer, Mr. M. J. Lansdown, 53 Clarendon Road, Trowbridge, Wiltshire.

XXVII   *Wiltshire Returns to the Bishop's Visitation Queries, 1783.* Edited by Mary Ransome (1972). Folder

XXVIII *Wiltshire Extents for Debts Edward I–Elizabeth I.* Edited by Angela Conyers (1973)

XXIX   *Abstracts of Feet of Fines relating to Wiltshire for the reign of Edward III.* Edited by C. R. Elrington (1974)

XXX   *Abstracts of Wiltshire Tithe Apportionments.* Edited by R. E. Sandell (1975)

VOLUMES IN PREPARATION

Wiltshire Glebe Terriers, edited by Susan Avery; *Salisbury General Entry Books*, edited by Alan Crossley; *The Charters of Lacock Abbey*, edited by K. H. Rogers; *The Edington Cartulary*, edited by Janet Stevenson; *Wiltshire Clergy of the Seventeenth Century*, edited by Barrie Williams; *Dean Chaundler's Register*, edited by T. C. B. Timmins; *The Bradenstoke Cartulary*, edited by Vera C. M. London; *Wiltshire Gaol Delivery Rolls for the reign of Edward I*, edited by R. B. Pugh

A leaflet giving fuller details may be obtained from Mrs. Steele, Milestones, Hatchet Close, Hale, Fordingbridge, Hants.